Your Identity in the Trinity

Your Identity in the Trinity

Discovering God's Grace in the Gospel

SEAN COLE
Foreword by Jeff Iorg

WIPF & STOCK · Eugene, Oregon

YOUR IDENTITY IN THE TRINITY
Discovering God's Grace in the Gospel

Copyright © 2019 Sean Cole. All rights reserved. Except for brief quotations in critical publications or reviews, no part of this book may be reproduced in any manner without prior written permission from the publisher. Write: Permissions, Wipf and Stock Publishers, 199 W. 8th Ave., Suite 3, Eugene, OR 97401.

Wipf & Stock
An Imprint of Wipf and Stock Publishers
199 W. 8th Ave., Suite 3
Eugene, OR 97401

www.wipfandstock.com

PAPERBACK ISBN: 978-1-5326-7385-6
HARDCOVER ISBN: 978-1-5326-7386-3
EBOOK ISBN: 978-1-5326-7387-0

Manufactured in the U.S.A.   APRIL 8, 2019

Scripture quotations are from the ESV® Bible (The Holy Bible, English Standard Version®), copyright © 2001 by Crossway, a publishing ministry of Good News Publishers. Used by permission. All rights reserved.

To the generous and loving congregation
of Emmanuel Baptist Church.
You have taught me how to pastor, lead, and love God's church.

To our two wonderful boys, Aidan and Zachary.
You are treasured gifts from Jesus.

And especially to my wonderful wife, Dawn.
Your patience, kindness, and gentle spirit
have been used by the Lord to encourage me
as a husband, father, and pastor.
I appreciate your sacrifice and love.

Contents

Foreword by Jeff Iorg | ix
Introduction | xiii

1. The Chief End of Man—God's Glory | 1
2. The Power of Salvation—God's Gospel | 12
3. Essentials of your Identity | 22
4. Your Identity in the Father | 35
5. Your Identity in the Son | 48
6. Your Identity in the Holy Spirit | 69
7. The Deception of Indwelling Sin | 88
8. The Intense Struggle with Sin | 100
9. Killing Sin | 112
10. The Authoritative Word | 124
11. The Intimacy in Prayer | 147
12. The Celebration of the Ordinances | 170
13. Practicing the Gospel "One Anothers" | 185
14. Obeying the Great Commission | 202
15. Your Identity in Suffering | 219
    Conclusion | 232

Bibliography | 237
Subject Index | 245
Scripture Index | 249

Foreword

THE MOST CRUCIAL DISCOVERY leading to satisfaction in the Christian life can be summarized in this short phrase—being before doing. It seems so simple, yet requires a lifetime to master. God wants us to discover our identity in him—not in what we do for him or for others. He wants us to experience his ultimate purpose—transformation and conformation to the image of Jesus Christ. God is relentless in pursuing his relationship with us—motivated by his great love for us and devoid of anything we can do to earn that love.

My friend Sean Cole discovered these great truths through studying profound writings by prominent theologians, diving deeply into personal Bible study, unlearning myths and mistakes he once believed about being a Christian, and basing his daily behavior on his newfound insights. He has discovered his identity in the Triune God and wants you to do the same. He has now pulled together what he has learned in this very helpful and insightful book.

Identity is an important issue—not just for Christians, but for everyone. People search and struggle to define themselves. Young adults are often described as "trying to find themselves." Teenagers mimic each other and pop culture idols, all while falsely claiming they are "just doing me." Pseudosophisticated adults, who pride themselves on being beyond superficial or childish influences, nevertheless chase achievements, possessions, pleasures, and relationships to find the self-satisfaction they crave. Many people of all ages turn to philosophy, politics, or religion to define themselves and make sense of their place in the world. All of these are futile exercises in self-actualization.

God, who created humankind, is our source of identity. He defines humanity and delineates his purpose for each person. In short, God and

God alone is the source and substance of the answer to the questions "Who am I?" and "Why am I here?"

The answers to these questions are grounded in God himself, revealed as the Father, Son, and Holy Spirit. God is Triune. This book explains that complicated doctrine clearly and uses those theological parameters to answer, in very practical ways, questions about your identity and purpose. This is the best part of this book—grounding who we are in God himself and showing the practicality of theological reflection brought to life.

Another very helpful aspect of this book is the connection between identity and solving difficult dilemmas like handling temptations and persistent sin. This book is more than a treatise on ethereal doctrinal concepts. It shows how understanding those concepts is the ground source from which lasting life change emerges. One of the strengths of this book is how tightly it connects theological truth with practical application. Your identity in the Trinity really does impact how you relate to your spouse, the kind of employee you are, and the contribution you make as a church member. Good theology is practical theology and this book shows how what we believe impacts what we think, say, and do.

While reading this book, I reflected on my struggles with these issues. Many years ago, God helped me to discover my identity in him and change my perspectives on what it meant to serve him. I wish this book had been available to me thirty years ago! It would have helped me make sense of my struggles, questions, and doubts. It would also have helped me understand more about the depth of God's love for me, the identity I have in him, and the peace he has given me as a result. Too many years of my early Christian life and ministry were spent trying to earn God's love, prove my worth to him, or otherwise meet legalistic standards others created for me to validate my allegiance to God.

What a pointless treadmill-like race to nowhere! Fortunately, God helped me understand that being matters more than doing. He taught me that service results from God's love, not an effort to obtain it. God graciously and patiently taught me to delight in him, not in what he does for me or what I do for him, but just *in him* as Father, Son, and Spirit. My prayer is reading this book will lead to a similar breakthrough for you.

Sean Cole has done a lot of the hard work for you in setting the stage for your breakthrough on these issues. He has written a book with doctrinal depth and biblical breadth, while at the same time always connecting his theological discoveries to practical realities. Do not read this book as a critic taking apart a textbook. Read it devotionally, asking God to speak to you and change you as a result of what you learn.

May God's glory encompass you as you read!

JEFF IORG
President, Gateway Seminary

Introduction

LATE AT NIGHT AFTER his wife and children go to bed, Frank surfs the Internet and finds himself trapped in a hollow world of pornography. Entangled in lust, he fights a battle deep in his heart to understand his true identity in Christ.

Michelle's husband recently left her and the children for a more attractive, younger woman. She tirelessly works two jobs trying to make ends meet and cannot bring herself to forgive her ex-husband. She is entangled in bitterness in this internal battle to understand her true identity in Christ.

Ron is driven by success to climb the corporate ladder at all costs. On the surface, he appears calm, cool, and collected to his co-workers, but when he gets home to his family, he erupts like a volcano. His anger and frustration with life boil under the surface in this battle to understand his true identity in Christ.

Melanie is a social butterfly. She is the life of the party who always seems to be "in the know" about everyone's business. Most people keep their distance because of her insatiable need to gossip. She's trapped in a web of lying and backstabbing. She's in a battle for her heart and does not understand her true identity in Christ.

Darren grew up in a household that didn't have much money. Now as a recent college graduate, he makes good money. He competes with his friends by accumulating more toys—new cars, boats, and game systems. He's unaware of this spiral into materialism, greed, and envy. His appetite for stuff has led him into major credit card debt. Swimming in uncertainty and fear, he's in a battle to understand his true identity in Christ.

Frank, Michelle, Ron, Melanie, and Darren are fictional people, but they illustrate a pervasive reality—there are many Christians who struggle to understand their gospel identity in Christ.

WHY A BOOK ON DISCOVERING YOUR IDENTITY IN THE TRINITY?

For many years I struggled with understanding my identity in Christ. I knew that Jesus saved me by grace and that I would one day spend eternity with him in heaven, but I did not have a full grasp on the richness of the gospel. As a teenager and young adult, I lived my life trying to please God through my own effort, to somehow achieve this higher plane of spirituality and victory over all known sin. After numerous failures and trips to the altar to "rededicate my life," I often questioned my salvation. I lacked both the assurance that God had saved me and also wondered if I would ever make any progress in holiness. Through my own personal Bible study, struggle with sin, the encouragement of godly mentors, and the writings of great theologians, I have grown in understanding my identity in the Trinity. In the opening pages of his famous book *The Confessions*, St. Augustine writes, "You stir man to take pleasure in praising You, because you have made us for Yourself, and our heart is restless until it rests in You."[1] That described me for many years. I was restless because I did not entirely rest in what the Triune God accomplished for me in redemption.

We exist to display God's glory, declare God's gospel, and disciple for God's Great Commission. Instead of embracing these truths, many Christians have believed the lie that their identity in Christ does not affect how they live their lives in obedience to him. The gospel tells us that being (identity) comes before doing (obedience). This lack of understanding our gospel identity frequently results in either legalistic pride or frustrating guilt. The purpose of this book is to help believers understand their identity in the three persons of the Trinity and then joyfully serve God with gospel obedience. The gospel indicatives in the Bible serve as the fountain, motivation, and power for obeying the moral imperatives in the Bible. The gospel roots our assurance of salvation and motivation to obey God in our identity, not in moralism, which elevates our performance instead of exalting the finished work of Christ.

I am indebted to the works of the Puritan John Owen, who has dramatically influenced my theology as well as my understanding of the process of Christian growth in godliness. Over a decade ago, I read his book, *Communion with God: Fellowship with Father, Son, And Holy Spirit*, which opened my eyes to the riches of our gospel identity in each person

---

1. Augustine, *Confessions*, 3.

of the Trinity. Written in 1657, this extensive treatment of the subject has heavily impacted my thinking and theology and put me on a trajectory to learn more about who we are in the Triune God. Owen motivated me to study the doctrine of the Trinity more deeply; not only for biblical orthodoxy but also for personal doxology. In other words, the more I learned about my identity in each Person of the Trinity, the more my heart became inflamed to worship and submit to our great God.

There is no shortage of books on the gospel, Christian growth, and sanctification. What sets this book apart is that no other modern work specifically demonstrates how Christians find their identity in each person of the Trinity. Also, this book will give practical application of how to obey Christ out of the overflow of that Trinitarian identity. In chapters 1 and 2, we will explore how the chief end of man is to glorify God and enjoy him forever, as well as the truths surrounding the gospel of Christ. Chapter 3 serves as the thesis and heart of the book, which addresses the importance of discovering our identity in the Trinity. In chapters 4 through 6, we will focus on the Father, the Son, and the Holy Spirit respectively, and show how we find our assurance of salvation in this gospel identity. Our identity in the Trinity is not without its struggles. Chapters 7 and 8 will address the deceitfulness of indwelling sin and how we struggle daily between our flesh and the Spirit. In chapter 9, we will learn how to grow in Christ by decisively killing sin through the power of the Holy Spirit. Chapters 10 through 13 will center on the positive way we obey the Lord through an examination of how the early church in Acts 2 practiced the means of grace. We will explore four practices to help us grow in our Trinitarian identity: Scripture saturation, the intimacy of prayer, the celebration of baptism and the Lord's Supper, and practicing the gospel one anothers (fellowship). Chapter 14 will encourage us to obey the Great Commission as we seek to live out our gospel identity in a lifestyle of evangelism. In chapter 15, we will explore how God ordains our suffering as a means to strengthen us in our identity in the Trinity.

WHO SHOULD READ THIS BOOK?

If you struggle with assurance of salvation this book is for you. If you tend to approach obedience to God out of either guilt or legalism, this book is for you. If you struggle to overcome temptation and habitual sin, this book is for you. I hope that this book helps those who have experienced frustration in their walk with Christ, do not have a sound theological grasp on the gospel, and have possibly embraced some false doctrines. If you desire to grow spiritually in Christ and serve him with joyful obedience, this book provides a practical theology for how to practice the means of grace (word, prayer, fellowship, baptism and Lord's Supper, and evangelism) as joyful responses to whom the Triune God has called and promised us to become—conformed to the image of Christ.

I am the first to admit that I am not an expert in fully understanding my identity in the Trinity. I am also not an expert in wholehearted and joyful obedience to the Lord, as I fail many times. Yet I am a pilgrim on a journey to go deeper into the depths of the gospel so that I can fully enjoy the One God who has revealed himself to us in three distinct persons—namely, the Father, the Son, and the Holy Spirit. As a fellow sojourner, I invite you along on this pilgrimage so that together we can rest and rejoice in all that our great God has done for us in the gospel. I am a preacher at heart and love to stand before God's people every Sunday and exposit his word. This book is a product of over fifteen years of preaching expositionally through the Bible. Much of the material in this book comes from sermons I preached at Emmanuel Baptist Church in Sterling, Colorado. I have seen these truths transform God's people firsthand, and I am excited to share them with you. In his book, *The Supremacy of God in Preaching*, John Piper quotes Scottish preacher, James Stewart: "The aims of all genuine preaching are to quicken the conscience by the holiness of God, to feed the mind with the truth of God, to purge the imagination by the beauty of God, to open the heart to the love of God, to devote the will to the purpose of God."[2] I pray that what you read in this book will do just that!

SOLI DEO GLORIA

---

2. Piper, *Supremacy of God in Preaching*, 23.

1

The Chief End of Man—God's Glory

"Please show me your glory."
MOSES IN EXODUS 33:18

HAVE YOU EVER WONDERED why you and I exist? A Google search for the phrase "*Why do I exist,*" produces 11.8 million hits. Amazon has dozens of books with the title *Why Do I Exist*? The French mathematician Rene Descartes took the Western world by storm in the late 1600s with his famous line from his *Discourse on a Method*: "I think; therefore I am."[1] This one phrase helped launch the Enlightenment in Europe and has been the center of many philosophical debates for centuries. As humans, we have a fascination with trying to figure out our ultimate purpose and meaning in life. The opening line from the *Westminster Shorter Catechism* sums up the comprehensive and biblical answer to that lingering question of why you and I exist: "The chief end of man is to glorify God and enjoy him forever."[2] You will not hear this answer from the culture. The world says that selfish pursuits of pleasure define life's meaning with this mantra:

---

1. Descartes, *Discourse on the Method*, 28.
2. http://www.westminsterconfession.org/confessional-standards/the-westminster-shorter-catechism.php

"The chief end of man is to worship myself and enjoy as much selfish pleasure in the here and now as I possibly can!"

Think of all the commercials you see in a given week that sell the message that you are the center of the universe and you deserve to have whatever trinkets they have to offer. Even within the church we are often coddled into thinking that we exist for our glory and not for God's. We may often think that God resembles a genie in a bottle that exists for our comfort. As A. W. Tozer asserts,

> The purpose of God in sending his Son to die and rise and live and be at the right hand of God the Father was that he might restore to us the missing jewel, the jewel of worship; that we might come back and learn to do again that which we were created to do in the first place – worship the Lord in the beauty of holiness, to spend our time in awesome wonder and adoration of God, feeling and expressing it, and letting it get into our labors and doing nothing except as an act of worship to Almighty God through his Son, Jesus Christ.[3]

Do you agree with his radical claim that worship is missing in our churches today? Could the body of Christ indeed be guilty of not worshipping God? The Puritan Thomas Watson gives this rebuke to the church: "Many heathens have worshipped their false gods with more seriousness and devotion than some Christians do the true God. Oh, let us chide ourselves; did I say chide? Let us abhor ourselves for our deadness and formality in religion, how we have professed God, and yet have not worshipped him as God."[4] Could the contemporary church be so entrenched in deadness and formality that we have lost sight of the true meaning of worship? John Calvin said, "The human mind is a perpetual factory of idols . . . daily experience shows that the sinful mind is always restless until it finds something that looks like itself, in which it finds vain comfort as a representation of God. As a result of this blind passion, men have in almost all ages since the world began, set up imaginary idols before their eyes to take the place of God."[5] If the chief end of man is to glorify God and enjoy him forever, yet the human mind is a perpetual idol factory, what is the answer to this conflict? What does displaying God's glory mean?

---

3. Tozer, *Treasury of A. W. Tozer*, 284.
4. Watson, *Ten Commandments*, 54.
5. Calvin, *Institutes of the Christian Religion*, 97.

We exist to bring glory, honor, and majesty to God in all aspects of our lives. God created us for his glory, as evidenced in Isaiah 43:6–7, which reads, "Bring my sons from afar and my daughters from the end of the earth, everyone who is called by my name, whom I created for my glory, whom I formed and made." Why has the sovereign God of the universe created us? Was he lonely up in heaven and needed companionship? Absolutely not! We must never think of God as needful of anything. He is the self-existent powerful God who created all things.

THE GREAT I AM

The LORD revealed himself to Moses in Exodus 3:14: "God said to Moses, 'I am who I am.' And he said, 'Say this to the people of Israel: I am has sent me to you.'" There is no way to do justice to how the Hebrew language translates this phrase, but the word for "I AM" sounds very similar to the word "YHWH," which means "LORD." We can translate this interesting phrase in three ways that show us some profound truths about the nature and character of our great God. First of all, we could translate this as: "*I have always been who I have always been.*" This wording emphasizes the eternal nature of God, who has no beginning or no ending as the everlasting God. Second, this title can also mean: "*I AM who I AM*" meaning that God alone defines who he is. For example, I can say, "I am tall" or "I am blond" or "I am Dawn's husband" or "I am the pastor of Emmanuel Baptist Church" or "I am a created being." Everything about me is defined in relation to something else. I can't just say emphatically, "I AM . . ." Period! My total existence has been defined by and depends on God as my Creator. My identity is never in a vacuum. I can't be defined without depending on others. I was born to Greg and Cheryl Cole, and therefore I am their son. As a created being, I am contingent on others for my very existence. My existence and identity are also limited and constrained by factors outside my control. I've always wanted to be 6'6" like Michael Jordan so I could easily dunk; that has never happened since I am only 6'2". I've always wanted to fly like Superman, and that's never happened as well. No matter how hard I try, I cannot overcome the major limitations as a finite human as to who I am or who I want to be. But that cannot be said about God. The LORD's existence and identity have no limits and cannot be restrained because he is the sovereign Creator and he is absolutely free to do whatever he wants. No one or force in all the universe can dictate to him what he can or cannot do. He is not contingent on anything for his existence. Third, we can translate this title as "*I will be, who I will be*" which stresses that God will act in the future and continue to exist from everlasting to everlasting.

Interestingly, the way the Hebrew language utilizes this phrase can also mean that God causes, creates, and sustains all things. Scholar D. K. Stuart says, "The name should thus be understood as referring to YHWH's being the creator and sustainer of all that exists and thus the Lord of both creation and history, all that is and all that is happening—a God active and present in everything."[6] The word YHWH means more than just "I am," or "I exist"; it also means, "I cause things to be in existence, and I sustain those things so they continue to be." In other words, the LORD, the Great I AM, is the unchanging God who has no needs! Listen to how Job 26:14 describes the majesty of the LORD in creating the world: "Behold, these are but the outskirts of his ways, and how small a whisper do we hear of him! But the thunder of his power who can understand?" The psalmist echoes this mysterious God who has no needs in Psalm 102:25–27: "Of old you laid the foundation of the earth, and the heavens are the work of your hands. They will perish, but you will remain; they will all wear out like a garment. You will change them like a robe, and they will pass away, but you are the same, and your years have no end." When confronting the "unknown god" of the Athenians, Paul declares the self-existence of YHWH in Acts 17:24–25 where he says, "The God who made the world and everything in it, being Lord of heaven and earth, does not live in temples made by man, nor is he served by human hands, as though he needed anything, since he himself gives to all mankind life and breath and everything." Paul concludes eleven chapters in the book of Romans by declaring the glories of God in our salvation with an eruption of praise in Romans 11:34–36: "For who has known the mind of the Lord, or who has been his counselor? Or who has given a gift to him that he might be repaid? For from him and through him and to him are all things. To him be glory forever. Amen."

Our LORD is the inexhaustible God. He never tires. He has no beginning and no end. He is infinite. He is limitless. He is self-existent. He is sovereign. He is eternal. He is incomprehensible. Moses captured God's identity as the great I AM in Psalm 90:2, which states, "Before the mountains were brought forth, or ever you had formed the earth and the world,

---

6. Stuart, *New American Commentary*, 121.

from everlasting to everlasting you are God." Theologian Geerhardus Vos gave this excellent description: "The name gives expression to the self-determination, the independence of God, we call his sovereignty ... The name signifies primarily that in all God does for his people, he is self-determining, not moved upon by outside influences."[7] Now, here's the paradox of this beautiful truth of God as the great I AM. If God is absolutely sovereign, has no needs, is self-existent, is all-knowing, is all-powerful, and cannot be moved by outside influences, then why does he command us to worship him? Why give him glory? Isn't he already intrinsically glorious? Does God even need us to praise him? One concept you should get out of your vocabulary is that God needs anything. God doesn't have any needs—especially anything we as sinful humans can offer him.

The LORD, the great I AM, YHWH, sovereignly rules over heaven and earth, yet in his amazing providence, has created us for his glory. He made us as his children so that we would display his glory back to him in joyful worship. Isaiah 42:8 reads, "I am the LORD; that is my name; my glory I give to no other, nor my praise to carved idols." This word for "glory" (*kabod*) in the Old Testament Hebrew means "weighty" or "to be heavy." As his creation, we should view God as weighty and worthy of honor. The glory of God consists of his splendor, majesty, weightiness, holiness, and power that comprise his intrinsic nature as the great I AM.

Even though God is inherently glorious, the Scriptures call us to reflect, display, or ascribe to him the glory due his name. Psalm 29:2 says, "Ascribe to the LORD the glory due his name; worship the LORD in the splendor of holiness." What does it mean to ascribe glory to God? Do we add to his glory? Do we somehow make him more glorious than he already is? Is there some deficiency in God that we must correct so that he can somehow become glorious? Absolutely not! To ascribe glory means to give him what he alone deserves. We don't add a measure to his glory, but we reflect back to him the glory that he inherently has. The word for "glory" (*doxa*) in the New Testament means to honor someone's reputation or to make much of his name. A comprehensive view of the Scripture demands that we make much of God by giving proper honor to him with our worship. He is worthy. He is majestic. He is powerful and glorious. As a result, the Scriptures call us to consistently display God's glory with the totality of our lives. John Piper defines worship this way:

---

7. Vos, *Biblical Theology*, 134.

> Worship is a way of gladly reflecting back to God the radiance of his worth . . . It doesn't mean making him honorable or increasing his honor. It means recognizing it and feeling the worth of it and ascribing it to him in all the ways appropriate to his character . . . In the end, the heart longs for God himself. To see him and know him and be in his presence is the soul's final feast. Beyond this, there is no quest. Words fail."[8]

We don't just glorify God on Sunday mornings, but we worship him as a lifestyle. The most comprehensive verse on giving glory to God is 1 Corinthians 10:31: "So, whether you eat or drink, or whatever you do, do all to the glory of God." If you're a student, do your schoolwork in such a way that you honor the name of the LORD. As you do the dishes or change dirty diapers or talk on the phone to a friend or stand in line in at the grocery store or confront an employee or go out on a date with your boyfriend or girlfriend, are you doing these in such a way that you honor God the Father? You display God's glory so that others can see your priority for God's reputation as encompassing every aspect of your life. Paul exhorts us in Colossians 3:17: "And whatever you do, in word or deed, do everything in the name of the Lord Jesus, giving thanks to God the Father through him." Abraham Kuyper said, "There is not a square inch in the whole domain of our human existence over which Christ, who is Sovereign over all, does not cry, Mine!"[9] Every inch of our lives should come under the sovereign rule of God. Romans 12:1 gives this instruction: "I appeal to you therefore, brothers, by the mercies of God, to present your bodies as a living sacrifice, holy and acceptable to God, which is your spiritual worship." Displaying God's glory should become so essential to your life that it's like breathing. Are you conscious that you're taking breaths right now? Displaying God's glory is the heartbeat, the very breath, of the believer as we find our ultimate satisfaction in all that God supremely is.

THE GLORY OF GOD IN EXODUS

Exodus 33:12–23 records an intimate conversation between Moses and the LORD, which I have paraphrased here. Moses says, "God, you're commanding me to lead the Israelites to the Promised Land, but you are

8. Piper, *Desiring God*, 83, 89.
9. Bratt, *Sphere Sovereignty*, 488.

only sending an angel ahead of me. In the same breath, God, you say that you know me intimately and that I have received your grace. This sounds confusing, God. Why won't you go with us! Don't just send an angel in your place. God, I'm your chosen man, and these are your chosen people!" In other words, for Moses, an angel is not good enough to lead them into the Promised Land. He will settle for nothing less than the presence of God himself to guide them.

In verse 13, Moses prays: "Now therefore, if I have found favor in your sight, please show me now your ways, that I may know you in order to find favor in your sight. Consider too that this nation is your people." He pleads for God's direction and grace in leading the Israelites. He wants to know this great God more intimately and powerfully. Paul's prayer in Philippians 3:10 resembles Moses' desire: "I want to know him and the power of his resurrection, and may share his sufferings, becoming like him in his death." That's the way we should pray: "Lord show me your ways! Reveal yourself to me through your word. I want to know you. I want to walk with you, follow you, and have my eyes opened to your working around me. I desperately need you to lead me!"

The LORD responds to Moses' request in verse 14 with a reassuring and triumphant answer: "My presence will go with you and I will give you rest." The book of Exodus never mentions the angel from this point forward because God and God alone will lead them successfully to the Promised Land. In verse 15, Moses issues a heartfelt plea and cry of desperation: "LORD, if you personally do not go with me, then do not lead us from here!" Is that your heart's desire as well? Do you want to take one step forward in faith without the presence of God in your life? Let us also not settle for anything less than the empowering and gracious presence of the Lord leading us in his mercy and power.

In Exodus 33:18, Moses makes one of the boldest requests of all time: "Please, show me your glory!" God answers Moses in 33:20-22: "'But,' he said, 'you cannot see my face, for man shall not see me and live.' And the Lord said, 'Behold, there is a place by me where you shall stand on the rock, and while my glory passes by I will put you in a cleft of the rock, and I will cover you with my hand until I have passed by.'" Because God is a consuming fire (Heb 12:28-29) of holiness that will burn away our sinful eyes, nobody can see God's face and live. First Timothy 6:16 says, "God who alone has immortality, who dwells in unapproachable light, whom no one has ever seen or can see. To him be honor and eternal dominion. Amen." C. F. Keil and Franz Delitzsch state, "As our bodily eye is dazzled and its power of vision destroyed by looking directly at the brightness of the sun, so would our whole nature be destroyed by an unveiled sight of the brilliancy of the glory of God."[10] This holy and glorious God who has the name above all names graciously places Moses in the cleft of the rock. The LORD's glory passed by as he covered Moses with his hand, only allowing him to see his backside glory, but never his face.

In this intimate encounter, God gave two amazing promises to Moses. First of all, he said that he would make all of his goodness pass before Moses; and secondly, that he would proclaim to him his unique name. God's goodness comprises his divine character in all of his holy attributes—especially in salvation. Psalm 31:19 says, "Oh, how abundant is your *goodness*, which you have stored up for those who fear you and worked for those who take refuge in you, in the sight of the children of mankind!" Isaiah 63:7 says, "I will recount the steadfast love of the LORD, the praises of the LORD, according to all that the LORD has granted us, and the great *goodness* to the house of Israel that he has granted them according to his compassion, according to the abundance of his steadfast love." Titus 3:4–6 says, "But when the *goodness* and loving kindness of God our Savior appeared, he saved us, not because of works done by us in righteousness, but according to his own mercy, by the washing of regeneration and renewal of the Holy Spirit, whom he poured out on us richly through Jesus Christ our Savior."

The CREDO

In Exodus 34:6–7, we find one of the most glorious truths in the entire Old Testament:

> The Lord passed before him and proclaimed, "The Lord, the Lord, a God merciful and gracious, slow to anger, and abounding in steadfast love and faithfulness, keeping steadfast love for thousands, forgiving iniquity and transgression and sin, but who will by no means clear the guilty, visiting the iniquity of the fathers on the children and the children's children, to the third and the fourth generation."

We can call this statement the Credo of Israel, and the Old Testament repeats these truths on numerous occasions.[11] Let's look in detail at these

---

10. Keil and Delitzsch, *Pentateuch*, 476.
11. Neh 9:17–19; Pss 86:15, 103:8, 11:4; Joel 2:12–13; Jonah 4:2.

attributes of God and let them sink into your soul. Read them and think about them as if you've never heard of these before. Imagine that this is your first time to hear about the glory of God.

The LORD is *merciful*. The imagery conveys the way a nursing mother shows compassion toward her helpless baby. In the same manner, our tender-hearted LORD reveals himself as a loving, gracious parent who looks with compassion upon us as weak and needy sinners. In our sin, we have nothing to offer God, so he condescends to our utter spiritual bankruptcy and meets us at our point of desperation.

The LORD is *gracious*. God as the sovereign King bends down to rebels who in no way deserve his love or mercy. Overwhelmed by our sin, we cry out to him for help. He doesn't owe us anything but justice, but instead he acts liberally and graciously toward us, knowing all along we can never pay him back.

The LORD is *slow to anger*. God expresses extreme patience in snorting in exasperation. He does not execute immediate justice or discipline, but shows great restraint because he has a high threshold of tolerance for our disobedience. Aren't you thankful for the endless patience of our holy God?

The LORD is abounding in *steadfast love*. This Hebrew word, *hesed*, describes God's tenacious fidelity and resolve to maintain a relationship with sinful people. Our LORD obligates and swears upon himself that he will be faithful to his covenant and promise to love his people whom he has chosen. He*sed* is the most beautiful and powerful expression of God's unfailing love for sinners in the entire Old Testament.

The LORD abounds in *faithfulness*. The image implies that God holds us in his strong arms the way a parent would hold a helpless infant. God proves trustworthy as we can count on him as a firm foundation. He is immovable as our strong tower of confidence and hope.

The LORD is a *forgiving* God. He cancels the debt against us by wiping the slate clean. He tosses our sins and rebellious actions to the bottom of the sea. God forgives our sins as far as the east meets the west. He forgives us on account of the death of Christ on the cross.

The LORD is also a *just and righteous* God. Listen to this warning. God is loving, merciful, compassionate, faithful, and forgiving, but not indiscriminately. In the end, everybody doesn't, in fact, go to heaven. God will punish the wicked. If you don't have a personal relationship with Christ whereby you have trusted him alone as Savior and Lord and have repented of your sins, you are still under God's righteous condemnation.

He treats you as Judge, not as a loving Father. When you trust Christ, God adopts you into his family, and you are an object of his eternal love. But if you die without Christ, you will experience God's wrath.

I love the parental imagery that describes God as our Father. We are helpless babies who can't offer him anything, yet God lovingly takes us in his arms, cares for us, and shows us mercy. Isaiah 40:11 describes God's fatherly love as a shepherd: "He will tend his flock like a shepherd; he will gather the lambs in his arms; he will carry them in his bosom, and gently lead those that are with young." I remember the first time I held my firstborn son. His umbilical cord was tied around his neck when he was born, so he immediately had to go to an oxygen tent for a few hours. Neither my wife nor I got to hold him directly. I reached down in the tent, and he grabbed my finger. As a concerned father, I looked down on him with compassion and tenderness, praying for him in those first few hours of his precious life. And then I got to hold him for the first time! In this beautiful moment, I understood how God treated me as his child. I realized how helpless, clueless, and powerless of a sinner I was, someone who was entirely dependent on my heavenly Father for everything. That's just a small picture of how our great God loves us. We are imperfect parents, but we still love our children. How much more does God, the perfect parent, love his children immensely?

Think about the thoughts and feelings rushing through Moses' heart after this intimate encounter with the LORD in the cleft of the rock. He had seen the backside glory of God and heard God's goodness recounted to him in this credo. In light of all this, how did Moses respond to the glory of God in his midst? Exodus 34:8 says, "Moses quickly bowed his head toward the earth and worshipped." As God revealed his powerful, unchanging, miraculous character to Moses, Moses passionately bowed in worship.

Would that be your response as well? Would you urgently and passionately bow your entire life to the great I AM who is worthy of all your worship, and glorify his name in all the earth? Let Psalm 86:8–12 be the anthem of your life:

> There is none like you among the gods, O Lord, nor are there any works like yours. All the nations you have made shall come and worship before you, O Lord, and shall glorify your name. For you are great and do wondrous things; you alone are God. Teach me your way, O LORD, that I may walk in your truth; unite my

heart to fear your name. I give thanks to you, O Lord my God,
with my whole heart, and I will glorify your name forever.

The first and most crucial step in understanding your gospel identity comes through an overwhelming sense of the weighty majesty of God's glory. The chief end of man is to glorify God and enjoy him forever!

2

The Power of Salvation— God's Gospel

"I must take counsel of the gospel. I must listen to the gospel, which teaches me, not what I ought to do, but what Jesus Christ the Son of God hath done for me . . . Most necessary it is, therefore, that we should know the gospel well, teach it unto others, and beat it into their heads continually."

MARTIN LUTHER[1]

HAVE YOU HEARD OF the phrase "Pay it Forward?" This philosophy of life teaches that if someone performs a random act of kindness on your behalf, you may not immediately be able to pay them back. Instead, you return the favor by doing a random act of kindness for someone else. It's a creative way to "pay back" the goodness done to you by being kind to someone else. A few years ago, a movement called the "Karma Experiment" formed on Facebook and rapidly grew to over 1,000,000 members in 39 countries. In their own words, it is an "international kindness community that exists to serve and support the thousands of local organizations and millions of kindness advocates throughout the world."[2]

1. Luther, *Galatians*, 72–73.
2. http://www.karmaexperiment.com/about.

This organization believes that if enough people do random acts of kindness, then the world will evolve into a utopia of peace and harmony—ushering the end of social ills that plague society. It urges people to seize each opportunity to give selflessly to others so that the world can be a better place. The Karma Experiment desires to motivate people to do random acts of kindness by promoting this "pay it forward" mentality. This concept sounds very noble. It sounds reasonable. Who doesn't want to be kind to others? Who doesn't want the world to be a better place? Who doesn't want to be selfless and giving to others in the spirit of generosity? These are wonderful virtues. But here's a huge question: Why is it called the "Karma Experiment?" What's the catch? Does anybody do an act of kindness with no strings attached? Or do they hope to receive something in return?

What exactly is karma? It's a cosmic cause and effect. If you do enough good deeds or random acts of kindness, then over time good things will come back to you. But if you do bad deeds or fail to pay it forward over time, then eventually bad things will come back to haunt you. In other words, the more you pay it forward and show kindness, the more good karma you're stacking up, so things won't go badly for you in the future.

So, this Karma Experiment does have a catch—you better do enough good deeds and pay it forward to the extreme so that positive things will come your way. If you don't, you will face bad karma in the form of future suffering. This experiment is not as selfless as it appears. It's very self-centered. The only reason people perform acts of kindness is so that they will be blessed in the future with good karma. I would venture to say that millions of people around the world fundamentally operate on this worldview. Sadly, believers in Christ are not immune to this type of philosophy. You may think this is how life works. You may even approach your relationship with God as more of a pay it forward karma experiment than what the Bible teaches. Is this approach to life truly good news? Can you truly do enough good to pay it forward? How much kindness is enough kindness to make sure you have good karma coming back to you? What if your evil deeds outweigh your good deeds? Is there any hope at all in this belief system?

I have good news for you! The gospel of Jesus Christ stands in direct opposition to this idea of karma and paying it forward. What exactly is the gospel? If I were to go out today and stop people on the streets and ask them this fundamental question: "What is the gospel?" I would get a lot of different answers. "It is a type of music that my grandmother likes!" "It's that program on TV with that crazy televangelist!" "It means to ask Jesus into your heart." "It is something church people believe." "I don't know!"

I have a burning passion: As believers in Christ, we must never lose our appreciation for, or our love and understanding of, the gospel. The gospel is central to all we are and what we do. The gospel should affect both our thinking and our behavior. It should transform our hearts and bend our wills to the lordship of Christ. Most, if not all, of the battleground in the Christian life is found in the heart and mind. If we can have our thought life permeated by an accurate and clear picture of the gospel, then we will be sustained by his powerful grace to understand our identity. If we can have our hearts softened by the beauty of Christ in the gospel, we will bow humbly in gratitude because of his amazing grace. If we can have our wills reoriented to God's radical mercy in the gospel, then we will obey him consistently in daily repentance. In other words, the gospel should affect the totality of our lives—our deepest thoughts, our most intense affections, and in presenting our bodies as living sacrifices holy and acceptable to the Lord.

The word "gospel" itself means "good news!" It is an announcement of what God has done for us in the death, burial, and resurrection of Christ. It is not simply good advice that you can take or leave. It is not a mere suggestion to help improve your life. It is not a private spiritual experience with no grounding in historical facts and truth claims. Instead, we proclaim the gospel as news. We announce the gospel. People must hear the gospel. It would be similar to the leading story on cable news or the banner ad on a website. The gospel announces a historical fact that has happened such as "The Broncos Win Super Bowl 50!" or "Gas Prices Hit All-Time Low!" or "Donald Trump Wins Presidency."

OF FIRST IMPORTANCE

Paul summarizes the heart of the gospel in 1 Corinthians 15:1–4:

> Now I would remind you, brothers, of the gospel I preached to you, which you received, in which you stand, and by which you are being saved if you hold fast to the word I preached to you—unless you believed in vain. For I delivered to you as of first importance what I also received: that Christ died for our

sins in accordance with the Scriptures, that he was buried, that he was raised on the third day in accordance with the Scriptures.

At its core, the gospel manifests itself in the historical facts surrounding the life, death, and resurrection of Jesus and it centers on the substitutionary atonement. It proclaims that Jesus died in our place, bearing God's wrath, paying the penalty for sin that we deserved so that God could forgive, cleanse, and accept us. Paul reminds us that the gospel is not only the message that we have initially received, but also in which we are currently standing. The gospel serves as the foundation that determines everything for life and godliness. The way Paul uses the verb tense in our "standing" means that we took our stand on the gospel when we first believed, and yet we are continually taking our stand on it in the present. We are to hold fast to this gospel as our bedrock confession. We regularly find our confidence in a sovereign God when standing on the solid foundation of the gospel.

When we trust Christ for salvation, we embrace him wholeheartedly with our entire lives. We surrender to his lordship. We take him as our treasure. And this is not just a one-time decision where we signed on the dotted line. True saving faith means that you continually trust in Jesus as you hold fast to him, casting yourself continually upon his mercy to save you. While the gospel is, first and foremost, a historical fact, the Bible does provide us with some rich descriptions about the multifaceted nature of the good news.

THE POWER OF GOD

Paul proclaims the potency of the gospel in Romans 1:16: "For I am not ashamed of the gospel, for it is the power of God for salvation to everyone who believes, to the Jew first and also to the Greek." Since the gospel has inherent power, there is no greater truth that we can proclaim. We need to share the whole counsel of God's word, but the primary message we need to emphasize over and over again is the gospel. We often think that once we become Christians, we are to move on to more profound teachings that will grow us in our Christian walk. We go off on tangents like creationism, or end times teachings, or parenting techniques, or some new secret that the latest and greatest book or televangelist has come up with for us to grow. These teachings in and of themselves are not inherently wrong, but actual growth and true transformation always come back to a proper understanding of the gospel.

Jerry Bridges claims that as Christians we need to preach the gospel to ourselves daily:

> Why do so many believers live in quiet desperation? The reality of present-day Christendom is that most professing Christians actually know very little of the gospel, let alone understand its implications for their day-to-day lives. My perception is that most of them know just enough gospel to get inside the door of the kingdom. They know nothing of the unsearchable riches of Christ.[3]

As Christians, we need to hear the gospel over and over again. We need to preach it to ourselves over and over again. It is our bedrock. It is our ballast in the boat of our souls that prevents us from getting off course, and protects us from the onslaughts of the world. Why do we need the stability of the gospel in our lives? Because we are prone to wander! We can all relate to the words in that famous hymn "Come Thou Fount of Every Blessing" which says:

> "O to grace how great a debtor, Daily I'm constrained to be! Let Thy goodness, like a fetter, Bind my wandering heart to Thee. Prone to wander, Lord, I feel it, Prone to leave the God I love; here's my heart, O take and seal it, Seal it for Thy courts above."

We wander into either legalism or despair. If we lose track of the gospel in our lives, we tend to drift toward the performance trap. We tend to work for God's approval and do things so that God will love us. We become legalistic. We try hard to earn God's acceptance. We feverishly run on the treadmill performing so that we somehow obligate God to love us and forgive us. The other direction we can drift or wander manifests itself in despair or condemnation. We live in fear of God as a Judge instead of a loving Father. The insecurity of guilt makes us think that God is always upset with us and that we are so bad that he could never love us. We wallow in self-loathing, thinking we don't deserve his forgiveness. We fret that we've sinned beyond his reach or that somehow we've lost our salvation. We have feelings of condemnation that lead to despair.

Both of these ditches are treacherous. The gospel centers us back to the fact that as a loving Father, God accepts us on account of Christ. We don't have to prove our worthiness to him. We obey and serve him out of

---

3. Bridges, *Gospel for Real Life*, 14–17.

gratitude and joy, not legalism or fear. And when we do sin, we cry out for forgiveness, and we rest in the finished work of Christ on our behalf to cleanse us of all unrighteousness. In other words, being gospel-centered keeps us sane! Milton Vincent encourages us with these words: "There is simply no other way to compete with the forebodings of my conscience, the condemning of my heart, and the lies of the world and the devil than to overwhelm such things with daily rehearsings of the gospel."[4]

THE VALUABLE TREASURE

Where do we see the beauty of Jesus shine most brightly? What makes us worship Jesus more fervently? The answer: when we look at him in the gospel. The gospel informs our worship and inflames our hearts to love Jesus. Second Corinthians 4:4–7 reads,

> In their case the god of this world has blinded the minds of the unbelievers, to keep them from seeing the light of the gospel of the glory of Christ, who is the image of God. For what we proclaim is not ourselves, but Jesus Christ as Lord, with ourselves as your servants for Jesus' sake. For God, who said, "Let light shine out of darkness," has shone in our hearts to give the light of the knowledge of the glory of God in the face of Jesus Christ. But we have this treasure in jars of clay, to show that the surpassing power belongs to God and not to us.

Satan, as the god of this world, has blinded the minds of unbelievers from seeing something particular—the glory of Christ in the gospel. In this spiritual battle, we have the responsibility to proclaim or preach Jesus as Lord to those enslaved to sin. When we proclaim the gospel, God does something miraculous. He opens blind eyes through the power of the Holy Spirit, which is similar to God's creative work on the first day of creation where he said, "Let there be light!" He shines the light of the gospel into the hearts of unbelievers so that they can now see the glory of Christ in the gospel. An unsaved person steeped in spiritual blindness views Jesus and his gospel as outrageously foolish. His beauty becomes a royal waste of their time. Non-Christians may view Jesus as a guru or spiritual life coach who has some practical moral teachings, but Jesus is not worthy of their absolute devotion and worship. But when God sovereignly shines that light in nonbelievers' hearts and regenerates them by

---

4. Vincent, *Gospel Primer for Christians*, 14.

causing the new birth, they miraculously see Jesus as glorious, beautiful, and worthy to be treasured. He is worth pursuing as supremely valuable (for more on regeneration, see chapter six).

Paul calls the glory of Christ in the gospel a treasure in a jar of clay. Why a vulnerable, easy-to-break earthen jar? Why are we commissioned as feeble people to carry this treasure? God has entrusted to us the most significant message—the gospel of Jesus Christ—so that when all is said and done, God alone gets the credit, and people praise his name because the surpassing power belongs to him.

Let's follow the flow of how we have described the gospel thus far. The gospel is the most important message we could ever share. There is also inherent power in the gospel. When we proclaim the gospel, this power manifests itself in God transforming sinners to embrace the glory of Jesus. God has entrusted this gospel to people like us to share with others so that in the end he gets all of the glory. As a jar of clay, would you commit to declaring God's gospel to rebel sinners as the means God uses to open their eyes and grant them forgiveness that is only found in Christ?

THE WORD OF TRUTH

Paul provides two descriptions of the trustworthiness of the gospel. In Ephesians 1:13–14, he writes, " In him you also, when you heard the word of truth, the gospel of your salvation, and believed in him, were sealed with the promised Holy Spirit, who is the guarantee of our inheritance until we acquire possession of it, to the praise of his glory." He echoes this idea in Colossians 1:5–6: "Of this you have heard before in the word of the truth, the gospel, which has come to you, as indeed in the whole world it is bearing fruit and increasing—as it also does among you, since the day you heard it and understood the grace of God in truth." The gospel is the word of truth. It is absolutely true. The death, burial, and resurrection of Jesus are undisputed historical facts that God has come down from heaven in Jesus and bought us with his blood. Notice that Paul doesn't say the gospel is true. There would be nothing wrong with that statement, but there are many things that are true. I was born in Kansas City, Missouri. I have blond hair and blue eyes. I love a sizzling New York strip steak cooked medium with French fries. These descriptions of me are true. Many things in this world are true, but they have no inherent power to save or the sovereignty of God behind them. Paul says that the gospel is the word of truth. It is the truth with a capital "T." Many people base the validity of Christianity upon their subjective feelings or sentimentality. They may claim that the gospel is true for them, but they would never force someone else to accept it as true. We must remember that the gospel of Jesus Christ presents to the world a truth claim rooted in historical facts and numerous eyewitnesses. The gospel is not merely one of many good truisms in our society, but stands as the most pivotal event in history.

LIFE

Second Timothy 1:8–10 displays a passage that should blow our minds and soften our hearts. Paul writes,

> Therefore do not be ashamed of the testimony about our Lord, nor of me his prisoner, but share in suffering for the gospel by the power of God, who saved us and called us to a holy calling, not because of our works but because of his own purpose and grace, which he gave us in Christ Jesus before the ages began, and which now has been manifested through the appearing of our Savior Christ Jesus, who abolished death and brought life and immortality to light through the gospel.

According to the Scriptures, when did you and I receive grace in Jesus? In ages past before the foundation of the world, God set his electing love upon us and chose us for salvation to receive forgiveness. The gospel of Jesus Christ abolishes death and brings eternal life. We receive ultimate life through the gospel, and not only eternal life with Jesus in heaven, but life right now here on earth by experiencing the power and presence of God himself. The gospel is lifegiving. It destroys death. It defeats sin. It crushes Satan. It culminates in eternal life with Christ.

First and foremost, the gospel is the message of the death, burial, and resurrection of Jesus in order to save us from our sins and conquer death. The gospel has power. The gospel is the truth. The gospel gives life. That's what the gospel is. Would you never get over the gospel? Would you daily mine the treasures of the gospel as food for your soul? One of the moving prayers in the Puritan book called *Valley of Vision* reads: "Holy Trinity, continue to teach me that Christ's righteousness satisfies justice and evidences your love; help me to make use of it by faith as the ground of my peace and of your favor and acceptance of me, so that I may live always near the cross."[5] Would you make it your holy ambition to always live near the cross?

To understand the gospel, we must first get the message correct. The gospel message is the good news that Jesus lived a perfect life, died in our place by shedding his blood, and was raised on the third day to bring us into a relationship with God. First Peter 3:18 reads: "For Christ also suffered once for sins, the righteous for the unrighteous, that he might bring us to God." So not only must we get the message correct, but we must also let these truths sink deep into our souls by preaching the gospel to ourselves every day. This daily reminding ourselves of the realities of the gospel will reveal to us who we truly are in Christ. Do you rejoice that you have peace with God? Do you stand in awe that God has forever removed your guilt and condemnation? Do you rely on the power of God to give you all things needed to grow in Christ? These are only available to you because of the gospel!

NOTHING MORE PRECIOUS

Listen to the passionate words of Paul in Acts 20:24: "But I do not account my life of any value nor as precious to myself, if only I may finish my course and the ministry that I received from the Lord Jesus, to testify to the gospel of the grace of God." Paul confesses that his life would be one massive waste of time if he did not testify to the gospel of grace. His burning desire was to finish the course, to complete the task, to reach the finish line, to fulfill his ultimate purpose in life. And what was that purpose? To testify to the gospel of grace.

What is the gospel of grace? Grace is the glorious truth that we deserve the full measure of God's wrath, condemnation, and eternal hell, but that in Christ, who died as our sacrifice, we receive all of God's riches, blessings, and eternal life. We cannot earn this grace. Grace isn't something that God is obligated to give us. Instead, he gives this mercy to us because of his infinite love. The gospel message declares to us God's amazing grace toward hell-deserving sinners. Because of our sin and rebellion, we deserve hell. We are guilty; not simply neutral or undeserving, but "hell-deserving" sinners. We are helpless, hopeless, and hell-bound without the sovereign grace of God in the gospel. Martyn Lloyd-Jones

---

5. "Election," 49.

said, "There is only one thing I know of that crushes me to the ground and humiliates me to dust, and that is to look at the Son of God, and especially contemplate the cross."[6] John Stott adds,

> Every time we look at the cross Christ seems to be saying, I am here because of you. It is your sin I am bearing, your curse I am suffering, your debt I am paying, your death I am dying. Nothing in history or the universe cuts us down to size like the cross. All of us have inflated views of ourselves, especially in self-righteousness, until we have visited a place called Calvary. It is there, at the foot of the cross, that we shrink to our true size.[7]

Walter Marshall gives this wisdom: "That we may receive life and strength whereby we are enabled for immediate performance, we must meditate, believing on Christ's saving benefits, as they are discovered in the gospel."[8] Would you never get over the beauty, glory, and unsearchable riches of the gospel? Would you make it a passionate priority to meditate on the majesty of Christ's saving benefits as you discover them in the gospel? You experience ultimate joy by understanding the vast depths of the good news. In the next chapter, we will explore what it means to find your gospel identity in the Trinity.

---

6. Swindoll, *So you Want to Be?*, 139.
7. Stott, *Message of Galatians*, 179.
8. Marshall, *Gospel Mystery of Sanctification*, 194.

3

Essentials of your Identity

"True saints have their minds, in the first place, inexpressibly pleased and delighted with the sweet ideas of the glorious and amiable nature of the things of God. And this is the spring of all their delights, and the cream of all their pleasures."

JONATHAN EDWARDS[1]

THE POPULAR *TRANSFORMERS* MOVIES dazzle audiences with over-the-top CGI cars and trucks converting into talking robots that engage in epic battles over the fate of the universe. If only the process of Christian transformation were that glamorous, exciting, and easy. In reality, the process of becoming more and more like Jesus may take time, may incur pain, and at times, seem like you're experiencing no growth at all. As we think about the glory of God in the gospel, our identity in Christ becomes extremely important. Paul explains this truth in Romans 8:29: "For those whom he foreknew he also predestined to be conformed to the image of his Son, in order that he might be the firstborn among many brothers." In this passage, Paul tells us that God has planned from the very beginning that he would conform his people to the image of his Son Jesus. In other words, our ultimate purpose in life is to look more and more like Jesus.

---

1. Edwards, *Religious Affections*, 103.

The word "conformed" means to "*morph*" or to "*be similar*" to Jesus. John Stott comments on this verse: "The transformation process begins here and now in our character and conduct, through the work of the Holy Spirit, but will be brought to completion only when Christ comes and we see him, and our bodies become like the body of his glory."[2] This gospel promise is not some vain hope based upon the amount of effort we put forward in our strength to somehow get ourselves to heaven. This promise does not claim that if we are faithful or obedient enough, then God will reward our energy with conformity to Christ. Instead, God sovereignly and powerfully promises to accomplish this transformation in us on account of his grace alone. John Murray gives us this confidence by stating, "God's love is not passive emotion; it is active volition, and it moves determinatively to nothing less than the highest goal conceivable for his adopted children, conformity to the image of the only-begotten Son."[3] Stop and ponder the amazing reality of God's sovereign work on your behalf! God receives ultimate glory through this promise to make you not only more and more like Jesus in the present, but he promises that you will be conformed to Christ's image on that final day and into eternity. Charles Hodge describes this conforming to Christ's image as, "more definitely that what Christ is we are to be!"[4]

You may look at your spiritual life today and question whether this can be a reality in your situation. You may be struggling in your walk with Christ. You may be frustrated with your current level of spiritual progress. You may feel internal angst that you are not growing to look more like Jesus. Here's the good news!! This passage tells us that God has made it his eternal priority to do this work of transformation in your life. This process may be long, painful, and grueling, but in the end, it will be well worth it. Our goal is to find our ultimate satisfaction and identity in knowing Christ more deeply. Rest securely in the promise from Philippians 1:6: "And I am sure of this, that he who began a good work in you will bring it to completion at the day of Jesus Christ."

---

2. Stott, *Message of Romans*, 252.
3. Murray, *Epistle to the Romans*, 318.
4. Hodge, *Romans*, 259.

LOOKING AT JESUS

Paul provides another critical verse that expounds on this idea of God conforming us to look more like Jesus. In 2 Corinthians 3:18, he writes, "And we all, with unveiled face, beholding the glory of the Lord, are being transformed into the same image from one degree of glory to another. For this comes from the Lord who is the Spirit." The major truth in this passage is this: *The more we look at Jesus, the more we will look like Jesus.* The word Paul uses for "behold" means to gaze or look into a mirror. When you spend time looking at yourself in the mirror, you go to great lengths to make sure that you don't walk out the door looking like a freight train hit you!! People in our culture spend a great deal of time looking at themselves in mirrors. In Greek mythology, Narcissus was so enamored with his beauty that he spent all his days staring at himself in a reflective pool. Narcissism occurs when you are self-absorbed, highly competitive, vain, and, fundamentally in love with yourself. Your gaze is continuously upon yourself rather than fixed on Christ alone.

Instead of looking at ourselves, Paul tells us in this passage to see the glory of the Lord—especially in the gospel. When we spend time looking at Jesus through his word and abiding in him through prayer, a beautiful thing happens to us. We begin to become transformed into his same image. The word for "transformed" is where we get our English word "metamorphosis." This verb denotes two realities: first, this process is a continual action; and second, we are passive in this process as the Holy Spirit does the work of transformation. As we continue to spend time with Jesus by looking at his glory in the gospel, we undergo this spiritual metamorphosis by the power of the Holy Spirit. We won't grow as much to look like Jesus if we don't spend the time necessary looking at Jesus. John Owen says, "One of the greatest privileges and advancements of believers, both in this world and to eternity, consists in their beholding the glory of Christ."[5] Do you believe this? One of your greatest privileges and the best way for you to advance in your spiritual growth is to gaze on the glory and beauty of Christ. It takes time. It takes adjusting priorities. It takes time reading the word and digesting its depths. It takes time praying and passionately pursuing Jesus. Our Lord taught this truth in John 15:5: "I am the vine; you are the branches. Whoever abides in me and I in him, he it is that bears much fruit, for apart from me you can do nothing."

---

5. Owen, *Glory of Christ*, 42.

We will explore this practice of spending time in the word and prayer in later chapters that discuss God's means of grace to help us grow in Christ.

GOSPEL GRAMMAR

You might think of the gospel merely as the information a non-Christian needs in order to be saved, or perhaps you see it as the entry requirements for the Christian life. Instead, the gospel is not just the entry ramp that gets us on the "Christian highway," but an intricate freeway system that spans from coast to coast. The gospel is meant to be explored and enjoyed—similar to a cross-country excursion. As believers, we need to hear the gospel preached every week as we gather on the Lord's Day for worship (see chapter ten). Listen to how Paul describes the impact of the gospel in Colossians 1:5–6: "Of this you have heard before in the word of the truth, the gospel, which has come to you, as indeed in the whole world it is bearing fruit and increasing—as it also does among you, since the day you heard it and understood the grace of God in truth." Paul wrote this letter to those who were already Christians and reminded them that the gospel was bearing fruit and growing in their lives. We need to saturate ourselves in the gospel so that we can overwhelm the temptations of this world with the glory and majesty of Christ.

A gospel-centered believer understands that who we are in Christ (identity) must come before what we do for Christ (obedience). The Bible addresses both issues. The Bible tells us who we are in Christ and what God has done for us (the gospel indicatives) and it also tells us how to obey Jesus with holy lives (moral imperatives). What happens if you're told to obey, but you're not given the basis or foundation for why and how you can obey based upon your identity in Christ? This reversing of the gospel order can lead to inflated pride on the one hand or deflating guilt on the other. You can become puffed up in thinking you can meet God's standard in your strength or you shrivel in despair thinking you can never please God. Christians can begin to believe that God merely desires behavior modification, keeping lists, and obeying rules without any connection to our dynamic relationship with Christ. The Holy Spirit changes our hearts and encourages us to obey Jesus because we want to, not because we have to. This reality has everything to do with our identity.

The gospel tells us that God accepts us on the basis of Christ's righteousness and that on our best days when we are living wonderfully holy lives and on our worst days when we are struggling with sin he does not love us any more or any less based upon our performance. On those days when you're arguing with your spouse, speeding in traffic, and getting frustrated with your dog, God does not love you less. Or on those days when you're hitting on all your spiritual cylinders and having your daily devotional time, serving at a soup kitchen, and volunteering at VBS, he does not love you more. He loves us constantly and permanently based upon Christ's performance and his finished work on the cross. When we trusted Christ for salvation, all of our sins were credited or transferred to him, and his perfect righteousness and perfect record of obedience were credited or transferred to us. Based upon what Christ alone has done, God the Father can now declare us not guilty, and permanently adopts into his family as dearly loved children. We will explore this truth called justification by faith alone in more depth in chapter five. Michael Horton gives this description:

> The gospel transforms us in heart, mind, will, and actions precisely because it is not itself a message about our transformation. Nothing that I am or that I feel, choose or do qualifies as Good News. On my best days, my experience of transformation is weak, but the gospel is an announcement of a certain state of affairs that exists because of something in God, not something in me; something that God has done, not something that I have done; the love in God's heart which he has shown in his Son, not the love in my heart that I exhibit in my relationships . . . Our only hope lies outside of us, from the God who rescues us in his Son![6]

GOSPEL IDENTITY IN THE TRINITY

Many Christians struggle with assurance of their salvation. They often wonder if God loves them less when they are struggling with sin and assume that he must love them more when they are living the victorious Christian life. Evangelicalism has been plagued by an overwhelming confusion between justification and sanctification as the grounds of our assurance, position, and acceptance in Christ. Richard Lovelace captures this sentiment:

---

6. Horton, *Gospel-Driven Life*, 77–79.

> Many have so light an apprehension of God's holiness and of the extent and guilt of their sin that they consciously see little need for justification, although below the surface of their lives they are deeply guilt-ridden and insecure . . . Few know enough to start each day with a thoroughgoing stand upon Luther's platform: you are accepted, looking outward in faith and claiming the wholly alien righteousness of Christ as the only ground for acceptance, relaxing in that quality of trust which will produce increasing sanctification as faith is active in love and gratitude.[7]

We must clearly understand how our assurance of salvation is rooted in what God alone has done for us in Christ through the power of the Spirit. In other words, our foundation for acceptance by God lies in the imputed righteousness of Christ given to us through justification; not in examining how well we are growing in holiness through progressive sanctification as the grounds for our acceptance. Many books or resources on growth in holiness focus on a deficient motivation for sanctification. In short, they leave the gospel entirely out of the discussion on spiritual growth. They encourage you as a believer to search within yourself so that you can analyze and measure your progress instead of looking by faith outside of yourself at your position in Christ as the motivation for growing in Christ.

Understanding your position in Christ (identity) and focusing on who you are concerning the Trinity will grant you more assurance because you become increasingly aware of God's riches of grace, which will give you a longer-lasting motivation to keep growing. Your position becomes more critical than your progress because it forces you to look outside of yourself to the finished work of Christ and what the Triune God has sovereignly accomplished on your behalf. In response to this amazing grace, you then joyfully live a life of worship, pursuing holiness out of gratitude to him instead of being motivated to prove your worth to him through your obedience. In other words, being (our identity) comes before doing (our obedience).

Our assurance of salvation is rooted in our gospel identity. Whenever you experience doubts, anxiety, or stress about your performance as a Christian, do not look within yourself to evaluate your acceptance by God based on your growth. Instead, by faith, look outside of yourself to Christ and find your identity in who he is and who you are in his imputed righteousness. The Reformers and Puritans differentiated between two

---

7. Lovelace, *Dynamics of Spiritual Life*, 101.

kinds of faith—a *reflective* faith that looks inward for signs of personal faithfulness, as opposed to a *direct* faith that looks outside to Christ alone as the basis for your assurance. We should not look to our level of obedience for the assurance of God's love and acceptance for us. The Bible calls us to obey the Lord faithfully, but before we get busy doing things for Jesus, we must first find comfort and assurance in the gospel as our motivation for that obedience. When you attempt to find your assurance or identity in a reflective faith that searches within for evidence of gospel growth you can become frustrated and often lose that assurance because of the sin that overwhelms you at times. We may be tempted to think that we can somehow lose our salvation, which the Bible emphatically denies.[8] We can lose our assurance of salvation. D. A. Carson defines Christian assurance as "a believer's confidence that he or she is already in a right standing with God, and that this will issue in ultimate salvation."[9] When we question our assurance, we wonder if we have placed ourselves outside of God's love. We wonder if we have done enough good works to keep ourselves in God's good graces. How do we renew or maintain our assurance in the gospel? Walter Marshall instructs us "to get your assurance, and to maintain it, and to renew it upon all occasions by the direct act of faith, by trusting assuredly on the name of the Lord, and staying yourself upon your God."[10]

Understanding the nature of saving faith also helps anchor us in our identity. John Calvin defined faith as, "A firm and certain knowledge of God's benevolence toward us, founded upon the truth of the freely given promise of Christ, both revealed to our mind and sealed upon our hearts through the Holy Spirit."[11] Calvin's understanding of the gospel affirms a Trinitarian view of our identity and faith. He focuses on God the Father's benevolence and love toward us rooted in Christ the Son's redemptive work for us graciously applied to us through the Holy Spirit. Our gospel identity is intrinsically linked to faith in the Trinitarian God. J. C. Ryle made this claim:

> I lay it down fully and broadly as God's truth, that a true Christian, a converted man, may reach such a comfortable degree of

---

8. John 10:27–30; Rom 8:35–39; 1 Cor 1:7–9; Phil 1:6; Eph 1:13–14; 1 Thess 5:23–24; 1 Pet 1:3–5, Jude 24–25

9. Carson, "Reflections on Assurance," 248.

10. Marshall, *Gospel Mystery of Sanctification*, 133.

11. Calvin, *Institutes of the Christian Religion*, 499.

faith in Christ, that in general he shall feel entirely confident as to the pardon and safety of his soul, shall seldom be troubled with doubts, seldom be distracted with fears, seldom be distressed by anxious questionings, and in short, though vexed by many an inward conflict with sin, shall look forward to death without trembling, and to judgment without dismay.[12]

Do you believe this? Can you truly be so confident in your relationship with Christ that you rest in this solid assurance of your true identity as a child of God? Charles Leiter claims, "This is the New Testament method of teaching growth in grace: 'Realize who you really are, and then be who you are.' The call to believers is not, 'Try to be who you are not,' as many Christians supposed, but rather, 'Be who you are!'"[13] Second Peter 3:18 commands us to: "Grow in the grace and knowledge of our Lord and Savior Jesus Christ." One of the ways we grow spiritually comes in comprehending our gospel identity.

CRUCIAL DEFINITIONS

To understand our fundamental Christian identity, we must possess a biblically orthodox understanding of the doctrine of the Trinity. Faulty views of the Triune God not only lead to defective worship, but also lead believers to embrace heresies which prove disastrous to real spiritual growth. Louis Berkhof defines the Trinity as such: "There is in the Divine Being but one indivisible essence; in this one Divine Being there are three persons—the Father, Son, and Holy Spirit; the whole undivided essence of God belongs equally to each of the three persons."[14] The Bible provides three foundational truths concerning the doctrine of the Trinity. If we distort or remove one of these three crucial tenets, we cease to have a biblical definition of the Trinity. We can compare this definition to an equilateral triangle; if you take one side out, it ceases to be a triangle. We can also think about a three-legged stool. If we remove one of the legs, the seat falls over and fails to support those who would sit on it. If we remove any of these three truths about the Trinity, we no longer have God as he has revealed himself in Scripture and our faith comes tumbling down with no support.

---

12. Ryle, *Holiness*, 101.
13. Leiter, *Justification and Regeneration*, 58.
14. Berkhof, *Systematic Theology*, 87–88.

Truth One: There is only one God, not a plurality of gods

The Bible teaches that God is one in essence or being. Deuteronomy 6:4–5 reads, "Hear, O Israel: The Lord our God, the Lord is one. You shall love the Lord your God with all your heart and with all your soul and with all your might." When this passage describes the LORD as "one," it means not only that God is the unique King above all other so-called gods, but that he is also the one, singular God. The LORD who reveals himself as "one" signifies his uniqueness as well as a singularity. This wording also stresses God's consistent and unchangeable nature. Numerically, there is only one God. Uniquely, there is only one God above all other gods. Sovereignly, there is only one God who alone is Creator and ruler of the universe. John Frame asserts, "God's unity, therefore, is not merely a numerical fact, but a central concern of piety. Before God's presence we confess that he alone is God."[15] Moses captures the uniqueness and power of God in Exodus 15:11: "Who is like you, O Lord, among the gods? Who is like you, majestic in holiness, awesome in glorious deeds, doing wonders?" Isaiah 45:21–22 says, "Declare and present your case; let them take counsel together! Who told this long ago? Who declared it of old? Was it not I, the Lord? And there is no other god besides me, a righteous God and a Savior; there is none besides me. Turn to me and be saved, all the ends of the earth! For I am God, and there is no other." Michael Horton says, "Personal faith without a clear understanding of the object of that faith is idolatry . . . To worship God apart from worshipping the Triune being who exists in three persons is to worship an idol."[16]

Truth Two: Three distinct persons, namely, the Father, the Son, and the Holy Spirit, share the same essence of Godhood.

John's prologue teaches this truth. John 1:1 states, "In the beginning *was* the Word, and the Word was *with* God, and the Word *was* God." John employs an imperfect past tense verb in the Greek language for "was," which means *continual action in the past*. We can translate this passage as Jesus "has always existed." There has never been a time when Jesus did

---

15. Frame, *Doctrine of God*, 625.
16. Horton, *Law of Perfect Freedom*, 53, 67.

not exist as the eternal Son. Also, Jesus, or the Word, was "with God." In other words, Jesus is not the same person as the Father. They are two distinct persons. Think about it this way: How can you be with yourself? The preposition "with" denotes two separate persons. If Jesus and the Father are the same person, then how can they be with one another? That's like saying yesterday I was with myself at the store, and we had a great time. You would think twice about my mental condition if I spoke like that. The little preposition (*pros*) that John uses for "with" conveys the idea of being face to face, or in intimate fellowship. We could also translate this as "at home with" or "close to." Jesus has always existed as the eternal Son of God and has done so in a perfect and intimate face-to-face fellowship and communion with God the Father. We do not worship many gods. We also do not worship one God who merely assumes roles. God is not playing two roles—one role of the Father and one role of the Son. That is a heresy called "modalism" where God is not distinct in three different persons, but is one God playing three different roles or exists in three different modes. The Bible teaches that there is one God who exists in three distinct persons.

We see this clearly at Jesus's baptism in Matthew 3:16–17: "And when Jesus was baptized, immediately he went up from the water, and behold, the heavens were opened to him, and he saw the Spirit of God descending like a dove and coming to rest on him; and behold, a voice from heaven said, 'This is my beloved Son, with whom I am well pleased.'" As the incarnate Son, Jesus is the only person of the Trinity who came to earth with a physical body. At his baptism, the Spirit of God descends like a dove, and then a voice from heaven calls Jesus his Son. Now unless Jesus is a fantastic ventriloquist who throws his voice, why would the Father speak to his Son from heaven if they are the same person?

Truth Three: All three persons of the Trinity are co-eternal and are co-equal

We often impose ideas on God that come from corporate America or the military, which operate with flowcharts and chains of command. The Father is not more superior than Jesus, nor is Jesus subordinate to the Father, nor is the Holy Spirit inferior to the other two persons. All three persons are co-eternal and co-equal in essence, being, and substance. In John 20:28, Thomas confesses that the risen Christ is God, which provides one of the most explicit statements on the deity of Jesus. Paul affirms in Colossians 2:9, "For in him the whole fullness of deity dwells bodily." The Father has always existed, the Son has always existed, and the Holy Spirit has always existed. Arius was a pastor in Alexandria, Egypt, in the early 300's AD who widely popularized the idea that Jesus was at one point in time created by God the Father. He argued that while Jesus is far greater than the rest of creation and has God-like qualities, he is not the eternal Son of God. The Council of Nicaea condemned his views as heresy in AD 325. His heresy is called *Arianism*. It's crucial that you as a Bible-believing Christian embrace this truth that Jesus has always existed as the eternal Son of God. He was never created. He has always existed in eternity past. The Holy Spirit has always existed and was never created. He is not some impersonal force or misty fog, but a divine person who shares all the attributes of deity. Bruce Ware summarizes,

> The Christian faith affirms that there is one and only one God, eternally existing and fully expressed in three persons, the Father, the Son, and the Holy Spirit. Each member of the Godhead is equally God, each is eternally God, and each is fully God—not three gods but three persons of the one Godhead. Each person is equal in essence as each possesses the identical same, eternal divine nature fully, yet each is also an eternal and distinct person of the one undivided divine nature.[17]

Theologians make a distinction between the ontological essence of the Trinity in relation to the economic functions of each divine person. By ontological essence, we mean that all three persons share the same being or substance as fully God. The Father, the Son, and the Holy Spirit are one or unified in being. The economic function, on the other hand, describes the activities and roles that the three persons play regarding creation, providence, and our salvation. From all eternity, the Father decided to send the Son, and the Son willingly agreed to be sent by the Father. Jesus doesn't send the Father to earth, but instead, the Father sends the Son. Also, the Son sends the Holy Spirit after his ascension back to the Father in heaven. Even though the Father, Son, and Spirit share equality and eternality in power, glory, and essence, and there is no hierarchy or subordination in their shared oneness as God (ontological essence), nevertheless, each person plays a distinct role (economic function) in how they accomplish our redemption. John Owen asserts, "Each Person of the

---

17. Ware, *Father, Son, and Holy Spirit*, 43.

Trinity was involved in this great work of salvation. The love, grace, and wisdom of the Father planned it; the love, grace, and humility of the Son purchased it; and the love, grace, and power of the Holy Spirit enabled sinners to believe and receive it."[18] In eternity past, the Father elected and predestined his people for adoption. The Son, as the incarnate God-Man, redeemed his people by dying on the cross and physically rising again with a glorified body. The Holy Spirit regenerates, seals, and indwells his people at a point in time. J. I. Packer summarizes this distinction between the ontological essence and economic function of the Trinity: "God is triune; there are within the Godhead three persons, the Father, the Son, and the Holy Ghost; and the work of salvation is one in which all three act together, the Father purposing redemption, the Son securing it, and the Spirit applying it."[19]

GRACE, LOVE, AND FELLOWSHIP

Second Corinthians 13:14 summarizes this truth about our identity in the Trinity. Paul writes, "The grace of the Lord Jesus Christ and the love of God and the fellowship of the Holy Spirit be with you all." Do you see all three persons of the Trinity in this passage? As a Christian, we have this uniquely dynamic intimacy with the Triune God. We have grace upon grace in Christ. The Father profoundly loves us. We enjoy the indwelling and sanctifying fellowship with the Holy Spirit. This Trinitarian reality defines who we are. Our feelings don't determine our identity nor what others may say about us. What God objectively says about us in his word ultimately determines who we are as Christians. We can rest assured that if we've trusted Christ for salvation, these truths define our permanent identity in the Trinity. Henry Scougal gives this insight: "We know by experience that true faith is a union of the soul with God, a real participation in the divine nature, the very image of God drawn upon the soul."[20] This statement is an amazing truth to ponder. As a believer in Christ, the Triune God has powerfully knit your soul to his in a dynamic relationship of faith.

---

18. Owen, *Holy Spirit*, 1.
19. Packer, *Knowing God*, 20.
20. Scougal, *Life of God*, 3.

In the Chronicles of Narnia series by C. S. Lewis, Aslan the lion represents Jesus. In the second book, *Prince Caspian,* Lucy engages in a dialogue with Aslan:

> *"Aslan," said Lucy "you're bigger."*
> *"That is because you are older, little one," answered he.*
> *"Not because you are?"*
> *"I am not. But every year you grow, you will find me bigger."*[21]

As we grow in understanding our identity in the Trinity, we will find our great God to be "bigger" than we ever imagined. The joyful reality is that you have experienced a change wherein the more you look at Jesus, the more you begin to become like Jesus. How we relate and interact with the Father, the Son, and the Holy Spirit impacts our Christian identity. Our understanding of the Trinity dramatically influences our understanding of the gospel itself. Fred Sanders argues, "Nothing we do as evangelicals makes sense if it is divorced from a strong experiential and doctrinal grasp of the coordinated work of Jesus and the Spirit, worked out against the horizon of the Father's love. Personal evangelism, conversational prayer, devotional Bible study, authoritative preaching, world missions, and assurance of salvation all presuppose that life in the gospel is life in communion with the Trinity."[22] In the following chapters, we will explore these beautiful truths concerning each person of the Trinity which will affect how we worship, pray, fellowship, evangelize, and find our security in the gospel. We will focus on this comprehensive statement regarding our identity and relationship with the Triune God.

We are:

> Chosen, adopted, and accepted by the Father;
> Purchased, forgiven, and righteous in the Son;
> Regenerated, indwelt, and sanctified by the Spirit.

---

21. Lewis, *Prince Caspian,* 148.
22. Sanders, *Deep Things of God,* 9.

4

Your Identity in the Father

"I believe the doctrine of election, because I am quite certain that, if God had not chosen me, I should never have chosen him; and I am sure he chose me before I was born, or else he never would have chosen me afterwards; and he must have elected me for reasons unknown to me, for I never could find any reason in myself why he should have looked upon me with special love."

CHARLES HADDON SPURGEON[1]

ALBERT EINSTEIN IS CONSIDERED one of the most brilliant men ever to live. When asked this question: "What is the most difficult thing in the world to understand?" guess what his answer was? The income tax! The Johns Hopkins magazine website provides a list of the most difficult things for humans to understand or perform. For example, Japanese is the most challenging language for Americans to learn. The most difficult math problem to solve involves using only a compass and an unmarked straightedge to divide a 60-degree angle into three equal parts. In other words, the task involves constructing a 20-degree angle with no protractors allowed. You can't do it. Scientists declare the concept of "dark matter" the most challenging mystery of astronomy to grasp. The Whipple procedure, or removal of pancreatic cancer, proves the most intricate

---

1. Spurgeon, C.H. *Spurgeon's Autobiography*, 170.

surgery to perform because the pancreas is the most deeply embedded organ in the human body. Are there some specific teachings or doctrines in the Bible that are equally difficult to understand? Theologically, the doctrine of election and predestination may be one of the most challenging teachings to discern or embrace, but this truth is crucial to finding our identity in the Trinity.

CHOSEN BY THE FATHER

One of the most profound truths that affects our gospel identity comes in the reality that the Father has sovereignly chosen us in Christ before the foundation of the world. Ephesians 1:3–6 reads,

> Blessed be the God and Father of our Lord Jesus Christ, who has blessed us in Christ with every spiritual blessing in the heavenly places, even as he chose us in him before the foundation of the world, that we should be holy and blameless before him. In love he predestined us for adoption to himself as sons through Jesus Christ, according to the purpose of his will, to the praise of his glorious grace, with which he has blessed us in the Beloved.

Throughout the Bible we see God choosing both individuals and nations. In Genesis 6, God chose Noah to build the Ark. In Genesis 12, God chose Abraham to be the father of many nations and to bless him. He chose Jacob over Esau. He chose the nation of Israel to be his treasured people. He chose David to be king of Israel. God has the sovereign right to choose based upon his will alone. Psalm 135:6 states, "Whatever the LORD pleases, he does, in heaven and on earth, in the seas and all deeps." In Isaiah 46:9–10, God emphatically states, "Remember the former things of old; for I am God, and there is no other; I am God, and there is none like me, declaring the end from the beginning and from ancient times things not yet done, saying, 'My counsel shall stand, and I will accomplish all my purpose.'" Job 42:2 states, "I know that you can do all things, and that no purpose of yours can be thwarted." The Scripture is very clear that God is sovereign and can do whatever he wants to do. No force in the universe moves God's hand or stops his plans.

In mercy, the LORD chose individuals simply because he wanted to choose them. In addressing the nation of Israel, God says in Deuteronomy 7:6–8:

> For you are a people holy to the LORD your God. The LORD your God has chosen you to be a people for his treasured possession, out of all the peoples who are on the face of the earth. It was not because you were more in number than any other people that the LORD set his love on you and chose you, for you were the fewest of all peoples, but it is because the LORD loves you and is keeping the oath that he swore to your fathers, that the LORD has brought you out with a mighty hand and redeemed you from the house of slavery, from the hand of Pharaoh, king of Egypt.

There was no merit, goodness, strength, or anything positive in Israel that moved the LORD to choose them as his people. He merely set his electing love on Israel because he was pleased to do so. We need to have this perspective when it comes to sovereign election. There is nothing positive within us that motivated God to choose us. In eternity past, God didn't look down the corridors of time and foresee anything good, worthy, or honorable in us that would prompt him to choose us as his children. He merely chose us because he wanted to choose us. Paul echoes this truth in 2 Thessalonians 2:13–14: "But we should always give thanks to God for you, brethren beloved by the Lord, because God has chosen you from the beginning for salvation through sanctification by the Spirit and faith in the truth. It was for this he called you through our gospel, that you may gain the glory of our Lord Jesus Christ."

The Timing of Election

When did this election or choosing occur? Ephesians 1:4 tells us that it was "before the foundation of the world," and 2 Thessalonians 2:13 tells us that it was "from the beginning." God made his choice before any of us were even born or he created the world. Second Timothy 1:8–9 reads, "Therefore do not be ashamed of the testimony about our Lord, nor of me his prisoner, but share in suffering for the gospel by the power of God, who saved us and called us to a holy calling, not because of our works but because of his own purpose and grace, which he gave us in Christ Jesus before the ages began." Paul affirms that God gave us grace in Christ Jesus before the ages began. This truth is just another way of saying that God's sovereign choice of his people to be saved occurred before the creation of the world. Revelation 13:8 affirms this reality: "And all who dwell on earth will worship it, everyone whose name has not been written before the foundation of the world in the book of life of the Lamb that was slain." The names of all those who would believe in Jesus as Lord have already been written down in the book of Life before the creation of the world.

In eternity past, God decided to save a massive number of people—millions upon millions (Rev 7:9–10). This unconditional election considered the total depravity of humans. Since humans are sinful and dead in transgressions, we will never make the first move toward God in saving faith. God must initiate our salvation from first to last. Jesus gives us some great insight into this doctrine of sovereign election in John 6:37–39: "All that the Father gives me will come to me, and whoever comes to me I will never cast out. For I have come down from heaven, not to do my own will but the will of him who sent me. And this is the will of him who sent me, that I should lose nothing of all that he has given me, but raise it up on the last day." Jesus makes an emphatic statement that the Father has given to him a people—his sheep or the elect. As a result of the Father's giving these people to Jesus, they will infallibly come to him in saving faith. Also, Jesus will not lose any of them nor will he ever cast them out, but he will raise them up on the last day. Jesus could not be clearer on the sovereignty of the Father in election. God graciously gives the elect to Jesus as a love gift. These and only these will most certainly come in faith to Jesus. Our Savior will permanently keep these chosen ones, and he will bring them to the completion of their salvation in heaven on the last day. This electing love of the Father giving the Son a particular people before time has historically been called the Covenant of Redemption. The Second London Baptist Confession provides a good definition of the covenant of redemption as "that eternal covenant transaction that was between the Father and the Son about the redemption of the elect."[2] Theologian Louis Berkhof explains this eternal covenant as "the agreement between the Father, giving the Son as head and Redeemer of the elect, and the Son, voluntarily taking the place of those whom the Father had given him."[3]

ADOPTED BY THE FATHER

What is the goal of this election? Ephesians 1:4–5 says that God made a choice of certain people and that he made this choice before creation—but to what end or purpose? Paul claims that the Father chose us to be

---

2. https://www.1689.com/confession.html.
3. Berkhof, *Systematic* Theology, 271.

holy and blameless before him. Election is an incredible privilege of God's mercy and grace, but there is also a responsibility and purpose behind God's choosing. God's purpose in electing us was not just to save us from the damages of sin and grant us eternal life, but his choice of us involved creating for himself a people conformed to the likeness of his Son Jesus—a treasured people to be holy and blameless.

In verse 5, Paul introduces us to God's act of predestination. You may ask: "What is the difference between election and predestination?" Election focuses on God's sovereign choice. Predestination focuses on our destiny or destination. The word "predestined" means to determine our destiny beforehand. What exactly is our future? This verse gives us our destination: to be adopted as the Father's children through Jesus Christ. The heavenly Father not only chose us but has set his eternal love on us—especially in the doctrine of adoption. What exactly is adoption? Adoption signifies our entry into a privileged position as children of the Father. Think about the staggering implications of this! Before time began, God in his infinite mercy chose you—a helpless, hopeless, and hellbound sinner—not because you were any good or had anything positive to offer God. In light of this fallen condition, he predestined us for adoption as his children. We have the glorious privilege of being sons and daughters of the living God who created the universe. J. I. Packer states, "If you want to judge how well a person understands Christianity, find out how much he makes of the thought of being God's child, and having God as his Father. If this is not the thought that prompts and controls his worship and prayers and his whole outlook on life, it means that he does not understand Christianity very well at all."[4]

Before God redeemed us, who was our "natural" father? What was our identity as sons and daughters before salvation? Paul addresses this in Ephesians 2:1–3:

> And you were dead in trespasses and sins in which you once walked, following the course of this world, following the prince of the power of the air, the spirit that is now at work in the sons of disobedience—among whom we all once lived in the passions of our flesh, carrying out the desires of the body and the mind, and were by nature children of wrath, like the rest of mankind.

This verse tells us that we were once sons of disobedience and children of wrath due to our sin. We belonged to our father the devil, the ruler of

---

4. Packer, *Knowing God*, 201.

the air. But now what has happened? God has taken us from our natural state of rebellion and sin and adopted us into his family forever! You may often hear people say that everybody in the world is God's child. Is that true? Who specifically are God's children? Only those who are in Christ by sovereign election and adoption. Only those who have trusted Christ for salvation. God created all people in his image, and they have dignity as his creation, but they are not his children. Only those who have faith in Christ are children of God. The prologue to John's Gospel affirms this truth: "But to all who did receive him, who believed in his name, he gave the right to become children of God" (John 1:12). Notice how becoming a child of God is now a "right" that we possess, which means before we believed in Jesus we had no right to be a child of God. We had no access to him, and we were under his just condemnation. But now, we have the right to become children of God. And with that privilege comes the intimacy of walking with him as our Father.

Paul describes our new status as adopted children in Galatians 3:26: "For in Christ Jesus you are all sons of God, through faith." What does it mean to be a son of God? We did not have to work for or earn this sonship, but God adopted us out of his good pleasure for us before the world even began. In that ancient culture, daughters had no rights and could not inherit property. The "son" would be the legal heir of the father's estate or wealth. Women were legally forbidden to have this status. Paul makes a radical statement that all believers in Jesus—both men and women—are legal heirs to eternal life because God has adopted us into his family. As a Christian woman, you may find being called a "son" of God a little awkward. You would think that Paul should have said we are "sons and daughters" of God. We miss the radical nature of Paul's statement concerning sonship in that ancient world that would have shocked his original audience. In both the Jewish and Roman culture of his day, one would never call women "sons of God." Here's the beauty of our adoption as "sons." Before you were "in Christ" you were under the law. You were imprisoned by sin. You were dead in your transgressions. You were in the bondage of despair with no hope of getting out. You were hopeless, helpless, and hell-bound. But through faith in Christ, God adopts you into his family with all the rights and privileges of a son—an heir.

Paul continues this line of thought concerning adoption in Galatians 4:6-7: "And because you are sons, God has sent the Spirit of his Son into our hearts, crying, 'Abba! Father!' So you are no longer a slave, but a son, and if a son, then an heir through God." On the cross, Jesus objectively, by his blood, purchased our adoption as sons as a bona fide reality. He secured for us a legal status before God as full heirs of eternal life. The Father legally adopts us because of the cross of Christ. It is an objective reality that is once and for all. Because of the pressures of the world, the flesh, and the devil, we often don't experientially feel or sense that security or assurance of God's love for us in Christ. Sometimes as adopted children, we forget our Father's love for us. We start thinking of ourselves as slaves again instead of as sons. Because of Christ's redemption, we are adopted sons of God whether we feel like or not. Romans 5:5 tells us that "hope does not put us to shame, because God's love has been poured into our hearts through the Holy Spirit who has been given to us." The Holy Spirit secures our internal subjective experience of this adoption leading us to cry out passionately "Abba!" The Holy Spirit does this internal work in our hearts to bring us assurance, comfort, and confidence to sense the overwhelming love of the Father. When you experience doubt or despair, and feel weak and overcome by sin, the Holy Spirit who lives inside of us comforts us, encourages us, and empowers us to seek the Father in prayer. Because the Holy Spirit has reminded us that we are indeed children of God, we cry out to him with this profoundly emotional response of intense joy from the recesses of our heart.

In our adoption, Jesus secures our permanent status as sons, while the Holy Spirit guarantees our daily experience of it. How does the Holy Spirit make us aware of our adoption? We can approach our heavenly Father with a freedom that comes through this affectionate, intimate, confident access we have as his children. We don't relate to God as a slave to a master, but as a son to a father. Hebrews 4:16 encourages us: "Let us then with confidence draw near to the throne of grace, that we may receive mercy and find grace to help in time of need." Rejoice in this freedom of adoption. Find satisfaction in having intimate access to the Father. Never forget that the Holy Spirit empowers you to cry out "Abba!" As our loving Shepherd, the Father loves to give good gifts to his adopted children. Jesus tells us of the heart of the Father in Matthew 7:11:: "If you then, who are evil, know how to give good gifts to your children, how much more will your Father who is in heaven give good things to those who ask him!" James 1:17 says, "Every good gift and every perfect gift is from above, coming down from the Father of lights with whom there is no variation or shadow due to change." As our Father, God lavishes us with good gifts because it flows from his very nature as a merciful God.

He has adopted us into his family, and therefore we have all the rights and privileges that come with being a child of the King.

The Basis for Election

What is the foundation behind all of God's sovereign activity in predestination and adoption? In Ephesians 1:5, Paul tells us that the Father chose us according to the purpose of his good pleasure. God took great joy in his election of sinners. This truth is staggering to me. I know that there is nothing good in me. I know that I was once dead in my sins and an enemy of God. I know that I was a child of wrath. I know that I was once blinded by Satan and enslaved to the passions of my flesh. I know that I was a rebellious, outrageous lawbreaker. To think that God took great pleasure and joy in choosing me is beyond belief or explanation. None of us can honestly explain why the Father chose us. The only answer we can give is that it is a result of God's sovereign joy and desire to do so, and in the end he merely wanted to do it for his good pleasure.

Our heavenly Father profoundly loves us as his children. Romans 5:8 captures the essence of this love: "But God shows his love for us in that while we were still sinners, Christ died for us." God did not wait for us to get our act together or clean ourselves up to save us. God did not give us the impossible task of earning our salvation through good works to redeem ourselves. Instead, he loved us while we were still ungodly and alienated sinners, and took the initiative to send Jesus to die on the cross for us. Paul continues this theme of God's great love in Ephesians 2:4–7:

> But God, being rich in mercy, because of the great love with which he loved us, even when we were dead in our trespasses, made us alive together with Christ—by grace you have been saved—and raised us up with him and seated us with him in the heavenly places in Christ Jesus, so that in the coming ages he might show the immeasurable riches of his grace in kindness toward us in Christ Jesus.

God overcame our spiritual deadness by making us alive in Christ. This new birth results from God's richness of mercy, great love, and the immeasurable riches of his grace. The apostle John describes God's love in 1 John 3:1–2: "See what kind of love the Father has given to us, that we should be called children of God; and so we are. The reason why the world does not know us is that it did not know him. Beloved, we are

God's children now, and what we will be has not yet appeared; but we know that when he appears we shall be like him, because we shall see him as he is." John begins by saying "See!" "Pay attention!" "Let this truth grip your hearts!" John wants us to stop dead in our tracks. Are you blown away that the infinite holy majestic God of the universe has loved us and adopted us as his children? This is our identity!

ACCEPTED BY THE FATHER

Not only has the Father chosen and adopted us, but he has also accepted us on account of Christ. Zephaniah 3:17 paints a beautiful picture of how the Father tenderly receives us: "The Lord your God is in your midst, a mighty one who will save; he will rejoice over you with gladness; he will quiet you by his love; he will exult over you with loud singing." The LORD made this promise to the nation of Israel during a time of intense rebellion and military oppression. This passage portrays God as a "mighty one" which conveys the image of a powerful warrior who will conquer all of our enemies. Poetically, this verse gives three ways in which God shows his fatherly compassion to his people: by *rejoicing, quieting,* and *singing*! One commentator makes this statement: "To consider Almighty God sinking in contemplations of love over a once-wretched human being can hardly be absorbed by the human mind."[5] Can you genuinely fathom how the Creator of the universe rejoices over you as his child? Do you find bedrock assurance in the truth that our Father will quiet you by his love? This Hebrew word for "quiet" can also mean that God will "renew" you with strength by granting you a sense of peace that passes understanding! This verse may be the only incident in the Bible where God himself is said actually to sing, and he bursts into joyous singing over his children!

The writings of John Owen have profoundly influenced my understanding of this Trinitarian identity. One paragraph in his book, *Communion with God: Fellowship with Father, Son, and Holy Spirit*, had a dramatic impact on me when I first read it many years ago, and it continues to resonate with me:

> So much as we see the love of God, so much shall we delight in him, and no more . . . but if the heart be once much taken up with this eminency of the Father's love, it cannot choose but to

---

5. Barker, *New American Commentary*, 497.

be overpowered, conquered, and endeared to him . . . Exercise your thoughts upon the eternal, free, and fruitful love of the Father, and when you do this, you will find that your heart is wrapped up in delight for him . . . Sit down a little at the fountain, and you will quickly discover the sweetness of the streams. You who have run from him, will not be able to keep a distance from him for a moment.[6]

I love his imagery! He calls us to sit down with God by spending quality time in his presence to be overwhelmed by his love. Draw near to him, and he will draw near to you! And when you draw near and sit at the fountain of his love, you experience a sweetness in his presence. You won't want to run away anymore. You won't want to hide from God, become distracted by the world, or experience feelings of guilt and defeat. You will not be able to keep your distance from him at all because his love has overpowered your heart and you desperately want to bask in his breathtaking affection for you in Christ. This is the greatest mystery in the universe, that the sovereign God in all of his blazing holiness, perfect righteousness, and sovereign power would dare save sinners such as you and me! This love is grace unknown. It is unthinkable. It is unimaginable. It is a love beyond degree. What is our identity in the Father? We are chosen, adopted, and accepted by the Father.

OUR JOYFUL RESPONSE

Since we are chosen, adopted, and accepted by the Father, how then should we respond to the Father? What should these truths produce in us as adopted, chosen, predestined children who were once his enemies and children of wrath? Praise! That's why Paul erupts with worship in Ephesians 1:6: "to the praise of his glorious grace!" Sovereign election should result in praise for God's grace. How does Paul describe this grace? He calls God's grace "glorious!" Sovereign grace reflects the Father's full glory, which shone brightly when he chose to save rebel sinners by electing them before the foundation of the world, predestining them to be adopted children, and lavishing them with inexhaustible love.

---

6. Owen, *Communion with God*, 69.

Our identity in the Father produces a deep humility

The LORD wasn't forced to choose us. He didn't have to love us. If he had not selected anybody for salvation, he would still be just and righteous. We could never lay a claim against God that he was unjust if he chose not to save anybody because all of us deserve hell. We are the worst of sinners who only deserve wrath. So, we should never go around boasting about our election. We should never take our election for granted because God was never obligated to give us grace in the first place. This mercy should drive us to our knees in humility. It should make us humbly praise God for his glorious grace. Galatians 6:14 gives us this attitude: "But far be it from me to boast except in the cross of our Lord Jesus Christ, by which the world has been crucified to me, and I to the world." God's grace in election should never lead us to arrogance or an air of superiority that somehow, we are worthier than others to receive salvation. We should never believe that somehow, God has given us some special treatment because of something innate within us. Instead, from first to last, God elected us as a free gift of grace. Our loving Father was under no obligation to shower us with mercy. Our joyful response should overflow with deep humility.

Our identity in the Father produces assurance of salvation

Since God determined in eternity past to save us infallibly by his unthwartable purpose, he assures us that we will never lose our salvation or fall away from this state of grace. Why would God go to great lengths from before time to elect us, adopt us, send Christ to die for us, and send the Holy Spirit to live in us, just to let us falter and leave it up to us as the final determiner of our eternal salvation? The Father's eternal decree to rescue us from sin should give us the solid confidence that he will continue in both the present and the future to keep us saved. God's eternal, immutable love for us serves as the basis of our assurance. D. A. Carson explains,

> God's love does not function exactly like ours. How could it? God's love emanates from an infinite Being whose perfections are immutable . . . God does not 'fall in love' with the elect; he

does not 'fall in love' with us, he sets his affection on us. He does not predestine us out of some stern whimsy; rather in love, he predestines us to be adopted as his sons.[7]

Theodora Beza wrote, "The love that is in God is no passion arising of some good that it apprehends, but it is the very simple essence of God . . . The cause of that love of his, is not in the creatures, as though they were such as could allure God to love them, but it is rather in God, who of himself is good, and pours goodness upon his creatures."[8] God's love for us never changes or fluctuates. Geerhardus Vos made this powerful statement: "The reason God will never stop loving you is that he never began."[9] The LORD reassures us in Jeremiah 31:3, "I have loved you with an everlasting love; therefore I have continued my faithfulness to you."

Our identity in the Father produces a desire for holiness

An unbalanced or hyper view of God's sovereignty in election may lead us to believe that we can engage in a lifestyle of rebellion and disobedience because God will automatically forgive us and doesn't care about how we live. Remember the truth that we have been chosen to be holy and blameless in Christ. The doctrine of election is not a license for us to live in blatant sin against God's law, because "after all, I'm elect and God's going to save me no matter how I live." This notion reflects pagan fatalism and not Christianity. You demonstrate evidence of your election by growing in holiness with a life that is pleasing to the Father. First Peter 1:15–16 instructs us, "But as he who called you is holy, you also be holy in all your conduct, since it is written, 'You shall be holy, for I am holy.'" Hebrews 12:14 also admonishes us: "Strive for peace with everyone, and for the holiness without which no one will see the Lord." Our identity fuels our obedience. Our election serves as the impetus for our practice of godliness.

---

7. Carson, *Difficult Doctrine*, 60–61.
8. Beza, in Renihan, *God without Passions*, 69.
9. Vos, *Redemptive history and Biblical Interpretation*, 298.

Our identity in the Father leads us to seek his glory above all

Jesus gave us the Greatest Commandment in Mark 12:28–30:

> And one of the scribes came up and heard them disputing with one another, and seeing that he answered them well, asked him, "Which commandment is the most important of all?" Jesus answered, "The most important is, 'Hear, O Israel: The Lord our God, the Lord is one. And you shall love the Lord your God with all your heart and with all your soul and with all your mind and with all your strength.'"

This commandment involves loving God with the totality of our lives. Since he first loved us, the Father frees us by grace to respond to his love for us with a reciprocal love for him. Because God is a gracious Father who has chosen, loved, and accepted us, we passionately love him back. Our greatest desire in life should be to love God. First John 4:10 says, "In this is love, not that we have loved God but that he loved us and sent his Son to be the propitiation for our sins."

God commands us to love him without equivocation and to seek his glory above all else. Everything comes back to the glory of God. Remember from chapter one that God is first and foremost interested in himself. That may sound abnormally foreign to our self-centered psyches, but God cares most about his glory alone, and he will not share it with anyone else (Isa 42:8). Since God is majestically sovereign, he has chosen us, adopted us, and accepted us. In turn, we pursue his glory above all else as our ultimate desire in life (1 Cor 10:31; Col 3:17). As transformed believers who find our identity in this beautiful relationship to the Father, everything in our thoughts, words, and deeds should redound to the glory of God. Are you passionately seeking the glory of God? Have you lost that child-like wonder and awe for the Father? Does your life's passion consist in making much of him instead of making much of yourself? Are you daily amazed and assured by the glorious truth that you are chosen, adopted, and accepted by the Father? You discover your gospel identity by understanding your privileged status in the Father! Rest securely in that permanent position!

5

Your Identity in the Son

"Behold, the Lamb of God, who takes away the sin of the world!"
JOHN THE BAPTIST IN JOHN 1:29

IN A WONDERFUL SCENE toward the end of John Bunyan's book *The Pilgrim's Progress*, the two main characters, Christian and Hopeful, have just escaped Doubting Castle where Giant Despair brutalized them and left them for dead. Christian is at the point of committing suicide when he remembers that he has a key called Promise that will get him out of this terrible prison. After an intense period of struggle, they travel to the Delectable Mountains where the four Shepherds refresh them. The Shepherds lead the two men to the top of the mountains to a spot called Clear and give Christian what is called a Perspective Glass so that he can see the Celestial City off in the distance. Peering through the glass, they see the gate to the city and the glory of heaven. As a result of seeing their future home in heaven with Jesus, they go on their way joyously singing.

Having a clear view of our future is rather compelling. I wonder how often you think about heaven and the anticipation of one day seeing Jesus face to face? My prayer for you in this chapter is that you would take the time to see Jesus for who he is. I pray that the Holy Spirit would give you eyes to see the majesty of Jesus in all of his splendor; and that by truly seeing him, your hearts will be inflamed with both worship and obedience. Are you prepared to behold the Lamb of God who takes away your sins? What is our identity in Jesus? *We are purchased, forgiven, and righteous in the Son.* John Owen writes this:

> Many love this world too well, and have their minds too much filled with the things of it, to entertain our desires of speeding through it to a state in which they may behold the glory of Christ . . . hence perplexing fears, vain hopes, carnal designs, cursed, self-pleasing imaginations, feeding on, and being fed by the love of the world and self, do abide and prevail in them. But we have not so learned Christ Jesus.[1]

Have you "learned Christ Jesus?" We desperately need to learn more about our identity in Jesus the Son. What has our glorious Savior accomplished for us in our gospel identity?

PURCHASED BY JESUS

Hundreds of years before the death of Christ, the prophet Isaiah graphically depicted his sufferings on the cross: "All we like sheep have gone astray; we have turned—every one—to his own way; and the Lord has laid on him the iniquity of us all" (Isa 53:6). This passage describes the total depravity of humans who have rebelled in our sin as well as the substitutionary atonement of Christ in our place. In 2 Corinthians 5:21, Paul expresses this unfathomable truth as well: "For our sake he made him to be sin who knew no sin, so that in him we might become the righteousness of God." We find the key to understanding what it means to be purchased by Jesus in the prepositional phrase "for our sake." The little preposition is *hyper* in the Greek, which means "in the place of or as a substitute for." The gospel proclaims that Jesus died *in place* of sinners as our sacrificial substitute. Paul also describes how Jesus purchased us for himself in Galatian 3:13: "Christ redeemed us from the curse of the law by becoming a curse for us—for it the is written, "Cursed is everyone who is hanged on a tree." What does it mean that Jesus redeemed us from the curse by becoming a curse for us? Paul does not say Christ was simply cursed, but notice carefully that he says Christ "became" a curse.

How can the sinless, spotless Jesus, as the Lamb of God, become a curse on our behalf? Let us begin by stating what it does not mean. It doesn't mean that Jesus became a sinner. Jesus was absolutely perfect in thought, word, and deed, and obeyed his Father completely. Hebrews

---

1. Owen, *Glory of Christ*, 187.

4:15 affirms this truth: "For we do not have a high priest who is unable to sympathize with our weaknesses, but one who in every respect has been tempted as we are, yet without sin." His sinless perfection qualified him to go to the cross for us as a one-of-a-kind substitute. When Paul says that Jesus became sin, it means that our sins were imputed or credited to Christ so that at the moment he hung on that cross, God treated him as if he were a sinner in our place. Matthew 27:45–46 describes the spiritual torment Jesus suffered on the cross: "Now from the sixth hour there was darkness over all the land until the ninth hour. And about the ninth hour Jesus cried out with a loud voice, saying, '*Eli, Eli, lema sabachthani?*' that is, 'My God, my God, why have you forsaken me?'" What does it mean that the Father abandoned the Son? In those three hours of darkness, Jesus bore the full brunt of God's wrath against us for our sins. Jesus felt the tremendous weight of being a curse because the Father imputed or credited to him our sins as if he committed the transgressions we committed. This is staggering because Jesus never once sinned. As he bore our transgressions and paid the penalty of the Father's justice, God treated Jesus as a sinner in our place.

Wrath Removed

How do we comprehend this idea that God expresses wrath against our sin? Jesus gave a dire warning for those who would reject him in unbelief and die in their sins in John 3:36, saying, "Whoever believes in the Son has eternal life; whoever does not obey the Son shall not see life, but the wrath of God remains on him." Our Lord assumes that before we place our faith in him, the wrath of God abides or remains on all people. J. I. Packer gives one of the best definitions: "God's wrath is not the capricious, arbitrary, bad-tempered, and conceited anger that pagans attribute to their gods. It is not the sinful, resentful, malicious, infantile anger that we find among humans. It is a function of that holiness which is expressed in the demands of God's moral law . . . it is a righteous anger."[2] God must respond in anger to the breaking of his law. He can't just brush our sin under the carpet and give it a little wink! He has to punish our evil. He did this in Christ! Jesus stood in our place as a substitute in that God treated him as condemned––not because of his own sin, but because of our wicked infractions perpetrated against a holy God. Theologically, we

---

2. Packer and Dever, *In My Place*, 35.

call this propitiation, which involves the turning aside from or appeasing of God's wrath. While on the cross, Jesus experienced the full justice of God in his body against our sin by absorbing God's righteous anger against sin. Listen to how Martyn Lloyd-Jones describes propitiation:

> On the cross, God did not spare his Son any of the punishment. He did not say, because he is my Son, I will modify the punishment. I will hold back a little; I cannot do that to my own Son. I cannot regard him as a sinner. I cannot smite him; I cannot strike him. He did not say that! He did everything he had said he would do. He poured out all his divine wrath upon sin, upon his own dearly beloved Son.[3]

First Peter 2:24 describes how Jesus bore this penalty on the cross: "He himself bore our sins in his body on the tree, that we might die to sin and live to righteousness. By his wounds you have been healed." Martin Luther comments on what it meant for Jesus to "become a curse" for us:

> Being made a sacrifice for our sins he is not now as an innocent person without sins, but a sinner who carries the sins of Paul, who was a blasphemer, Peter who denied Christ, of David, who was an adulterer and murderer . . . It was not he himself who committed these sins, but he received the sins that we had committed; they were laid on his own body, that he might make satisfaction for them with his own blood . . . In short, our sin had to become Christ's own sin, or else we will perish forever.[4]

Since God's law requires impeccable obedience, Jesus, as the perfect God-Man, was the only one qualified to take our place and satisfy the payment for our sin. John Calvin said this, "When we behold the disfigurement of the Son of God, when we find ourselves appalled by his marred appearance, we need to reckon afresh that it is upon ourselves we gaze, for he stood in our place."[5] God will exercise his wrath in one of two ways. The first way comes in Jesus bearing that wrath in our place as a substitute. Since we are united to Christ by faith, we are spared God's wrath, as Romans 8:32 states, "He who did not spare his own Son but gave him up for us all, how will he not also with him graciously give us all things?" The second way God expresses his wrath is eternal hell where unbelievers receive the due punishment for their rebellion. All praise and glory belong

---

3. Lloyd-Jones, *Cross*, 81.
4. Luther, *Galatians*, 151–52.
5. Calvin, in Mahaney, *Living the Cross Centered Life*, 53.

to Jesus who experienced being forsaken by God so that we would never have to suffer the abandonment and wrath that we rightfully deserve.

In Galatians 3:13, Paul introduces the word "redeemed," which leads us to ask another question: What does it mean for Christ to redeem us from the curse? The word "redeem" or "redemption" comes from the marketplace of Paul's day where people traded slaves. To redeem means to buy someone out of slavery with a ransom price. We were all in spiritual bondage to sin and Satan, and powerless to release ourselves from this prison. Jesus paid for us with his precious blood buying us out of bondage and welcoming us into his family. First Peter 1:18–19 explains this redemption: "Knowing that you were ransomed from the futile ways inherited from your forefathers, not with perishable things such as silver or gold, but with the precious blood of Christ, like that of a lamb without blemish or spot." Because of Jesus' death on the cross in your place, he bought you out of spiritual bondage and liberated you from the devastating curse of sin and guilt.

I want you to think about two trees for a moment. In the garden of Eden, Adam and Eve disobeyed God and ate from the tree of the knowledge of good and evil. What resulted from eating from this tree? A universal curse on all creation. Adam and Eve were separated from God, guilty, and deserving of punishment. By eating from the first tree, the curse of sin came into the world and has infected us all with spiritual deadness, depravity, and rebellion against God, which renders us guilty before him and deserving of full punishment. Romans 5:12 recounts the tragic consequences of Adam's cosmic trespass: "Therefore, just as sin came into the world through one man, and death through sin, and so death spread to all men because all sinned."

Now think about the second tree—the old rugged cross. When Jesus hung from the second tree, he reversed the curse that came into the world from the first tree. Jesus is the Second Adam who overturned what the first Adam did. Jesus lived a perfect life and died a sinner's death in our place by becoming a curse for us. Jesus overturned the cosmic consequences that have defiled all of us from the curse of the first tree in the garden of Eden by becoming a curse for us on the second tree called Calvary. In Romans 5:17, Paul further explains this truth: "For if, because of one man's trespass, death reigned through that one man, much more will those who receive the abundance of grace and the free gift of righteousness reign in life through the one man Jesus Christ." George Smeaton provides this insight: "The Lord descended into the lowest abyss of that curse which we had incurred, and tasted death, the penalty of sin, so that we might never taste of it ourselves."[6] The Son has purchased us out of slavery to sin and has given us a new identity as blood-bought children of the Father.

FORGIVEN BY JESUS

The movie *Bella*, set in New York City, tells the story of a star soccer player named Jose. As he drives home one afternoon celebrating his victory, he accidentally hits a little girl who dies immediately on impact. Jose, crushed with grief and guilt, tries for years to find the mother of the child and beg her forgiveness. When he finally has the opportunity to ask her forgiveness, she refuses, leaving Jose as a shell of a man. Jose eventually meets Nina, a pregnant young woman who works as a waitress at his brother's restaurant. As a single woman struggling with the thought of bringing a child into the world, she contemplates having an abortion. By the end of the movie, Jose talks her out of having an abortion, adopts her baby, and the end credits show them as a new family enjoying a day at the beach. This adoption is Jose's way of dealing with the guilt of killing the little girl. He doesn't want another child to be killed, so he does everything in his power to stop Nina from having an abortion.

This film demonstrates the crippling and agonizing effect guilt can have on us when we sin. Many of us struggle with extreme guilt. We may feel guilty for not spending enough time with our spouse. We may feel guilty for how we have treated our children when they disobeyed us. We may feel guilty for a habitual sin that we can't shake. We may not even know why we experience these feelings of guilt, but they are there deep inside of us. This guilt haunts us. It never lets us sleep. And maybe we even get to the point where this guilt cripples us. We not only have feelings of guilt, but the Scripture is very clear that before we were Christians, we all stood guilty and condemned before God as lawbreakers. Not only do we feel guilty, but without Christ, a death sentence hangs over our heads that loudly pronounces us as objectively guilty. The effects of guilt prove devastating. As condemned sinners, we desperately need to hear the good news that Jesus can forgive the greatest of sinners. John Owen proves extremely helpful in helping us understand how our assurance of salvation and identity comes in Christ's forgiveness: "Faith's discovery of

---

6. Smeaton, *Apostles' Doctrine of the Atonement*, 257.

forgiveness in God is the great encouragement of a sin-perplexed soul."[7] The second aspect of our gospel identity comes in realizing that God entirely forgives us in the Son.

The Ultimate Denial

Have you ever wondered what the difference was between Judas, who committed suicide after betraying Jesus for thirty silver pieces, and Peter, who denied Jesus three times? Judas never repented. He loved his silver and his sin more than he loved Jesus. Judas may have said all the right things, fooled all the other disciples, and looked very religious, but fundamentally he did not love Jesus. On the other hand, Peter repented with godly grief, confessed his love for Jesus, and was restored by God's amazing grace. We see this restoration of Peter in John 21:15–17,

> When they had finished breakfast, Jesus said to Simon Peter, "Simon, son of John, do you love me more than these?" He said to him, "Yes, Lord; you know that I love you." He said to him, "Feed my lambs." He said to him a second time, "Simon, son of John, do you love me?" He said to him, "Yes, Lord; you know that I love you." He said to him, "Tend my sheep." He said to him the third time, "Simon, son of John, do you love me?" Peter was grieved because he said to him the third time, "Do you love me?" and he said to him, "Lord, you know everything; you know that I love you." Jesus said to him, "Feed my sheep."

This scene takes place as the disciples are eating fish and bread around a charcoal fire. What else happened around a charcoal fire? We find the answer in John 18:18: "Now the servants and officers had made a charcoal fire, because it was cold, and they were standing and warming themselves. Peter also was with them, standing and warming himself." It was the very spot where Peter cussed angrily that he did not know Jesus as the rooster crowed. Jesus asks Peter the ten-million-dollar question: "Do you love me more than these?" In a sense, Jesus asks, "How does your love surpass the love of these other disciples? How does your love for me compare to these guys who did not publicly deny me three times? Peter, what exactly is the intensity of your love for me in comparison to these other men?" How can Peter accurately answer this question after his denial of Jesus three times? What can he say? What did Peter say about his

---

7. Owen, in Ferguson, *John Owen on the Christian Life*, 100.

love and commitment to Jesus before the cross? What does Peter pledge to Jesus? I will follow you to the death! I will lay down my life for you! I will never abandon you or deny you! I don't know about the rest of these guys, but I can prove my love for you is greater than theirs is! I will die for you, Jesus! Peter answered Jesus in Matthew 26:33–35, "'Though they all fall away because of you, I will never fall away.' Jesus said to him, 'Truly, I tell you, this very night, before the rooster crows, you will deny me three times.' Peter said to him, 'Even if I must die with you, I will not deny you!' And all the disciples said the same."

He was a self-sufficient, zealous, immature man who was always comparing his love with the other disciples to outdo them in terms of his passionate commitment to Jesus. Peter bragged that he was more on fire for Jesus than these guys. Peter had a pretty high opinion of himself, and Jesus confronts this attitude head on. Beware of comparing your spiritual commitment to others as it leads to legalism and pride. This often happens with young, immature Christians who think that once they get saved, they will never struggle with sin, will never fail, and always be absolutely committed to Jesus. They have this unrealistic view of sin and often compare their level of commitment to others.

After his failure in denying Jesus, Peter can't compare himself to these other disciples because they did not deny Jesus three times. They didn't sin as grievously as he did. They didn't face plant publicly like Peter. Peter cannot appeal this time to his prideful zeal, self-sufficiency, and commitment with all the other guys staring right at him. He's been humbled. He's been through the fire of guilt, conviction, and brokenness. Notice how Peter does not answer the question. He doesn't compare his love to these other disciples. He merely says, "Lord, you know that I love you." Period—not more than these or less than these. Peter is a changed man. The three denials have humbled him. This miserable failure has transformed him. He has gone from a prideful, overzealous, overconfident, passionate man who fell hard into sin, to a humbled, broken, and contrite man who cannot appeal to his level of commitment or compare himself to the others.

Jesus' three questions are in relation to Peter's three denials. On the last time, Peter is grieved—he's cut to the heart—he's broken because Jesus has asked him three times. To what does Peter appeal? He can only submit himself to the sovereign knowledge of Jesus who knew all things. Jesus knew what was in Peter's heart. Peter again can't appeal to his efforts, his past resume, or his track record. All he can do is to appeal to

Jesus' knowledge of all things. When you sin grievously and stand guilty before a holy God, all you can do is cast yourself at his mercy and trust in his amazing grace to save you. You are brokenhearted, humbled, and you dare not appeal to your resume or stellar record of past faithfulness. God does not accept you based on your faithfulness but forgives you on account of Christ's work on the cross.

Based upon Peter's answer, Jesus graciously restores him to public ministry in front of these disciples and tells Peter to shepherd his people. How would Peter do this? What's the rest of the story for Peter? Does he go down as the man who denied Jesus three times, sealing his fate as the greatest failure in human history? No, Peter was forgiven. Humbled by amazing grace, Peter would preach the first Christian sermon at Pentecost, see the power of the Holy Spirit show up, and 3,000 people repent and trust in Jesus. He would share the gospel with Cornelius who became the first Gentile convert in Acts. He would write 1 and 2 Peter, and also serve as the major source of material for Mark's Gospel. He would feed the flock through teaching, preaching, loving, and ministering to God's people. The restoration of Peter serves as a powerful illustration of how Jesus forgives sinners.

Being forgiven in the Son should result in deep, inner joy that stirs your affections for Jesus because he's saved you by amazing grace. Like Peter, Christ has cleansed and transformed you by his mercy. Hebrews 7:25 says, "Consequently, he is able to save to the uttermost those who draw near to God through him, since he always lives to make intercession for them." This word "uttermost" means "completely, forever, absolutely, once and for all." Think about the implications of this! Jesus saves us absolutely and to the uttermost from all our sins, all our weaknesses, all of our trials, all of our temptations, death itself, and final judgment. Because he is the resurrected Christ who is exalted and enthroned in heaven, he is always living to make intercession for you. Romans 8:34 gives us this assurance: "Who is to condemn? Christ Jesus is the one who died—more than that, who was raised—who is at the right hand of God, who indeed is interceding for us." F. F. Bruce said, "His once-completed self-offering is utterly acceptable and efficacious; his contact with the Father is immediate and unbroken; his priestly ministry on his people's behalf is never ending, and therefore the salvation which he secures to them is absolute."[8]

---

8. Bruce, *Epistle to the Hebrews*, 175.

RIGHTEOUS IN JESUS

J. I. Packer calls justification by faith the "storm center of the Reformation."[9] Charles Spurgeon went so far as to say: "Any church which puts in the place of justification by faith in Christ another method of salvation is a harlot church."[10] Paul articulates the glory of what it means to be counted righteous in Jesus in Romans 3:21–26:

> But now the righteousness of God has been manifested apart from the law, although the Law and the Prophets bear witness to it—the righteousness of God through faith in Jesus Christ for all who believe. For there is no distinction: for all have sinned and fall short of the glory of God, and are justified by his grace as a gift, through the redemption that is in Christ Jesus, whom God put forward as a propitiation by his blood, to be received by faith. This was to show God's righteousness, because in his divine forbearance he had passed over former sins. It was to show his righteousness at the present time, so that he might be just and the justifier of the one who has faith in Jesus.

Martyn Lloyd-Jones called this passage the "Acropolis of the Bible and the Christian faith."[11] What kind of righteousness is this? Paul tells us what kind of righteousness it is not. It is not righteousness based upon doing good or through perfect obedience to the Ten Commandments or church attendance or anything that we can do in our strength to somehow make ourselves right with God. Isaiah 64:6 says, "We have all become like one who is unclean, and all our righteous deeds are like a polluted garment. We all fade like a leaf, and our iniquities, like the wind, take us away." So then what kind of righteousness is it? It is imputed righteousness or outside righteousness that God credits or reckons to us. The third description of our new identity is that we are righteous in the Son.

The Need for Justification

In Romans 3:23, Paul describes our depravity by stating that we "fall short" of God's glory. We can translate this word, in the present tense, as we are constantly, as a condition, falling short of God's glory. The phrase

---

9. Packer, *Concise Theology*, 164.
10. Spurgeon, *Spurgeon at his Best*, 116.
11. Lloyd-Jones, *Romans*, 65.

"fall short" means to "lack or to be deprived of." In essence, due to our nature as sinners, we are continually lacking, falling short, or being deprived of God's glory. Paul emphasizes the insidious nature of sin as an offense to God's glory, as it is a failure to praise him for who he is in all of his majesty and beauty. Every single person is born dead in sin and by nature continuously exhibits a lifestyle of sin that at its core is a failure to glorify God. We are idolaters who have exchanged the glory of God for a lie (Rom 1:18–32). We can't produce enough positive righteousness to be acceptable in God's sight or to deal adequately with the seriousness of our sin. We need alien righteousness which comes not from within us as sinners, but from outside of us as a gift of God's grace.

The Definition of Justification

The original language is important here for understanding the depth of this issue. In verse 22, this righteousness comes "from" God, which denotes that he alone is the source of this righteousness. As sinners, we cannot produce this righteousness in and of ourselves. The righteousness that the Father requires is not inherent in us. The cause of this justification—God's declaring us righteous or having the imputed righteousness of Christ—must come from God alone, who grants it to us as a gift of grace. What exactly does "justified" mean? The word comes from both the legal as well as the banking world. It means to declare that somebody is in the right. God as the Judge of the universe renders a positive verdict to sinners that gives us a new standing as not guilty. Before the bar of God's justice, we stood condemned with a negative balance of sin in our spiritual bank account. We could never do enough good to get ourselves out of this enormous debt. We needed the accounting and the positive balance of Christ deposited into our account. When we believed in Jesus for salvation, all of our sins were credited or imputed to Christ's account, and God credited his perfect righteousness to our account. Because of this transaction, God the Judge can now look down on our life, and he sees our sins attributed to Jesus and Jesus' perfect righteousness imputed to us. As a result, the Father makes a legal verdict or declaration that we are righteous. We stand accepted in a permanent new position. Romans 3:24 describes us as "justified by his grace as a gift" which is a one-time action; not a process, but a unique event. The moment we trust Christ for salvation, the Father permanently justifies us. In this new status, God treats us not only as if we had never sinned, but also as if we had perfectly lived the life of righteousness that Jesus lived.

Historically, justification by faith has been a called a "great exchange." Question 60 of *The Heidelberg Catechism* beautifully describes our identity as being righteous in the Son:

> *Question: How are you right with God?*
>
> Answer: Only by true faith in Jesus Christ. Even though my conscience accuses me of having grievously sinned against all God's commandments and of never having kept any of them, and even though I am still inclined toward all evil, nevertheless, without my deserving it at all, out of sheer grace, God grants and credits to me the perfect satisfaction, righteousness, and holiness of Christ, as if I had never sinned nor been a sinner, as if I had been as perfectly obedient as Christ was obedient for me. All I need to do is to accept this gift of God with a believing heart.

The Means of Justification

How does God impute or credit the righteousness of Christ to you? How are you justified? The answer: By faith alone in Christ alone. Faith is the instrument, not the grounds, of our justification. God justifies us by the merits of Christ, not by the exercise of our faith. We must understand this carefully. You and I need to place our trust in Jesus for salvation; yet our faith is not what counts us righteous before God. Instead, the righteousness of Christ imputed to us counts us righteous before God. Saving faith is the means or instrument by which we get united to Christ in salvation, but faith is not the grounds or foundation of our right standing with God—only Christ is.

What is this saving faith? Sometimes we as Christians focus more on the quality of our faith than on the object of our faith. In other words, we substitute the word "faithful" for "faith." We often wonder how strong, intense, or radical our faith is regarding its quality. Is my faith good enough or powerful enough to keep me saved? Do I even have enough faith, and if so, how much faith is enough? We think of faith more like a substance that we can measure rather than as receiving and resting in Christ alone as the object of our faith. You can have weak faith and still be justified. We are not justified based on the level of our faith, but on the one-time declaration the Father made that secures our position on account of the righteousness of Christ. I want you to picture in your mind two bridges that go across a canyon. The first is an old, wooden, rickety bridge. As you stand there, you have confidence in your ability to cross the bridge if you're careful. You measure the quality of your faith and step out boldly on a weak bridge hoping it will keep you from plunging to your death. The second bridge is solid concrete. As you stand there before it, your fear of heights overwhelms you as you cautiously step out with fear and trembling. In the first bridge scenario, the focus was on the quality of your faith, not the strength of the bridge. In the second scenario, you may have weak faith but can have confidence that the bridge will hold you up; not your faith. It's not the quality of your faith but the trustworthiness of the bridge. Justification by faith is not measured by the quality of our faith or the intensity or degree of our faithfulness or how well we repent or how much we truly trust in Jesus. The object of our faith is what is of utmost importance, and that is Jesus Christ alone. We must remember that the faith itself that we exercised when we trusted in Christ for salvation was in and of itself a gracious gift of God (Eph 2:8–9; Phil 1:29). Faith is a receiving and resting in Jesus personally, and what he accomplished in his death, burial, and resurrection.

The Benefits of Justification

What benefits do we receive from our justification by faith alone in Christ alone? Paul answers this question in Romans 5:1–2: "Therefore, since we have been justified by faith, we have peace with God through our Lord Jesus Christ. Through him we have also obtained access by faith into this grace in which we stand, and we rejoice in hope of the glory of God."

We have peace with God

What does this promise assume? Before our justification, we were hostile enemies of God who by nature continually fell short of his glory. Colossians 1:21–22 describes this warfare: "And you, who once were alienated and hostile in mind, doing evil deeds, he has now reconciled in his body of flesh by his death, in order to present you holy and blameless and above reproach before him." This peace with God is not a subjective feeling, but an objective reality based upon what he has done for us in Christ. It means that we have the confident assurance to know that we are no longer guilty as Romans 8:1 gives us this certainty: "There is therefore now no condemnation for those who are in Christ Jesus."

WE ALSO HAVE PERMANENT ACCESS TO GOD

The word "access" in Romans 5:2 describes how we were once outsiders unfit to enter God's presence because of our sin and that we needed a Mediator to bring us into his presence. The Father overcame our guilt by taking the initiative to declare us righteous. This access to God is permanent and does not fluctuate based upon our performance. Martin Luther likened our sinful condition to that of a pile of manure stinking up the hillsides of Germany. We're corrupt, stinky, and rotten to the core! During winter, the falling snow covers the rotten dunghill in a pristine white blanket. Underneath the snow, the dunghill is still a dunghill, but from above it looks white. That is how justification works. The LORD covers us with the perfect righteousness of Christ so that when he looks down upon us as spiritual dunghills, he doesn't see a stinking pile of manure, but instead sees pure white snow. In our justification, our condition as sinners does not internally change, but our status does. We go from being guilty in sin to being declared righteous in Christ. This great exchange is not an internal cleansing, but an external and permanent reality. It's a legal declaration, not a change in us. One of the ways we rest in our identity in Christ and his righteousness comes in grounding our assurance of salvation in the imputed righteousness of Christ. J. C. Ryle says, "Christ's work, not our own work—either in whole or in part, either directly or indirectly—is the only ground of our acceptance with God: that justification is a thing entirely without us, for which nothing whatever is needful on our part but simple faith, and that the weakest believer is as fully and completely justified as the strongest."[12]

THE BLESSING OF PSALM 32

Psalm 32 beautifully combines all three aspects of our identity in the Son—purchased, forgiven, and righteous. This was Augustine's favorite psalm, and he had it written on a plaque above his bed to meditate upon every night before bed. He said, "The beginning of knowledge is to know

---

12. Ryle, *Holiness*, 113.

oneself to be a sinner."[13] That is so true. We can never truly experience the depths of God's mercy and grace unless we have a realistic view of who we truly are. In Psalm 32:1–2, David writes, "Blessed is the one whose transgression is forgiven, whose sin is covered. Blessed is the man against whom the Lord counts no iniquity, and in whose spirit there is no deceit."

David uses three specific Hebrew words to describe sin. First, "transgression" means a breaking loose or rebellion in that we have committed treason against our Infinite Creator. Second, David uses the basic Hebrew word for "sin" which conveys a deviation, falling short, missing the mark, or turning from the right path. This word describes how archers would shoot arrows and miss the target. "Sin" describes how we fall short of God's holy standard of the law. Third, David employs the word "iniquity" which connotes our spiritual condition as distorted, twisted, and corrupt to the core. These three expressions of sin sum up the totality of what it means to stand condemned under God's wrath. Not only have we offended him personally and rebelled against his law, but we are radically depraved by nature.

How does the LORD respond to this overwhelming sinfulness inherent in humans? David describes three particular ways that God deals with our sin that reflect our identity—we are purchased, forgiven, and righteous in the Son. First of all, God pronounces the blessing of *forgiveness*. This Hebrew word means to be lifted off or carried away. Psalm 103:12 beautifully captures this idea: "As far as the east is from the west, so far does he remove our transgressions from us." Isaiah 43:25 reads, "I, I am he who blots out your transgressions for my own sake, and I will not remember your sins." We are forgiven in the Son!

Second, David describes the LORD as "covering" our sin which refers to the Day of Atonement. The word "cover" means to propitiate God's wrath against sin. On that special day, the high priest would take blood from an animal that had been sacrificed into the Holy of Holies which was in the very center of the tabernacle. He would then sprinkle the blood on the mercy seat, which was the lid or covering of the Ark of the Covenant. The Ark represented God's presence, and it also contained the two tablets of the Ten Commandments. The cherubim, or flaming creatures inscribed in gold on the lid, represented the absolute holiness of God. The seat, or lid, showed the clear separation between a holy God and the broken law inside the Ark. The blood sprinkled on the mercy

---

13. Augustine, quoted in Keil and Delitzsch, *Psalms*, 251.

seat covered or appeased God's wrath, shielding the Israelites from his rightful judgment because they had broken his law. Again, propitiation, or the covering of sin, means that on the cross Jesus as our substitute fully absorbed the wrath of God that stood against us. He deflected this justice that should have been aimed directly at us by becoming a curse for us.

Third, David expresses how the LORD does not "count" our sin against us. This is none other than an Old Testament reference to the doctrine of justification by faith alone. The Father does not count or credit our sins against us in his courtroom because the righteousness of Christ declares us not guilty through justification. Paul quotes this psalm in Romans to support the doctrine of imputed righteousness of Christ. Romans 4:5–8 reads, "And to the one who does not work but trusts him who justifies the ungodly, his faith is counted as righteousness, just as David also speaks of the blessing of the one to whom God counts righteousness apart from works: 'Blessed are those whose lawless deeds are forgiven, and whose sins are covered; blessed is the man against whom the Lord will not count his sin.'" Psalm 32 reaffirms our identity in Jesus the Son. We are purchased (our sins are covered); we are forgiven (a wonderful blessing); we are righteous (God does not count our sins against us). Martin Luther is so helpful here: "Learn to know Christ and him crucified. Learn to sing to him and say, 'Lord Jesus, you are my righteousness, I am your sin. You took on you what was mine; yet set on me what was yours. You became what you were not, that I might become what I was not!'"[14] That's profoundly stated. What was Jesus not? A sinner! And yet what did he become? A sin offering in our place condemned by God. And yet what were we not? Righteous and accepted by God. But yet, now because of this beautiful transaction, we can stand in the righteousness of Christ.

OUR JOYFUL RESPONSE

How do we respond to Jesus as those who are purchased, forgiven, and righteous in him? *First of all, we treasure Jesus as supremely valuable!* I'm not the world's most romantic husband. Imagine that my wife and I are celebrating our twenty-fifth wedding anniversary—the silver anniversary where many husbands go all out for their wives. And here's what I do—I forget to make reservations at a nice restaurant and instead take her out

---

14. Luther quoted in Stott, *The Cross of Christ*, 197.

to a local fast food restaurant. While biting into a greasy hamburger, I tell her that she is relatively pretty and at least she's not gotten fat over the past twenty-five years. As I pull out a gift, she waits in expectation for this glorious moment and I hand her a generic greeting card and tell her, "Well, I thought since this was our twenty-fifth anniversary I might as well get you a card to tell you I love you because that's what we husbands kind of have to do on these anniversaries." Would she be mesmerized with my romantic prowess? Would my wife be swept away in a moment of joy that her devoted husband has made every detail of this great evening so perfect? Or would she resent me and slap me in the face, feeling dejected and hurt. I may be saying that I love her and that our marriage is the most important thing in my life, but by my actions and my attitude I am only giving her sloppy leftovers. This scenario shows that I have no wholehearted passionate commitment to her as I fail miserably to express my devotion to and joy in who she is. In the end, our anniversary has become an obligation. A ritual. Something I have to do instead of celebrating my wife for who she is and enjoying twenty-five years of marriage. Now, why do I bring up this idea of loving my wife and treasuring and valuing her?

Treasuring Jesus

Jesus tells a parable in Matthew 13:44–46: "The kingdom of heaven is like treasure hidden in a field, which a man found and covered up. Then in his joy he goes and sells all that he has and buys that field. Again, the kingdom of heaven is like a merchant in search of fine pearls, who, on finding one pearl of great value, went and sold all that he had and bought it." In this parable, Jesus compares himself to both a buried treasure and this extraordinary pearl of great price. When we enter into a saving relationship with Jesus, he becomes our ultimate treasure. We value and prize him above everything else. He becomes our chief joy. He becomes our magnificent obsession. Everything else in all the world pales in comparison to treasuring Jesus as our precious, most valuable passion. You honor, value, and spend a lot of time on what or who you cherish. You reorient your life around those things or persons you value, and they become your primary preoccupation. In essence, Jesus says that he is to be our infinite treasure of surpassing worth.

In 1997, Billie Bob Harrell won the $31 million jackpot in the Texas lottery. He bought a ranch, six homes for himself and family, and an assortment of new cars. Yet he lost everything. He ended up divorcing his wife. After two years of becoming an instant millionaire, he committed suicide. "Winning the lottery is the worst thing that ever happened to me," he is quoted as saying shortly before his death.[15] *Worldly treasures never satisfy!* Jesus says that he is to be our infinite treasure of surpassing worth. Tim Keller defines what we often treasure:

> The real god of your heart is what your thoughts effortlessly go to when there is nothing else demanding your attention. What do you enjoy daydreaming about? What occupies your mind when you have nothing else to think about? What do you habitually think about to get joy and comfort in the privacy of your heart? When you pull your emotions up by the roots as it were, you will often find your idols clinging to them. Jesus must become more beautiful to your imagination, more attractive to your heart, than your idol. That is what will replace your counterfeit gods. If you uproot the idol and fail to plant the love of Christ in its place, the idol will grow back.[16]

Charles Spurgeon said, "He is to be enthroned, the royal One within your heart, as the king of your affections."[17] Is Jesus the King of your affections? Does he dominate your heart? Does he rule your thoughts? We should devote ourselves to the Lord in reckless abandon. Psalm 73:25–26 captures what it means to treasure Jesus: "Whom have I in heaven but you? And there is nothing on earth that I desire besides you. My flesh and my heart may fail, but God is the strength of my heart and my portion forever." David treasured the Lord deeply in Psalm 42:1–2: "As a deer pants for flowing streams, so pants my soul for you, O God. My soul thirsts for God, for the living God. When shall I come and appear before God?" In Philippians 3:8, Paul's chief desire was to treasure Jesus: "Indeed, I count everything as loss because of the surpassing worth of knowing Christ Jesus my Lord. For his sake I have suffered the loss of all things and count them as rubbish, in order that I may gain Christ." Paul makes this startling and crude statement that he has suffered the loss of all things and counted them as "rubbish," a coarse word that means a lump of manure, rotten food, or what one throws to a dog.

15. Field, "Ten Tragic Lottery Stories," para. 7.
16. Keller, *Counterfeit Gods*, 168–72.
17. Spurgeon, *Complete Sermons of C. H. Spurgeon*, 467.

Does this passion for Jesus characterize you? Do you have a burning desire to know Jesus more deeply and to gain him as your all in all? Thomas Watson pleads with us: "Oh, then, let us have endearing thoughts of Christ, let him be accounted our chief treasure and delight. This is the reason why millions perish—because they do not prize Christ."[18] We can never go overboard on valuing Christ. We can never go too far in desiring him. Do you always focus your thoughts and imagination on Jesus? Do you treasure him above anything else? Walter Marshall gives this encouragement: "Such a persuasion as this will allure and incline your wills and affections to choose and embrace Christ as the chief good, and never to rest satisfied without the enjoyment of him; and to reject everything that stands in competition with him or the enjoyment of him."[19] Hear the prayer of John Owen: "Blessed Jesus! We can add nothing to you, nothing to your glory; but it is a joy of heart to us that you are what you are, that you are so gloriously exalted at the right hand of God; and we do long more fully and clearly to behold that glory, according to your prayer and promise."[20]

Submitting to Jesus

In addition to treasuring Jesus, the Bible calls us to submit to him as Lord which means to align our lives under his kingly rule as our Sovereign Master. A.W. Tozer warns, "The Lord will not save those whom he cannot command. He will not divide his offices. You cannot believe in a half-Christ. We take him for what he is—the anointed Savior and Lord who is King of kings and Lord of lords!"[21] Jesus demands ultimate allegiance to him as Lord in John 12:23–25: "The hour has come for the Son of Man to be glorified. Truly, truly, I say to you, unless a grain of wheat falls into the earth and dies, it remains alone; but if it dies, it bears much fruit. Whoever loves his life loses it, and whoever hates his life in this world will keep it for eternal life." In this parable, the grain of wheat represents Jesus, who will die alone on the cross, be buried in the tomb, and three days later will rise again. Here's the main point of this teaching: The death of Jesus will bring about much fruit resulting in the salvation of a multitude

---

18. Watson, *Godly Man's Picture*, 54.
19. Marshall, *Gospel Mystery of Sanctification*, 149.
20. Owen, *Glory of Christ*, 128.
21. Tozer, in MacArthur, *Gospel According to Jesus*, 35.

of sinners. In other words, spiritual death is always the path to spiritual life. We experience salvation by dying to sin and being raised to new life with Christ.

Jesus explains what it means to submit to him as Lord in that we must lose our life. We must die to self. We must follow him. Submitting to Jesus does not involve signing a card, raising a hand, or walking an aisle. There is nothing inherently wrong with these evangelistic practices, but one can go through the motions of asking Jesus into their heart and yet never be soundly saved by grace. Many people today believe that all one has to do is accept Jesus as Savior, and then someday down the road, they can later make Jesus Lord. We as sinners do not make Jesus Lord; he is already Lord by virtue of his nature as the eternal Messiah who died on the cross, rose again, and reigns in heaven at God's right hand. Authentic saving faith involves trusting in Christ as Savior and submitting to him as Lord.

Jesus repeats this charge in Luke 9:23–25: "If anyone would come after me, let him deny himself and take up his cross daily and follow me. For whoever would save his life will lose it, but whoever loses his life for my sake will save it. For what does it profit a man if he gains the whole world and loses or forfeits himself?" Genuine faith means more than just accepting some facts about Jesus. Genuine faith is more than just wanting a "get-out-of-hell-free" card. Many people like the idea of Jesus as their Savior. Who doesn't like his or her sins forgiven and having eternal life in heaven? But how many people at the same time find Jesus so wonderful and glorious that they bow to him as Lord and King. Charles Spurgeon asserts, "Another proof of the conquest of a soul for Christ will be found in a real change of life. If the man does not live differently from what he did before, his repentance needs to be repented of, and his conversion is a fiction."[22] Jesus is very clear. You must follow him as the King by dying to yourself. There is no such teaching in Scripture that you can receive Jesus as your Savior, but it is somehow optional to accept him as Lord. It's all or nothing. The call to follow Christ is costly. It means that you cannot be so in love with your life, agenda, plans, sin or priorities. Submitting to the lordship of Christ is not optional. Repentance is not optional. Again, Spurgeon gives this warning: "Do not suppose that the Gospel is magnified or God-glorified by going to lost people and telling them that they may be saved at this moment by simply 'accepting Christ' as their Savior,

---

22. Spurgeon, *The Soul Winner*, 32.

while they are wedded to their idols, and their hearts are still in love with sin. If I do so, I tell them a lie, pervert the Gospel, and insult Christ."[23] Let us not merely give lip service to Jesus as king but let us bow before him in humility, joy, and worship as we daily die to ourselves and follow him wherever he leads. The hymn "Be Thou My Vision" demonstrates this daily submission to Jesus:

> Be Thou my Vision, O Lord of my heart;
> Be all else but naught to me, save that Thou art;
> Be Thou my best thought in the day and the night,
> Both waking and sleeping, Thy presence my light.
>
> Riches I heed not, nor man's empty praise;
> Be Thou mine inheritance, now and always;
> Be Thou and Thou only the first in my heart,
> O high King of heaven, my Treasure Thou art.

Is this hymn the song of your life? Jesus has given you a beautiful identity in that you are purchased, forgiven, and righteous in him. In joyful response, do you treasure and submit to the King as the greatest desire of your heart? May Hebrews 12:2 become your soul's anthem: "Keep looking to Jesus, the founder and perfecter of our faith, who for the joy that was set before him endured the cross, despising the shame, and is seated at the right hand of the throne of God."

---

23. Spurgeon, in Reisinger, *Today's Evangelism*, 25–26.

6

Your Identity in the Holy Spirit

"Without the Spirit of God we can do nothing. We are as ships without wind or chariots without steeds. Like branches without sap, we are withered. Like coals without fire, we are useless."

CHARLES H. SPURGEON[1]

IMAGINE THIS SCENARIO: YOU'RE going through your Facebook feed, and you come across a friend's post about the practice of "grave sucking," and in curiosity, you click on the link. You've just entered the world of the extreme prophetic hypercharismatic movement where people go to people's graves and try to suck the anointing from their dead bodies. For example, one pastor and his wife physically laid on C. S. Lewis's grave in an attempt to suck out his anointing. As you continue to surf the internet, you come across another teacher who is famous for his YouTube clips of smoking or toking the Holy Ghost. He compares the Holy Spirit to a drug that you shoot up, or like marijuana that you smoke, so that you will get closer to God. And then it links you to another website where a woman passionately gives a testimony about getting closer to the Holy Spirit through gold dust coming down in a church meeting, out-of-body astral projections, and angel orbs. After you shake your head in both shock and disbelief, you wonder what any of this has to do with the Holy Spirit.

1. Spurgeon, "Revival Promise," 3.

Now imagine this second scenario: you get a knock on your door, and two young men with white shirts and nice black slacks show up and inquire about what you believe about Jesus. You begin to question them about the tenets of their faith and find out that they believe in a prophet who allegedly received golden tablets in upstate New York in the mid-1800s. They think of the Holy Spirit as a force, or fog, or some ethereal power as they refer to the Holy Spirit as an "it." In scenario one, you've seen the wildest and most extreme abuses of the Holy Spirit through the Word-Faith theology, and in the second scenario, you've been confronted by a major cult that denies the personhood of the Holy Spirit. And then you begin to think to yourself: "you know what, I am not sure what I believe about the Holy Spirit. I can't remember the last time I heard a sermon on the person and work of the Holy Spirit." In some evangelical churches, there is a heavy emphasis upon the Father and the Son to the neglect of the Holy Spirit. On the other hand, there may be an overemphasis on the Holy Spirit in some of the more radical manifestations you may see in the Word-Faith movement. Much confusion exists on this matter of who the Holy Spirit is and how we relate to him in our salvation. What exactly is our gospel identity in the Holy Spirit? Who are we in relation to the Spirit? *We are regenerated, indwelt, and sanctified by the Holy Spirit.*

REGENERATED BY THE SPIRIT

In the last chapter, we explored the doctrine of justification whereby God declares us not guilty on account of the imputed righteousness of Christ. When we placed our faith in Jesus alone for salvation, God permanently, instantaneously, and completely justified us. Why did you believe in Jesus? What enabled your response to place your faith in Christ? Can sinners who are spiritually dead come to Christ unaided? The reason you believed in Jesus was that the Holy Spirit caused you to be born again or regenerated you. Before we understand the concept of the Spirit's regenerating power, we must understand the depravity and spiritual inability of humans due to sin. Let us explore three truths related to regeneration.

Truth Number One: You are born spiritually dead and unable to come to Christ due to the guilt of sin

In John 6, Jesus reveals some of the most explicit statements about the sinfulness of humans and the regenerating power of the Holy Spirit. In John 6:44, Jesus says, "No one can come to me unless the Father who sent me draws him, and I will raise him up on the last day." Jesus repeats this reality in John 6:65 by emphasizing that no one can come to him unless the Father has granted it. The wording here in the original language (*dynamis*) describes our inherent inability. No one has the ability in and of themselves to believe in Jesus or come to him in faith. Why do sinners lack the ability to believe in Jesus? Maybe you think we were all born as a blank slate and that we choose to sin because of our environment. Perhaps you think that we are not born sinners as a result of Adam's first trespass in the garden. Maybe you believe that we sin from time to time, but that we're really not that bad.

Does the Bible teach that we are in bondage to sin and unable to come to Christ if left to ourselves? Romans 8:6–8 affirms this spiritual inability: "For to set the mind on the flesh is death, but to set the mind on the Spirit is life and peace. For the mind that is set on the flesh is hostile to God, for it does not submit to God's law; indeed, it cannot. Those who are in the flesh cannot please God." Paul describes the condition of non-Christians as those who are "in the flesh," which means total domination by indwelling sin. This self-centered depravity characterizes the fundamental nature of unsaved people and is not something people can float in and out of. Also, all the verbs in this passage are in the present tense which denotes an ongoing reality. An unregenerate sinner's mind is currently spiritually dead and separated from God. Paul uses the same word (*dynamis*) that we saw in John 6 in that sinners *cannot* submit to God's law and *cannot* please God. This passage doesn't simply say that they *won't* please God, but that they *cannot*—they lack the ability. What is the one thing the pleases God the most? Coming to faith in his Son Jesus. In bondage to sin, you cannot please God by doing the greatest act of worship and devotion—trusting in Christ alone for salvation. First Corinthians 2:14 echoes this truth: "The natural person does not accept the things of the Spirit of God, for they are folly to him, and he is not able to understand them because they are spiritually discerned." The natural person, or the unsaved person, is again *not able* to understand the things of the Spirit. This inability does not mean a non-Christian cannot understand the facts concerning the gospel or that they cannot comprehend biblical concepts. They can receive the data cognitively, but spiritually they cannot exercise saving faith without the power of the Holy Spirit. Here's the fundamental problem that is universal to all people: we are all born spiritually dead, children of wrath, blinded by Satan, unable to understand spiritual truth, unable to please God, and unable to come to Christ. Simply put, all people are born totally depraved and are morally unable to come to Christ in the flesh.

Truth Number Two: The Holy Spirit must overcome your deadness by granting you new life and drawing you to Jesus

In John 6:44, Jesus says we cannot come unless the Father "draws us," and in verse 65, Jesus says we cannot come unless the Father "enables or grants" us the ability to come. What does it mean that God "draws" us? What does it mean that God "grants" us the ability to come? One lexicon defines this as "to draw, with the implication that the object being moved is incapable of propelling itself or in the case of person(s) is unwilling to do so voluntarily, in either case with the implication of exertion on the part of the mover."[2] The idea behind the word is that a person does not want to come to Christ and does not have the ability to come to Christ. As a result, God must overcome this unwillingness and inability by working sovereignly in the heart so that the sinner will indeed believe in Jesus.

In other words, this drawing is effectual in the sense that when God draws, the sinner will come. In verse 65, Jesus uses the same terminology but changes from "drawing" to "granting." The word here in the original language means to grant a gift. As one who is spiritually dead and in bondage, you cannot come in faith to Jesus unless the Father grants this ability to come as a gift of grace. Jesus teaches in John 6:63 that "It is the Spirit who gives life; the flesh is no help at all. The words that I have spoken to you are spirit and life." This is just another way of saying that God has to grant, draw, or enable you to place your trust in Christ alone. The Holy Spirit has to give you this new life. Why? Because in your flesh—in your bondage to sin—you are helpless. You are dead. You are incapable of coming. The flesh is of no help at all, which means that in your fallen condition you can't benefit or assist yourself in coming to Jesus unless the

---

2. Arndt et al., *Greek-English Lexicon*, 318.

Spirit gives you life. You cannot give yourself spiritual life. You lack the desire and ability to come to Christ if left to yourself.

The Bible uses various different terms and metaphors to describe this concept of drawing, granting spiritual ability, and giving life to sinners. Sometimes it's called being born again as Jesus tells Nicodemus in John 3:5–8:

> Truly, truly, I say to you, unless one is born of water and the Spirit, he cannot enter the kingdom of God. That which is born of the flesh is flesh, and that which is born of the Spirit is spirit. Do not marvel that I said to you, 'you must be born again.' The wind blows where it wishes, and you hear its sound, but you do not know where it comes from or where it goes. So, it is with everyone who is born of the Spirit.

Jesus gives an analogy of the wind over which no one has control. You can't see the wind. You can only look at the effects or results of the wind, but you sure know when it's windy. Wind is powerful and has a mind of its own. In comparison, the Holy Spirit, like the wind, blows new life into spiritually dead sinners, causing them to be born again.

Another metaphor for regeneration involves taking out a heart of stone as evidenced in Ezekiel 36:26–27: "And I will give you a new heart, and a new spirit I will put within you. And I will remove the heart of stone from your flesh and give you a heart of flesh. And I will put my Spirit within you and cause you to walk in my statutes and be careful to obey my rules." God sovereignly does all of the actions in the passage with the repeated phrase "I will . . ." You can't do this spiritual heart surgery yourself. Other times the Scriptures refer to regeneration as God making us alive. Ephesians 2:4–5 reads, "But God, being rich in mercy, because of the great love with which he loved us, even when we were dead in our trespasses, made us alive together with Christ—by grace you have been saved." Who makes whom alive? Do we make ourselves alive or does God make us alive? God makes us alive by grace. Why does God have to do it? Because we were dead in our trespasses.

Acts 16:14 describes regeneration: "One who heard us was a woman named Lydia, from the city of Thyatira, a seller of purple goods, who was a worshiper of God. The Lord opened her heart to pay attention to what was said by Paul." Lydia does not open her own heart to the gospel; God overcomes her spiritual inability and draws her to Christ. Titus 3:5 says, "He saved us, not because of works done by us in righteousness, but according to his own mercy, by the washing of regeneration and renewal of the Holy Spirit." Paul describes this internal cleansing using the term "regeneration" by the Holy Spirit. The Spirit gives life. The Spirit causes us to be born again. The Spirit makes us a new creation.

Here are some questions for you: Has the Father drawn you? Has the Spirit given you life? Has God replaced your heart of stone with a heart of flesh? Has God opened your heart? Has God made you alive in Christ? Have you been regenerated? If so, then you will come to Jesus. Regeneration comes before faith. You don't believe first and later get born again. You are born again, and the first thing you do is believe in Christ. How were you physically born as a baby? Did you do anything to birth yourself? Did you cause yourself to be born? What prompted you to be pushed out of your mother's womb? Under God's sovereign design, there is a nine-month pregnancy, and when the time is right, you are born. What is the first thing you do when you're born? You cry out! Now in our spiritual birth, do we initiate or cause ourselves to be born again? Do we give ourselves life? No, because we are spiritually dead. When the Holy Spirit grants life by regenerating us, the first thing we do once we are made alive is that we cry out in repentance and faith, and we come to Christ. Loraine Boettner explains regeneration as "something which is wrought in us, and not an act performed by us. It is an instantaneous change form spiritual death to spiritual life . . . If any person believes, it is because God has quickened him."[3]

Truth Number Three: When the Holy Spirit gives you new life, you will come to Jesus in saving faith.

If the Father has drawn you, you will come. If the Spirit has given you this life, you will come. Jesus affirms this in John 6:37, stating that all whom the Father has given him will come to him. Jesus does not say that you "may come" or that you "might" come, but that you will come. Here's the powerful truth: Nothing can stop you from coming to Jesus once the Spirit has given you life. No matter how sinful you have been. No matter how spiritually dead and rebellious you have been. No matter how guilty and helpless you are. No matter how much sin you've stacked up on your record. No amount of sin, guilt, shame, or rebellion can overcome God's sovereign power to save you when he gives you life. In an instant, he

---

3. Boettner, *Reformed Doctrine of Predestination*, 165–66.

powerfully overcomes all of those spiritual barriers and grants you life, and after this you will come in faith to Christ. You will repent of your sins. You will place all of your trust in Jesus. You will confess with your mouth that Jesus is Lord and believe in your heart that God raised him from the dead (Rom 10:9). Confessing Christ as Lord and believing in your heart that he rose from the dead is just Paul's way of saying that you have come to Jesus. Michael Horton says, "The new birth is from above, not from within. We do not cause or initiate regeneration. We are not born again because we believe. We believe because God reaches down from heaven and grants us the new birth."[4] Why did you confess Jesus as Lord? Why did you believe in your heart that Jesus rose from the dead? Why did you come to Christ in faith? Why were you saved? Because God overcame your spiritual deadness and rebellion by granting you the grace to come. John Murray describes God's grace in regeneration: "God's grace reaches down to the lowest depths of our need and meets the problem of the moral and spiritual impossibility which is inherent to our depravity and inability. And that grace is the grace of regeneration."[5] Your new identity in the Holy Spirit involves a radical inward change of heart whereby God renews, cleanses, and makes you alive in Christ. We can celebrate this reality in the words of 2 Corinthians 5:17: "Therefore, if anyone is in Christ, he is a new creation. The old has passed away; behold, the new has come."

INDWELT BY THE SPIRIT

On the night of his betrayal, Jesus gave some of the most in-depth teachings on the person and work of the Holy Spirit to his band of disciples in the Upper Room. Jesus says in John 14:16–17, "And I will ask the Father, and he will give you another helper, to be with you forever, even the Spirit of truth, whom the world cannot receive, because it neither sees him nor knows him. You know him, for he dwells with you and will be in you." What does our Lord instruct as about our identity as being indwelt by the Holy Spirit?

---

4. Horton, *Putting Amazing Back into Grace*, 125.
5. Murray, *Redemption Accomplished and Applied*, 96.

The Holy Spirit is a divine Person co-equal with the Father and Son

As we saw in chapter three concerning the doctrine of the Trinity, the Holy Spirit possesses all the attributes of God as well as divine personhood. Sometimes it is easier for us to think of God the Father as a person since we can relate to our earthly fathers. We also see Jesus the Son as a person because he came physically to earth as a man. Yet, it's a little more difficult for us to wrap our minds around viewing the Holy Spirit as a person—especially when referred to as the Holy Ghost. What comes to your mind when you think of a ghost? A phantom floating around or Casper the friendly ghost or some misty fog? I want you to notice the masculine pronouns Jesus uses for the Holy Spirit—"him" and "he." Jesus doesn't say "it" will be with you and "it" will dwell in you. First and foremost, the Holy Spirit is not an "it" but a "he"—a divine person who is co-equal and co-eternal with the Father and Son. The Holy Spirit was not created. He is not subservient to Jesus or the Father, but shares the same essence or being as God. I encourage you to be careful in how you speak of the Holy Spirit, and to do so as a "he" or "him," not an "it" or a force, energy, fog, mist, anointing, or anything else that is something you can easily manipulate or confer onto another person.

Jesus also describes the Holy Spirit as "another helper." It's important to understand the Greek word for "another," for it means another of the same kind—not another of a different kind. In other words, Jesus explains that the Holy Spirit is equal in deity to the Son. We can translate this word "helper" (*parekletos*) as "counselor" or "comforter" or "advocate." There is no good way to translate this unique Greek word into English and capture all of its nuances because it has multiple meanings where the context will determine how to best understand the term. When you think of a Counselor, today's usage of the word like a marriage counselor or a camp counselor may impact your thinking. This may cause some confusion in thinking about the Holy Spirit solely in therapeutic terms. In popular usage, one goes to a counselor for psychological help which does not convey the original meaning of the word "helper" or "counselor."

The word "helper" is a good translation, but it can also mislead you to think that you're the one in charge of your life and the Holy Spirit is more of your personal assistant to help you along whenever you need him. This may confuse the issue to think that the Holy Spirit is subordinate to you as merely your helper, but not a sovereign and divine person who is fully God. The word *parakletos* also describes the role of a legal advisor or an advocate who helps in the court of law, whether as a lawyer, witness, or representative. The word also denotes reinforcements sent to the front of the battle to help the struggling troops. Jesus does not simply say that he will ask the Father to give you some help now and then. He promises a divine person—a helper, an advocate, a strengthener. In this Upper Room discourse, Jesus is about to leave his disciples and ascend to heaven after his resurrection. How will Jesus mediate his presence and do what he has been doing the past three years while physically on earth? How will the ministry, help, encouragement, teaching, and leadership of Jesus continue in our lives if he is not physically there? Christ's presence will come through the gift of the Holy Spirit sent to strengthen, lead, guide, protect, and help us until he returns and brings us to heaven. The Holy Spirit will supply all of our needs and continue the ministry of Jesus in our hearts. While on earth in a physical body, Jesus guarded, protected, advocated, taught, ministered, and cared for the disciples. Now that he has ascended into heaven as the resurrected Messiah, the Holy Spirit will continue to carry on this work of Christ in our lives as well.

The Holy Spirit is also the divine Deposit who permanently lives in us guaranteeing our eternal life

In John 14:16, Jesus says the Holy Spirit "will be with you forever." In the original language, this verb is in continual action. The Holy Spirit will always, continually be with us forever. The word "with" means alongside, accompanying us. In verse 17, it says he will "dwell" with us, which means to take up residence, to abide, to permanently live with us. In the original language, we call this a timeless present-tense verb. This grammar is important because it does not mean that the Holy Spirit will come and go in and out of us. Instead, the verb "dwell" carries the idea that the relationship is permanent in that once the Holy Spirit takes up residence in you, he will never leave you. Interestingly, John employs three Greek prepositions to describe our relationship with the Holy Spirit. In your English translations, you may be tempted to glaze over little words like "with" and "in" and view them as insignificant. These prepositions are as follows:

- With you (*meta*)—this signifies intimate fellowship with the Spirit.

- With you (*para*)—this refers to the Spirit's presence as a divine person.
- In you (*en*)—this stresses that the Spirit is inside of you as the source of life.

This should give us great encouragement on many levels. If you are a Christian, then you have the fullness of the Holy Spirit living in you. You don't have to wait down the road for some second blessing or another experience to get more of the Holy Spirit. Romans 8:9 says, "You, however, are not in the flesh but in the Spirit, if in fact the Spirit of God dwells in you. Anyone who does not have the Spirit of Christ does not belong to him." If you're a Christian, you have the Spirit of God fully dwelling in you. First John 3:24 reads, "And by this we know that he abides in us, by the Spirit whom he has given us." First John 4:13 says, "By this we know that we abide in him and he in us, because he has given us of his Spirit."

ETERNAL SECURITY

In addition to Jesus' teaching about the Holy Spirit of truth living permanently inside of us, Paul also teaches that the Holy Spirit is the divine deposit or the down payment that guarantees you will have eternal life. He writes in Ephesians 1:13–14: "In him you also, when you heard the word of truth, the gospel of your salvation, and believed in him, were sealed with the promised Holy Spirit, who is the guarantee of our inheritance until we acquire possession of it, to the praise of his glory." What was the purpose of being "sealed" in Paul's day? A seal was a stamp of wax put on a document or a hot iron used to brand cattle or even slaves. Ancient seals had three essential functions.

First, seals were used to confirm that an official scroll was genuine or authentic. A scroll or a document that came from an important ruler or king would have his authoritative seal on it to show that it was legitimate. We have the official seal today that the President uses that visibly displays the authority of his office when he corresponds with Congress. Being sealed with the Holy Spirit conveys the idea that we are legitimate and authentic Christians. We have God's seal of approval on our lives to show that we are Christians whether we feel like it or not. The Holy Spirit seals us as officially belonging to the Father through adoption.

Second, a seal designated ownership. Cattle were marked with a brand to show that they belonged to the owners. Seals were even used on slaves to brand them with the specific marks to show that they were the property of their owner. When we are sealed with the Holy Spirit, it shows Jesus has bought us through his blood, and the heavenly Father owns us. The Spirit dwelling inside of us guarantees that we will forever belong to God as his treasured possession.

Third, people used a seal as a security device. If the seal on an ancient scroll was broken, it meant that someone had tampered with the contents. The seal was a way to show that the materials in the scroll were protected and secure. In other words, being sealed with the Holy Spirit is God's unbreakable promise that we will be eternally secure. Paul says here that the Spirit himself serves as the guarantee of our inheritance. In that culture, people used a warranty in commercial transactions to refer to the first installment or the down payment of the total amount due. For example, when you put a down payment on your house, you are in essence promising that you will fulfill your mortgage obligations to pay your monthly fees on time. It's the bank's way of knowing that you are serious about paying for your house. The Holy Spirit is the down payment, the guarantee, God has given us as a promise to live inside us. Will he ever fail? Will he cease to exist? Will he crumble under pressure? Will he not live up to his end of the bargain?

Absolutely not! The sovereign Spirit infallibly ensures us that we will get the final installment, namely heaven. We will get our full inheritance. We will be eternally secure. Paul affirms this idea in 2 Corinthians 1:21–22: "And it is God who establishes us with you in Christ, and has anointed us, and who has also put his seal on us and given us his Spirit in our hearts as a guarantee." The Spirit of God will never withdraw his presence. He will never nullify his guarantee. He is God's foolproof and unbreakable promise that we will be eternally secure. In other words, genuine believers in Christ will never fully nor finally fall away from the faith and lose their salvation. This is a great reason to feel secure. This is a great reason to thank God for the gift of the Holy Spirit. Romans 5:5 gives us this encouragement: "Hope does not put us to shame, because God›s love has been poured into our hearts through the Holy Spirit who has been given to us." The Spirit indwells you because of God's extravagant outpouring of love. Find great comfort in this security.

SANCTIFIED BY THE SPIRIT

In 1875, English poet William Ernest Hensley authored the poem *Invictus*, whose final stanza captures the heart of contemporary culture:

> It matters not how strait the gate,
> > How charged with punishments the scroll,
> I am the master of my fate;
> > I am the captain of my soul.[6]

This poem expresses the following sentiments: I don't care if the path to Christ is on the narrow road. I don't care if punishment awaits me on the final Day of Judgment. I don't care about anything except for "me!" I am in charge of my life. No one owns or controls me. I hold my future. I chart my course. I am the captain of my soul. Sadly, this self-absorbed ethos has infected many Christians who are tempted to believe that holiness in pleasing Christ is optional. As a Christian, you have been purchased with the blood of Christ to bow under the lordship of Christ by seeking to please him in everything. Second Corinthians 5:9–10 tells us: "So whether we are at home or away, we make it our aim to please him. For we must all appear before the judgment seat of Christ, so that each one may receive what is due for what he has done in the body, whether good or evil."

The Holy Spirit not only indwells us permanently, but he also sanctifies us as God's holy people. Do not be scared off by this word "sanctification." It simply means that the Holy Spirit sets us apart and works in our lives to make us more holy. Sanctification is what we have been exploring all along in this journey of understanding our gospel identity in this process of being conformed to the image of Christ. John Calvin has famously taught about the "Double Grace" in the gospel. He writes, "First being reconciled by the righteousness of Christ, God becomes to us, instead of a Judge, a loving Father; and secondly, being sanctified by the Spirit, we aspire to integrity and purity of life."[7] There is a double grace in the gospel. The first is justification by faith alone, which we explored in the previous chapter. This is the heart of the gospel. God no longer relates to us as a judge, but as a loving Father who can legally declare us not guilty on account of the imputed righteousness of Christ. Justification is a one-time declaration that settles our standing before God for all time.

---

6. Henley, *Selection of Poems*, 96.
7. Calvin, *Institutes of the Christian Religion*, 37.

We are permanently justified and always accepted and forgiven by God on account of Jesus. That is the first grace in the gospel. But there is a second grace. Because we have been justified, we will, as Calvin says, aspire to integrity and purity of life. We will grow to be more like Jesus. We will mature in Christ through obedience. We are new creations in Christ, and we are to walk in newness of life, bearing fruit for him. The Spirit is sanctifying us in our gospel identity.

Paul gives this instruction in 1 Thessalonians 4:1–3: "Finally, then, brothers, we ask and urge you in the Lord Jesus, that as you received from us how you ought to walk and to please God, just as you are doing, that you do so more and more. For you know what instructions we gave you through the Lord Jesus. For this is the will of God, your sanctification: that you abstain from sexual immorality." Paul specifically addresses sexual purity, but the overarching teaching is that God's prescribed will for believers is our sanctification. Peter also emphasizes this reality in 1 Peter 1:14–16: "As obedient children, do not be conformed to the passions of your former ignorance, but as he who called you is holy, you also be holy in all your conduct, since it is written, 'You shall be holy, for I am holy.'"

What does it mean that the Holy Spirit sanctifies you? It means that he has set you apart as distinctly different from the sinful world around you. Sanctification started when God saved you. He set you apart. He made you holy. You went from being a lost sinner to being part of the family of God. In our initial salvation, we were positionally sanctified in that God saw us as holy on account of Christ. We also grow in progressive sanctification in this process of becoming more like Jesus by walking in holiness throughout our lives. The Holy Spirit sanctified you at the new birth and continues to sanctify you or cleanse you as you grow in Christ. Paul exhorts us in Romans 12:1–2: "I appeal to you therefore, brothers, by the mercies of God, to present your bodies as a living sacrifice, holy and acceptable to God, which is your spiritual worship. Do not be conformed to this world, but be transformed by the renewal of your mind, that by testing you may discern what is the will of God, what is good and acceptable and perfect." First John 2:15–17 says, "Do not love the world or the things in the world. If anyone loves the world, the love of the Father is not in him. For all that is in the world—the desires of the flesh and the desires of the eyes and pride of life—is not from the Father but is from the world. And the world is passing away along with its desires, but whoever does the will of God abides forever."

J. C. Ryle defines sanctification as "that inward spiritual work which the Lord Jesus Christ works in a man by the Holy Spirit, when he calls him to be a true believer. He not only washes him from sins in his own blood, but he also separates him from his natural love of sin and the world, puts a new principle in his heart and makes him practically godly in life."[8] Wayne Grudem defines it as "a progressive work of God and man that makes us more and more free from sin and like Christ in our actual lives."[9] We must always remember that our standing, acceptance, and assurance of God's love for us is not in how well we perform in this process of sanctification. Our identity and security come in what Christ alone has done for us and how the indwelling Spirit of God applies that to us. David Peterson claims,

> Although God calls us to express the fact that we have been sanctified by the way we live, our standing with him does not depend on the degree to which we live up to his expectations. It depends on his grace alone. Those who are bowed down by the pressure of temptation and awareness of failure need to be reminded of the definitive, sanctifying work of God in Christ, by which he has established his holy people. On this basis, they should be urged to press on in hope and grasp again by faith the benefits of Christ's sacrifice.[10]

Completely Sanctified

Paul provides another powerful encouragement of God's sustaining grace in the sanctifying work of the Holy Spirit in 1 Thessalonians 5:23–24: "Now may the God of peace himself sanctify you completely and may your whole spirit and soul and body be kept blameless at the coming of our Lord Jesus Christ. He who calls you is faithful; he will surely do it." In 1 Thessalonians 5:23 above, Paul gives us the promise that God himself will sanctify us, not partially, but completely! We will never be sanctified entirely in this life, but God's desire for us is that we ever increase in holiness and ever grow in our sanctification by looking more like Jesus. Part of God's plan to keep us saved to the end involves the work of the Holy Spirit in our lives to sanctify us, grow us, and progressively make us more

---

8. Ryle, *Holiness*, 16.
9. Grudem, *Systematic Theology*, 746.
10. Peterson, *Possessed by God*, 48.

holy. Paul reminds us of God's faithfulness to surely accomplish this work of sanctification that he began at our initial salvation. The Holy Spirit will work in us holiness to make us ready to stand before Jesus on the day of his second coming. This standing is not something we can attain through our own works or righteousness, but is the working of the Spirit in our lives who will preserve us to the end. He will surely do it! He will make sure that we remain not only pure, holy, and ready for Jesus, but that we will ultimately be saved.

Think about the grandeur of the Golden Gate Bridge. This colossal structure stands 500 feet. The concrete used for each base pylon is 182,000 cubic yards dug deep into the bedrock of the cliffs jutting out of the Pacific Ocean. The load on each tower from the main cables is 61,500 tons. It is impressive, as each cable is made of 27,572 strands, which translates to 80,000 miles of wire that connects approximately 1,200,000 total rivets. This famous structure is a feat of engineering genius as the two towers on each end had to be built into the bedrock of the Pacific Ocean so that the foundation would be stable.

As powerful as it is; and as thick and massive as the concrete and bedrock go to support the two towers, it is still at risk. It took four years to complete back in the 1930s, and yet seismic engineers believe that it could take less than sixty seconds to destroy the bridge if an earthquake's epicenter hits near it. Experts estimate that it can only survive a magnitude seven earthquake. To address this threat, the city has ordered a $400 million retrofitting project that has taken almost a decade to complete that should help the bridge be able to tolerate an 8.3 magnitude quake. Even some of the world's most robust structures do not last forever. They cannot withstand hurricanes or tornadoes or earthquakes. Even those with the strongest foundations come crumbling down. And yet, when it comes to our salvation, we have something so strong that it can withstand anything. The foundation of our salvation is Christ, and he is our bedrock, and when the storms of life come and batter against us, we will not crumble, but he will make sure that we are safe to the end.

OUR JOYFUL RESPONSE

These truths about the Holy Spirit should bring joy to your hearts. Our hearts are prone to wander. The devil tempts us. We fail at times. The world batters us. Sometimes we get discouraged. We get tired. We wonder if being a Christian is even worth it. We often wonder if we're all alone in this fight of faith. We lose heart from time to time, and we need to remind ourselves that God is faithful to make sure we make it to the end. We need God's truth to tell us that the Holy Spirit is working powerfully in our lives to sanctify us and to prepare us for the second coming. What God begins, he will complete. He won't go halfway and then stop because somehow we have exhausted his patience or worn him out of his infinite grace poured out on us in the Holy Spirit. Philippians 1:6 reminds us: "And I am sure of this, that he who began a good work in you will bring it to completion at the day of Jesus Christ."

As we think about our relationship to each person of the Trinity, we have seen that we love and glorify the Father, and treasure and submit to the Son. What then is our joyful response to the Holy Spirit? We also in turn wholly depend on the power of the Holy Spirit. We express thankfulness for his overcoming our spiritual deadness by causing us to be born again. We declare our need for him to produce his fruit within us. We call upon him to do that deep work of transformation in our lives to make us look more like Jesus. He is the one who produces the fruit of the Spirit within you. He is the one who gives you the daily strength to face life's struggles. He provides you with God's grace to become more and more like Jesus. Again, the Holy Spirit is indispensable to your spiritual growth and gospel identity. Without him working in our lives, you and I are nothing!

MOTIVATION FOR OBEDIENCE

As a believer in Christ, you are chosen, adopted, and accepted by the Father! You are purchased, forgiven, and righteous in the Son. You are regenerated, indwelt, and sanctified by the Spirit. In short, you have a beautiful gospel identity in the Trinity! Each person of the Trinity has done a mighty work in your life. In thankfulness, you glorify and love the Father. You treasure and submit to the Son. You rely upon the Holy Spirit. If we only focus on our identity (being), we are just going half the distance to where God is taking us in the process of transformation. I said earlier in chapter three that "being comes before doing," and that is true, but to be faithful followers of Jesus, we also need to be "doing"—we need to obey. We need to respond to our great God for the love, grace, and power he's shown us. Walter Marshall succinctly captures the essence of how our gospel identity (being) flows outward into joyful obedience (doing):

> Holiness consists not only in external works of piety and charity, but in the holy thoughts, imaginations, and affections of the soul, and chiefly in love; from whence all other good works must flow . . . not only in refraining the execution of sinful lusts, but in longing and delighting to do the will of God, and in a cheerful obedience to God, without repining, fretting, grudging, at any duty, as it if were a grievous yoke and burden to you.[11]

Marshall shows how doing the will of God in "cheerful" obedience emerges from a heart that is not resentful toward God, but one that has been renewed to delight in conformity toward God's law. Finding our identity in the Trinity ignites a deep passion in us to obey God out of a sense of gratitude, instead of this obedience becoming a begrudging duty or unbearable yoke of frustrating guilt. This truth harkens back to understanding gospel grammar. If we get the moral imperatives before gospel indicatives, we have a disastrous recipe for growth in sanctification.

The gospel indicatives show us the reality of what the Triune God has perfectly accomplished for us in salvation and who we are in relation to him. Gospel indicatives do not tell us what to do, but instead, tell us what Almighty God has already done for us. On the other hand, moral imperatives tell us what to do in obedience to the LORD. As unregenerate sinners, we lacked the ability and desire to obey Jesus, and the Law of God threatened us with condemnation because we could not keep it perfectly. In regeneration, the Lord has graciously transformed us from the inside out whereby he has written or implanted the law within us. This incredible reality comes as a result of the new covenant promise in Jeremiah 31:33–34:

> For this is the covenant that I will make with the house of Israel after those days, declares the Lord: I will put my law within them, and I will write it on their hearts. And I will be their God, and they shall be my people. And no longer shall each one teach his neighbor and each his brother, saying, 'Know the Lord,' for they shall all know me, from the least of them to the greatest, declares the Lord. For I will forgive their iniquity, and I will remember their sin no more.

---

11. Marshall, *Gospel Mystery of Sanctification*, 1.

The LORD will put his law within us and write it on our hearts. What does this mean exactly? Before, in the old covenant, the law came externally on stone for the people to obey (Exod 31:18). God required them to obey and remain faithful to his holy standard, but yet his law was external. It wasn't an internal transformation whereby the Holy Spirit would take up residence in them and give them the power to obey. This desire to obey the Lord is a promise of regeneration or being born again. Moses likens this promise to spiritual circumcision in Deuteronomy 30:6: "And the LORD your God will circumcise your heart and the heart of your offspring, so that you will love the LORD your God with all your heart and with all your soul, that you may live." Sinclair Ferguson explains this truth, "In regeneration, the desires are renewed. In the work of giving us new spiritual life, God creates in us new tendencies and dispositions toward right living. He puts his law in our hearts so that the motivation to glorify and serve him in the paths of righteousness is no longer an external force, but an inward power."[12]

As those with a new identity in the Trinity, we now have both the ability and desire to obey due to the Spirit's work within us. We follow the Lord with a joyful willingness, not so that he will love and accept us in return. Instead, we diligently obey because, as dearly loved children, we rest in the security of a faithful Father who loves us, a righteous Savior who has bought us, and a powerful Spirit who has transformed us. John Owen writes, "This liberty of our Father's family, which we have as sons and children, being adopted by Christ through the Spirit, is a spiritual largeness of heart, whereby the children of God do freely, willingly, genuinely without fear, terror, bondage, and constraint, go forth to all holy obedience in Christ."[13] God never lowers the bar of obedience once we have been saved by grace. The law of God does not threaten us anymore nor are we under its penalty or power. We do not obey the law as a means of justification or acceptance by God. Instead, the law of God serves as a holy guide for living in glad obedience to him on a daily basis. Ernest Reisinger explains, "True, the Christian is not under the law as a covenant of works, nor as a ministration of condemnation, but he is under the law as a rule of life and an objective standard of righteousness for all people at all times."[14] The Puritan Samuel Bolton sums up what

---

12. Ferguson, *Christian Life*, 58.
13. Owen, *Communion with God*, 332.
14. Reisinger, *Law and Gospel*, xvii.

our response should be to the law of God: "Our obedience to the law is nothing else but an expression of our thankfulness to God who has freely justified us, that 'being redeemed, we might serve him without fear (Luke 1:74)."[15] Being (identity) does come before doing (obedience). The gospel indicatives come before the moral imperatives, but God still commands us as believers to obey him, not as a means to attain righteousness, but out of our new nature as adopted children. Even though we have this beautiful new identity in the Trinity, obedience to Jesus is not easy. The Bible describes the Christian life as constant warfare. In the next section, we will explore the insidious nature of indwelling sin and how the Bible commands us to kill it through the power of the Holy Spirit.

---

15. Bolton, *True Bounds of Christian Freedom*, 73.

7

The Deception of Indwelling Sin

"I am convinced that the first step towards attaining a higher standard of holiness is to realize more fully the amazing sinfulness of sin"
BISHOP J. C. RYLE[1]

IN THE SUMMER OF 2010, Lynn France received a shock to her system when she saw some wedding photos posted on Facebook. This scandalous discovery showed pictures of her husband, John France, marrying another woman at a ceremony at Disney World. This event was a classic case of deception and bigamy.[2] In 2005, John and Lynn exchanged vows in a storybook wedding on Italy's luxurious Amalfi coast. What started as wedding bliss quickly turned into a nightmare of unfaithfulness. Mr. France denied ever cheating on Lynn because he never considered their marriage to be legitimate in the first place. Her world came crashing down with a click of a mouse and a seemingly innocent visit to Facebook. We recoil in sickening confusion when we hear stories like this. We express disdain at the deception, manipulation, and secrecy of people whose entire lives are based upon one lie after another.

As we continue to discover our identity in the Trinity, we remember that the gospel indicatives come before the moral imperatives. Being

---

1. Ryle, *Holiness*, 14.
2. Martinez, "Lynn France Learns."

(identity) comes before doing (obedience). We now move into the section of this book which focuses on obedience to the Lord which should flow out of our gospel identity. As you rely on the power of the Holy Spirit to grow in grace, you quickly realize how difficult it is at times to obey the Lord. When it comes to our battle with sin, we face a foe whose deception, manipulation, and secrecy are far more insidious and destructive than the shenanigans of John France. We call this enemy sin—a tenacious opponent who promises us endless enjoyment and indulgent satisfaction, but in the end, leads us down a path of destruction. To grow in our gospel identity, we must understand what the Puritans often called the "exceeding sinfulness of sin."

Sin is a tricky foe. Sin is a manipulative enemy. Sin is a master of deception. Sin clouds our vision and keeps us from experiencing assurance of our salvation. Sin fights against us by hampering our ability to enjoy our identity in the Trinity. As John Owen says, "Sin always aims at the utmost: every time it rises up to tempt or entice, might it have its own course, it would go out to the utmost sin of that kind."[3] Thomas Brooks describes the seductive nature of sin by saying, "So a man bewitched with sin had rather lose God, Christ, heaven, and his own soul than part with his sin. Oh, therefore, for ever take heed of playing with or nibbling at Satan's golden baits."[4] In other words, we must not be mesmerized by the allurements of sin nor should we playfully dismiss sin as an impotent opponent. Sin is a powerful force that brutally thrives on deception. Over the next three chapters, I want to expose you to the evil nature of indwelling sin and explore how the Bible instructs us to put this sin to death. We will focus on growing in gospel obedience by learning how to kill this sin which so easily entangles.

HARDENED COMPROMISE

In Hebrews 3:12–13, the writer gives some of the strongest warnings in the New Testament about the exceeding deceitfulness of sin. He writes, "Take care, brothers, lest there be in any of you an evil, unbelieving heart, leading you to fall away from the living God. But exhort one another every day, as long as it is called 'today,' that none of you may be hardened by the deceitfulness of sin." This appeal comes in the context of a longer

---

3. Owen, *Mortification of Sin*, 32.
4. Brooks, *Precious Remedies against Satan's Devices*, 34.

discussion regarding that disobedient generation of Israelites who failed to enter the promised land due to their unbelief. As they wandered in the wilderness for forty years, the children of Israel hardened their hearts in rebellion, and as a result, the Lord barred them entry into the rest that he alone offered. Through the use of a powerful illustration from Israel's history, the writer of Hebrews shows us what happens when people disobey the voice of God. Disobedience ultimately leads to experiencing the wrath of God. He sharply warns us to stand up and pay attention to that unbelieving generation of Israelites so that we will not succumb to the same fate. He urges us to "take care"—which means to be on our guard against any upcoming hazards or pitfalls that would lead us into dangerous territory. In other words, be alert! Stand your guard! Pay careful attention!

When I was in college, I was somewhat of a dangerous driver (or so I'm told). It was an icy morning in Colorado Springs, and I was late for class. I impatiently decided not to scrape all of the ice off my windshield. Instead, I left a small circle right in front of me so at least I could see straight ahead, but chose not to scrape the passenger windows. In this act of impetuous stupidity, I drove to school and nearly got nailed by an oncoming car. In a fit of frustration, I sheepishly stopped the car, got out, and scraped all the windows this time. In my single-focused desire to get to school on time, I would have given my Driver's Ed teacher a stroke. I not only failed to look both ways but failed even to create space actually to look! I was not watching intensely for upcoming hazards. I was flippant, impatient, and dangerous. And it could have cost me my life, not to mention that of some other innocent soul.

This attitude stands in direct contrast to what the writer of Hebrews warns us about regarding the dangers of sin. He writes with intensity as a concerned pastor who genuinely cares for his people by reminding them of the impending dangers of apostasy. The Scripture calls us to take care or look intently to the exceeding deceitfulness of sin. We are to watch carefully that we do not have an unbelieving and hardened heart which would lead us away from faith in the living God.

This imagery of an unbelieving heart comes directly from Psalm 95:7–11:

> For he is our God, and we are the people of his pasture, and the sheep of his hand. Today, if you hear his voice, do not harden your hearts, as at Meribah, as on the day at Massah in the wilderness, when your fathers put me to the test and put me to the

proof, though they had seen my work. For forty years I loathed that generation and said, 'They are a people who go astray in their heart, and they have not known my ways.' Therefore, I swore in my wrath, 'They shall not enter my rest.'

From this psalm, a stark warning rings out to us that we should not harden our hearts in rebellion against God. As helpless sheep that are dependent upon the Great Shepherd Jesus, we must listen to the voice of our Savior and follow him. We must not harden our hearts in unbelief when we hear his voice. This unbelief is not just some passive lack of acknowledgment of God's voice or a casual disinterest in the things of God. Instead, this type of disbelief violently digs its heels into the ground in arrogant defiance and stubbornly refuses to believe in God. This frequent and persistent unbelief eventually leads to the deadly sin of apostasy.

The LORD himself describes to Moses this unbelieving and hardened generation in Numbers 14:11: "How long will this people despise me? And how long will they not believe in me, in spite of all the signs that I have done among them?" Later, in Numbers 14:27, God calls them a "wicked congregation." There exists a ruthless threat to a people who fail to heed the warnings from Scripture regarding the deceitfulness of sin. The potential of developing a hardened heart lurks wherever sin rears its ugly head. Where is the hope in this urgent warning? How do we come to terms with this enemy that threatens our gospel assurance?

THE DECEITFULNESS OF SIN

The writer of Hebrews warns us that we could become hardened by the deceitfulness of sin. By using the word "hardened" he again harkens back to Psalm 95 and its dire warnings concerning rebellion and disobedience. This word "hardened" was used to describe some of the Jews in Ephesus who scoffed at Paul's teachings as evidenced in Acts 19:9, which states, "But when some became stubborn (hardened) and continued in unbelief, speaking evil of the Way before the congregation, he withdrew from them and took the disciples with him, reasoning daily in the hall of Tyrannus." In classical Greek this word for "hardened" was a medical term used to describe the hardened swelling of a bone.[5] In current medical usage, we have a similar phenomenon called atherosclerosis, otherwise known as a hardening of the arteries. This condition occurs when cholesterol and fat

---

5. Kittel and Friedrich, *Theological Dictionary*, 5:1022–23.

collect and calcify in the arteries causing a tight restriction which eventually prevents the healthy flow of oxygen to our major organs. Too much sclerosis, or hardening, can eventually lead to either a stroke or a heart attack. Just as bad cholesterol can cause the hardening of arteries, the deceitfulness of sin can cause the spiritual hardening of our hearts.

In Ephesians 4:19, Paul describes the heart of an unregenerate sinner as one that has become callous. Callous is very similar to "hardened." Callous in the original language means to become insensitive to pain. In spiritual terms, it denotes a moral apathy whereby non-Christians are desensitized to sin. They no longer feel any shame or embarrassment at immorality. Their depravity and sinfulness no longer bother them since these things have become their lifestyle. Nothing shocks them. Persistent, habitual sin has a deadening effect on the human heart. What causes us to be hardened in our response to the living God? The answer lies in the exceeding deceitfulness of sin. Peter O'Brien says that "sin is viewed as a powerful agent that deceives."[6] If sin is such a powerful agent of deception, then we must understand how it deceives us. How does sin in and of itself pull the wool over our eyes? What makes sin so exceedingly deceitful?

THE ULTIMATE LIE

To answer these questions, we must return to the beginning when the serpent tempted Eve in the garden of Eden. In this tragic fall, we discover that the deceitfulness of sin comes primarily from a lie in Genesis 3:1–5:

> Now the serpent was more crafty than any other beast of the field that the LORD God had made. He said to the woman, "Did God actually say, 'you shall not eat of any tree in the garden?'" And the woman said to the serpent, "We may eat of the fruit of the trees in the garden, but God said, 'you shall not eat of the fruit of the tree that is in the midst of the garden, neither shall you touch it, lest you die.'" But the serpent said to the woman, "You will not surely die. For God knows that when you eat of it your eyes will be opened, and you will be like God, knowing good and evil.

---

6. Peter O'Brien argues that the Greek reading of the phrase "deceitfulness of sin" in the genitive case should be understood as objective ("sin deceives") rather than qualitative ("sinful deception") (O'Brien, *Letter to the Hebrews*, 149).

Jesus rebuked the Pharisees with this statement about the true nature of Satan in John 8:44: "You are of your father the devil, and your will is to do your father's desires. He was a murderer from the beginning, and has nothing to do with the truth, because there is no truth in him. When he lies, he speaks out of his own character, for he is a liar and the father of lies." As the father of lies, Satan deceived Eve by tempting her to question the very word of God. The most insidious words that anyone can utter are these: "Did God actually say . . . ?" By planting a seed of doubt and confusion in Eve's mind over the authority and validity of God's word, Satan told the biggest lie this world has ever known: that she could not trust the word of the living God.

He also tempts Eve to think that God may not be as good and generous as he says he is, and that he can't be trusted. God must be holding you back from experiencing maximum pleasure and joy. By twisting God's authoritative word, the devil is also questioning God's goodness. God was not being stingy or mean in the garden. He gave them a beautiful environment of lush beauty, brought them together in covenant marriage, they were naked and not ashamed, and they had perfect fellowship with God. Is this not an expression of God's goodness? God gave them all the food they wanted, all the beauty that they could enjoy, all the gold and resources that they would ever need, and the wonderful union of marriage with perfect sex and no arguments. To top it off, the two could walk with God in the cool of the day. That doesn't sound stingy or mean to me. That seems like God is giving them maximum pleasure and joy. Yet, he provided it under his terms and with his boundaries. God is not against pleasure and enjoyment. He created us to have passion and joy, but we only find that joy in him alone and through obedience to his law. We only experience the blessing and joy of God when we live on his terms. The terms of the covenant were straightforward. God in his bountiful goodness and generosity had given them everything that they could desire and yet withheld one tree from them. Do you fall for this ploy today? Do you fall for the lie that God is not good and generous and he's trying to hold you back from pleasure? Do you think all God wants to do is force rules down your throat, so you can live a stifled, hampered existence of bondage where you can't experience true freedom? That's the lie of Satan.

The devil also enticed them with the prospect that their eyes would be opened, and they would be like God. This is the epitome of pride. Satan tempted them to achieve what he tried to gain before he became a fallen angel (Isa 14:12–14). John Stott has said this: "At every stage of our

Christian development and in every sphere of our Christian discipleship, pride is the greatest enemy and humility our greatest friend."[7] Jonathan Edwards has said this: "Pride is the worst viper that is in the heart and the greatest disturber of the soul's peace and sweet communion with Christ . . . the most hidden, secret, and deceitful of all lusts."[8] Charles Spurgeon called pride "a brainless thing as well as a groundless thing; for it brings no profit with it. There is no wisdom in a self-exaltation."[9]

Satan also tells them a bald-faced lie that there are no dire consequences to sin; he flat out lies to them by saying, "You will not surely die." One of the most effective ways the devil tempts us as believers is to make us foolishly think that there will be no consequences to our sins. He tries to hide the outcome from us. He wants us to experience the pleasure of the now and to go ahead and take the bait and indulge in sin and worry about the fallout later. Go in blind to your sin and do not worry about the result. Click the mouse and watch pornography in the privacy of your house. Spend fifteen minutes of pleasure to reap a lifetime of sorrow. Say that hateful word! Gossip behind your coworkers back! Get angry! Explode! Lie! Cheat! Steal! Cuss! Harbor bitterness! Get out of control with your drinking! Do all those things because it's all about you and what brings you the most happiness and pleasure, and don't think for a moment that there are any consequences. That is the lie of Satan. Sin can be so devious because it presents to us a twofold lie: that we should not believe God's word and that there must be some better alternative rather than to obey him.

In 2 Corinthians 2:11, Paul reminds us of our ruthless enemy who stands behind all lies. He writes, "So that we would not be outwitted by Satan; for we are not ignorant of his designs." The word used here for "outwitted" means to be greedy with insatiable covetousness. Satan tries to take advantage of us by defrauding and cheating us. He has this lust for power and entices us with the deceitfulness of sin. And he also uses "designs"—those evil intentions, wicked plots, and strategies to keep us buying into the great lie that sin is better than obedience to God.

The infamous former investment broker Bernie Madoff pulled off the most massive Ponzi scheme ever in American history by defrauding investors of billions of dollars. Starting in the early 1990s, he orchestrated

---

7. Stott, in Mahaney, *Humility*, 29.
8. Edwards, "Advice to Young Converts," para. 10.
9. Spurgeon, "Pride and Humility," para. 5.

a plot that would eventually cause his clients to lose almost $65 billion. In June 2009, the court sentenced him to 150 years in prison. A Ponzi scheme is a con game where someone promises significant returns on investments that are paid out by new investors. Eventually, the money runs out, and everybody that invested loses his or her money. The hope is that the dishonest investor gets all of the unsuspecting victim's money before the money runs out or the authorities figure it out. While Madoff's scheme sent shockwaves through the financial world and caused irreparable damage to many, they come nowhere close to the damage inflicted by the wicked plots and evil intentions of the devil who deceives us with sin. All sin stems from a lie that obedience to God does not pay off in the end. Sin does a masterful job of deceiving us into believing the lie that it is good for us to surrender to our lusts. We buy into the myth that sin brings pleasure, enjoyment, satisfaction, and joy. Sin makes a tremendous promise that it cannot fulfill. Sin promises happiness, excitement, and fulfillment, but these benefits are not benefits at all. Sin has tricked us, and these are only fleeting pleasures.

FLEETING PLEASURES

The writer of Hebrews describes the active faith of Moses who refused to rush headlong into the bountiful pleasures of Egypt. Hebrews 11:24-25 states, "By faith Moses, when he was grown up, refused to be called the son of Pharaoh's daughter, choosing rather to be mistreated with the people of God than to enjoy the fleeting pleasures of sin." The word for "enjoy" in the original language means "to cling tightly." Moses did not want to hold on tightly to the fleeting pleasures of sin although he had every amusement at his disposal. As a member of the royal court of Pharaoh, he could have had all the women, money, food, and delicacies his heart desired. He had every pleasure imaginable at his fingertips. But instead of buying into the deceitfulness of sin, Moses understood that the comfort it offered was only fleeting.

This passage tells us that sin is pleasurable. We would not sin if we did not think it brought us pleasure. Sin feels good. Sin is fun. Sin promises excitement and allures us with the prospect of enjoyment. But these promises are empty. These pleasures of sin are fleeting. They are temporary. They only last for a season. Sin is so deceitful because it tricks us into believing that disobedience is fun. If we are honest with ourselves, we know all too well that sin can be fun. We happily rush into sin because we believe that we will experience ultimate pleasure at that moment. But what does iniquity reap in the end? We experience the crash and burn of this deception when the fleeting pleasure passes. Paul reminds us in Galatians 6:7–8: "Do not be deceived: God is not mocked, for whatever one sows, that will he also reap. For the one who sows to his own flesh will from the flesh reap corruption, but the one who sows to the Spirit will from the Spirit reap eternal life." Paul warns us not to fall into faulty thinking that sin will bring no real consequences. We do not find this word "mocked" anywhere else in the New Testament and it means "to turn your nose up in contempt or mockery." You can't outsmart God and how he has governed the universe with the law of reaping and sowing. There is an unstoppable law that always remains true in agriculture. If you plant corn seeds, you will not reap strawberries. You will receive a harvest of corn. In the same way, in the spiritual realm, you will always reap what you sow. The consequences or the harvest may not be immediate, but the harvest will eventually come.

Here's the adage: "Sow a thought, reap an act: sow an act, reap a habit; sow a habit; reap a character; sow a character, reap a destiny." This constant sowing to the flesh leads to corruption which in the original language means a rotting corpse that slowly decomposes over time. The more you sow to your flesh, the more sin gradually pollutes your life until eventually, it ends with destruction. What are some examples of sowing to the flesh? Maybe you surf the Internet and find yourself trapped in a hollow world of pornography. Perhaps you struggle with bitterness where you can't bring yourself to forgive those who have deeply hurt you. Maybe you're driven by success to climb the corporate ladder at all costs, which makes you irritable around your family. Perhaps it's an insatiable need to gossip where you lie and backstab to make yourself look better. Maybe it's a spiral into materialism, greed, and envy where your appetite for stuff has led you into major credit card debt.

HIDDEN CONSEQUENCES

We face an enemy who promises a great deal of enjoyment, but in the end, all we receive is destruction. In addition to sin deceiving us with fleeting pleasures, our adversary the devil also tries to hide the consequences of sin from us. Sin fools us into believing that there will be no real damaging consequences for our actions. We may suffer a little discomfort here or there and maybe have a guilty conscience for a while, but the payoff for the pleasures of sin far outweighs whatever consequences we might have to endure. Not only are we blind to the immediate results of sin, but we fail to see the ultimate future repercussions for giving in to this deceptive enemy. In Romans 2:5 we find these terrifying words: "But because of your hard and impenitent heart you are storing up wrath for yourself on the day of wrath when God's righteous judgment will be revealed." The end game for the unrepentant sinner who remains in a state of hardness is the fullness of God's fury. Ultimately it ends in eternal conscious torment which the Bible calls hell. Because sin is so deceitful, it tries to conceal this ultimate reality from us by diverting our attention from the pains of hell to the immediate pleasure we will experience if we give in to temptation.

One of the most heartbreaking illustrations manifests itself in the story of David and Bathsheba. Blinded by lust and power, David had no idea what the long-term ramifications of his illicit rendezvous with Uriah's wife would be:

> In the spring of the year, the time when kings go out to battle, David sent Joab, and his servants with him, and all Israel. And they ravaged the Ammonites and besieged Rabbah. But David remained at Jerusalem. It happened, late one afternoon, when David arose from his couch and was walking on the roof of the king's house, that he saw from the roof a woman bathing; and the woman was very beautiful. And David sent and inquired about the woman. And one said, "Is not this Bathsheba, the daughter of Eliam, the wife of Uriah the Hittite?" So David sent messengers and took her, and she came to him, and he lay with her. (Now she had been purifying herself from her uncleanness.) Then she returned to her house. And the woman conceived, and she sent and told David, "I am pregnant." (2 Samuel 11:1-5)

What started as an innocent walk on his roof devolved into a saga of treachery and betrayal. Did David truly understand the consequences of committing adultery with Bathsheba? Could he see the long-term violence and sexual perversion that would plague his family? He was blinded by the deceitfulness of sin and thereby chose not to fully examine the ramifications of taking that second look at the bathing beauty below. What started as a hot afternoon of "fun" resulted in murder, mayhem, and the menacing sting of the deceitfulness of sin.

"INNOCENT" DISTRACTIONS

Sin not only promises fleeting pleasure and tries to hide its consequences, but it also distracts us into committing idolatry. Sin may deceive us into taking good things such as a spouse or family or career that in turn become idols. That is why sin is so tricky. These gifts from God are not bad things in and of themselves, but we can elevate them to idol status if we exalt them above our love for Christ. Tim Keller says, "The greater the good, the more likely we are to expect that it can satisfy our deepest needs and hopes. Anything can serve as a counterfeit god, especially the very best things in life ... a counterfeit god is anything so central and essential to your life that, should you lose it, your life would feel hardly worth living."[10] For example, the driven workaholic who finds ultimate satisfaction in a career may not think he is committing the sin of idolatry. He has been deceived into taking a good thing such as a satisfying job and transforming it into his god. His job consumes him to the point where he finds his identity and ultimate purpose in climbing the corporate ladder instead of seeing that satisfaction and joy in Christ.

The deceitfulness of sin has also duped the doting mother who worships her children because she has taken God's precious gift of motherhood and elevated it to ultimate reality. Her children have become her idol, and she may not even know it because she has been so blinded by sin. While she may not be out committing adultery or cheating on her taxes or backstabbing her neighbor, she has a false sense of religious pride in that she is doing okay in her spiritual walk because she has not committed any grievous sins. Because sin has deceived her into making her children an idol, she, in turn, commits the gravest offense in the Bible—idolatry. She is living a false reality all because the deceitfulness of sin has hardened her.

THE BIG "WHY?"

Ultimately why do we buy the lie and get deceived by sin? As Christians who faithfully read and study God's word and are acutely aware of the devastating effects of sin, why do we go ahead and throw caution to the wind and give in? At the deepest level of our hearts, it all boils down to our desires. We have been tricked into believing that to desire sin is

---

10. Keller, *Counterfeit Gods,* xvii–xviii.

better than to desire Christ. We buy the lie that for the moment, sin is all-satisfying and Jesus is not. Instead of seeing the beauty, majesty, and excellencies of our Lord in his person and work, we see the temporary joy that might come from indulging our flesh. Our ultimate desire is for temporary pleasure instead of true lasting pleasure that only comes from Christ alone. C. S. Lewis captured this dilemma in his famous sermon "The Weight of Glory" when he wrote, "We are half-hearted creatures, fooling about with drink and sex and ambition when infinite joy is offered us, like an ignorant child who wants to go on making mud pies in a slum because he cannot imagine what is meant by the offer of a holiday at the sea. We are far too easily pleased."[11] The reason we are far too easily pleased is that the deceitfulness of sin has hardened us. We are content with the promise of temporary joy that comes from sin instead of finding our true contentment in the only One who can genuinely promise eternal joy. Sin is a ruthless enemy that has resulted from Adam's fall in the garden. Sin is insidious. It is manipulative, devious, and never rests for a moment. In the next chapter, we will discover that an intense battle wages deep within our lives between the remaining flesh and the Holy Spirit.

---

11. Lewis, *Weight of Glory*, 16.

8

The Intense Struggle with Sin

"This sanctification is throughout the whole man, yet imperfect in this life; there abides still some remnants of corruption in every part, from which arises a continual and irreconcilable war; the flesh lusting against the Spirit, and the Spirit against the flesh."

1689 SECOND LONDON BAPTIST CONFESSION

EVERY YEAR *MEN'S HEALTH* magazine comes out with its list of the most active cities in America. Usually, Denver, Colorado Springs, or Boulder shows up on this list as one of the most active, healthy, physically fit places to live. Living in Colorado, I see this all around me—cyclists, runners, hikers, kayakers, and mountain climbers. In contrast, Lexington, Kentucky, recently had the honor of being named America's most sedentary city.[1] This description was based upon how many hours a week the average person either watched cable TV or how many video games people purchased in a year. The article warned readers about the dangers of inactivity and prescribed some tips for getting more fit. Physicians and health experts have been warning us for years about the dangers of living a sedentary lifestyle which leads to obesity and many other serious health problems. Similarly, the sloth carries the reputation of being the slowest and laziest animal on the planet and even shares the name of one of the

---

1. Bar and Roberson, "Where Sit Happens."

seven deadly sins. These fascinating creatures live in the rainforests of Central and South America and sleep fifteen hours a day. On the ground, their maximum speed is 1.2 miles per hour.[2] The sloth epitomizes this idea of inactivity and passivity. While physical inactivity in humans can lead to potentially dangerous health issues, how does spiritual inactivity or passivity affect Christians in their pursuit of holiness? Should believers ever struggle with sin or should they instead move into a higher plane of spirituality often called "the victorious Christian life?" Is all effort in handling sin a work of the flesh and counterproductive to true spiritual transformation? Is instantaneous sanctification possible for those select few who have absolutely surrendered themselves in consecration to Christ by "letting go and letting God?"

THE BELIEVER'S DAILY REALITY

God has forever settled our identity in the Trinity by his sovereign grace. Once God justifies us, we are no longer under the penalty or tyranny of sin as our master. As believers, we are dead to sin's bondage and imperial rule in our lives through our union with Christ, and we now have a new identity in the Trinity. This does not mean that we no longer struggle with sin as a presence in our lives. While God destroyed sin's power and dominion through justification, the pollution and presence of indwelling sin remain. As such, God calls us to pursue holiness. In Romans 6:12–13, Paul writes, "Let not sin therefore reign in your mortal bodies, to make you obey their passions. Do not present your members to sin as instruments for unrighteousness, but present yourselves to God as those who have been brought from death to life, and your members to God as instruments for righteousness." Paul does not say that any struggle or striving to do this is sinful. He does not tell us to quietly and passively "let go and let God," but instead gives a strong imperative for us not to engage the flesh. Sin has no dominion or power over us as an active enslaving force in our lives, but we must still vigorously come to terms with its presence in our lives as justified believers.

Paul describes the painful reality all true believers experience on a daily basis in Galatians 5:16–17: "But I say, walk by the Spirit, and you will not gratify the desires of the flesh. For the desires of the flesh are against the Spirit, and the desires of the Spirit are against the flesh, for these are

---

2. "Sloths," 120–23.

opposed to each other, to keep you from doing the things you want to do." What are the desires of the flesh? The word means "over-desires," an all-controlling drive or longing. These cravings don't necessarily have to be sexual, but can be any desire that finds satisfaction and purpose in anything else besides Jesus. This passage clearly shows us that every Christian experiences an intense, ongoing battle between the desires of the Holy Spirit and the desires of the flesh.

The Bible describes two types of people in this world: (1) unregenerate, lost people without the Spirit, and (2) regenerate, saved people with the Spirit. Romans 8:8–9 says, "Those who are in the flesh cannot please God. You, however, are not in the flesh but the Spirit, if in fact the Spirit of God dwells in you. Anyone who does not have the Spirit of Christ does not belong to him." Romans 8:14 reads, "For all who are led by the Spirit of God are sons of God." Think about your life before God saved you by grace and before the Holy Spirit came to live in you. Your sinful nature was there alone on the throne of your heart ruling and reigning with no one to oppose it. However, the Holy Spirit entered into your life supernaturally and has begun this renewal in us. Now the flesh has an enemy—the Holy Spirit—and an intense battle rages in the life of every Christian. You will always have an impulse to sin because of the remaining flesh in you that has not been entirely eradicated. This impulse, craving, or desire no longer rules you, dominates you, or enslaves you as it did before your salvation, but this remaining sin can still exert a tremendous influence in this internal battle.

In Galatians 3:17, when Paul says that the flesh and Spirit "are opposed" to each other, this present-tense verb shows that this battle is a continual reality in the life of every believer. The flesh or sinful desires that remain in us are always at war with our new nature whether we like it or not. James 1:14–15 describes this struggle: "But each person is tempted when he is lured and enticed by his own desire. Then desire when it has conceived gives birth to sin, and sin when it is fully grown brings forth death." This passage shows a progression in how sinful desires and lusts take root in our hearts and eventually lead to action. First of all, a suggestion or lustful thought may pop into our minds. Secondly, we mull over that lustful thought, and think about the pleasures it will bring. Paul admonishes us in 2 Corinthians 10:5: "We destroy arguments and every lofty opinion raised against the knowledge of God, and take every thought captive to obey Christ." Third, we consent to engage this temptation. We agree in our hearts that acting out on this sin will benefit us greatly. Fourth, instead of resisting the temptation, we actually commit the sin. Because sin lurks deep inside our hearts, we need to be ever watchful, diligent and persistent in this battle. Jesus warns us in Matthew 26:41: "Watch and pray that you may not enter into temptation. The spirit indeed is willing, but the flesh is weak."

This intense struggle shows that you are indeed a believer. Perhaps you think that because you struggle and haven't gained a complete victory over sin and made this extreme progress in the Christian life, then you must doubt your salvation and wonder if God loves and accepts you. Because after all, if you were sinless and had complete victory, then God would look favorably upon you and you would be in his good graces. This intense and internal battle with sin is one of the most specific pieces of evidence that you are saved. Non-Christians do not struggle with sin. They may have a guilty conscience here and there, but they don't have the internal struggle because they don't have the Holy Spirit. They are powerless to do anything. They are in bondage to sin and don't have any help at all to say no. Only Christians struggle with sin. These competing desires within you prevent you from doing what you genuinely want to do. As an unsaved person, what did you genuinely want to do? You wanted to sin. You could not help but sin. You had no control over sinning because sin enslaved and dominated you as it was your master and your ultimate desire. However, as a saved person who has the Holy Spirit living in you, what do you genuinely want to do? You want to please Jesus and live for him in holiness. Your renewed heart desires to obey the Lord, but sometimes you give in to the cravings of your flesh. In other words, you are not walking by the Spirit, you are instead, giving in to the cravings of your flesh for temporary enjoyment.

IS EFFORT SINFUL?

Sadly, some distorted, subbiblical views in the evangelical world have made this teaching very confusing—namely, *sinless perfectionism*. This view came from John Wesley and has become very popular in modern-day Arminian churches that believe that it is possible actually to be free of all known sin. J. I. Packer critiques this view: "To teach Christians to infer from any present state of spiritual exaltation that all sinful desire is now permanently gone from them is a damaging mistake; the inference is false, and those who draw it thereby sentence themselves to some degree of moral and spiritual unreality."[3] Proponents of this view have reclassified or redefined sin as only intentional outward actions. The Bible teaches that we sin not only in what we do outwardly, but also in thoughts, imaginations, and words. This faulty view of Wesleyan or sinless perfectionism is not only subbiblical, but experientially we know that it is not true as we daily experience the pollution of sin in our lives. The idea that Christians can have complete and utter victory over known sins and never struggle is another defective view of sanctification. This view has its roots in the Keswick movement and is sometimes called the "Higher Life" or "Victorious Christian Life" theology.[4] The Keswick model of sanctification argues that any effort exerted on our part in struggling with sin or pursuing holiness stems from the flesh and proves counterproductive to experiencing true victory. What do the Scriptures teach about striving in our attempt to grow to become more Christlike? While this is not a comprehensive list, let us examine three key passages.

Philippians 2:12–13

First of all, in Philippians 2:12–13, Paul writes, "Therefore, my beloved, as you have always obeyed, so now, not only as in my presence but much more in my absence, work out your own salvation with fear and trembling, for it is God who works in you, both to will and to work for his good pleasure." This text more than any other clearly illustrates the apparent paradox in our progressive sanctification. At first glance, it can be confusing. When the word "work" shows up, we immediately get suspicious because we think Paul proposes works-based righteousness and that he throws salvation by grace out the window. That could not be farther from the truth. Paul's discussion does not focus on how sinners

---

3. Packer, *Keep in Step*, 145.

4. Andy Naselli's *No Quick Fix* is a helpful book that provides a comprehensive critique of this movement. The higher life movement began in 1858 when William Boardman's popular book *The Higher Christian Life* was released. Robert and Hannah Whitehall Smith popularized the theology in their influential book *The Christian's Secret of a Happy Life* (1885). Since 1875, the Keswick Convention in Keswick, England, has occurred every summer, teaching concepts such as "absolute surrender" and "let go and let God" theology. Influential proponents have been Evan Hopkins, H. C. G. Moule, F. B. Meyer, Andrew Murray, A. T. Pierson, Charles Trumbull, Robert C. McQuilkin, D. L. Moody, R. A. Torrey, and many from the Moody Bible Institute and Dallas Theological Seminary who hold to dispensationalism and the "Carnal Christian" theology.

receive salvation, but instead, shows us how saved persons live out the salvation they have already received. Paul focuses on the word "obedience" instead of "victory." The saints in Philippi have "always obeyed" which demonstrates that Paul's agenda centers on obedience to God's commands rather than instantaneous victory through passivity.

It is important for us to remember that God alone did all of the work in our initial salvation. He chose us before the foundation of the world. He adopted us into his family. He redeemed us through Christ's blood. He caused us to be born again. He transferred us from the kingdom of darkness to the kingdom of light. As sinners who were dead in our transgressions, we lacked the power to save ourselves and could not contribute one iota to our redemption. God alone gets all the credit for saving us. This is what theologians call the *monergistic* working of God. This word comes from two Greek words used together to create this idea—*mono* means "one or alone," while the word *ergon* means "to work." So monergistic salvation means that God alone does all the work in saving sinners. Once saved and given the gift of the indwelling Holy Spirit, he empowers us to live out this truth through this pursuit of holiness. This endeavor (post-salvation) is both monergistic and synergistic. Synergistic means "two or more working together." In other words, we as believers must do our part in this process, and God alone does his part. We must realize that if any fruit or transformation of eternal significance is to occur in our lives, it comes from the fact that God alone monergistically works in us to accomplish that growth.

In this passage, Paul gives us the command to work out our salvation. In the original language, this is a command we need to obey on a continuous basis. In other words, we could translate this as "keep on continually working out your own salvation." What exactly does it mean to work out our salvation? The word Paul uses for work out denotes active labor. In this process of growing to become more like Jesus, God commands us to exert continual energy. We do this with fear and trembling, which denotes a healthy fear and reverence of our awesome Savior. If we stop at verse 12 and use this in isolation to build a theology of sanctification, we would get depressed and suffer from guilt and frustration. In one sense, God commands us to take personal responsibility for our growth in godliness by working out our salvation. This requires diligence, obedience, urgency, and passion. If left to ourselves in this venture, we would never see any lasting fruit or experience gospel transformation. In and of ourselves, we cannot produce change. In his gracious provision, verse 13 displays for us the role God plays in our sanctification. It is synergistic in that we play a vital role in pursuing holiness through our initiative to work out our salvation. God keeps on continually working in us to do two things—will and work. God gives us the desire and the power to obey his commands. Those two realities were not part of us as unregenerate sinners before our salvation. In our lostness, we neither desired to obey God nor did we have the power to obey God. We wanted to feed our sinful pleasures, and because we did not have the Holy Spirit living within us, we could not follow the Lord's commands. However, through the new birth and the power of the gospel, God granted to us in our sanctification these two resources—the desire to obey and the ability to obey.

Ultimately, he receives all the glory for being the sole provider of our desperate need for grace. We work, but God also works. Our working may be feeble, inconsistent, and shallow at times, but behind the scenes, a sovereign God works to ensure that we perform his will through our good works according to his good pleasure. Jerry Bridges calls this cooperative effort between God and us "dependent responsibility" by saying that the responsibility to work out our salvation is one hundred percent our responsibility, but at the same time, we are one hundred percent dependent on the Holy Spirit actually to produce any fruit.[5]

First Timothy 4:7–8

First Timothy 4:7–8 serves as the second passage of Scripture which answers this question about striving or struggling in the Christian life. Here Paul writes, "Rather train yourself for godliness; for while bodily training is of some value, godliness is of value in every way, as it holds promise for the present life and also for the life to come." The word for "train yourself" comes as a command which we need to obey on a continuous basis. Also, this term comes from the world of athletics from where we get our word "gymnastics." When Olympic athletes in the first century would prepare for the games, they would go into strict physical training. Paul borrows this word from the athletic world to vividly illustrate the grueling nature in which we as Christians must strive to grow in holiness. Oscar Swahn from Sweden holds the record for the oldest person to win a Silver Medal in the 1920 Olympics at the age of seventy-two! He competed in the running deer shooting events. In the 2006 winter games

---

5. Bridges and Bevington, *Bookends of the Christian Life*, 95–97.

in Italy, Doug Gibson, age thirty-nine, won the skeleton race, which is similar to the luge and bobsledding. In skeleton racing, the athlete rides face down on a small sled flying down a track at forces up to 5Gs. For years, Gibson practiced on the ice, training his body for that one moment in history when he would finally win the gold medal. Think about the rigorous schedules athletes endure to prepare for the Olympics and how much time they put in the gym, or on the field, or on the slopes. First-class athletes are not haphazard even though they may have a great deal of natural talent. They discipline themselves every day to train with intensity and passion. This type of energy is what Paul describes when it comes to training ourselves for godliness. Instead of "letting go and letting God," Paul urges us to diligently go to the gym and work out spiritually so that we can grow in godliness.

Second Peter 1:5–8

In addition to Paul's teachings on the importance of exerting energy in our progressive sanctification, Peter also echoes this truth. In 2 Peter 1:5–8 he writes,

> For this very reason, make every effort to supplement your faith with virtue, and virtue with knowledge, and knowledge with self-control, and self-control with steadfastness, and steadfastness with godliness, and godliness with brotherly affection, and brotherly affection with love. For if these qualities are yours and are increasing, they keep you from being ineffective or unfruitful in the knowledge of our Lord Jesus Christ.

What does God command us to do in this passage? God calls us to make every effort to continually grow in godliness so that we will not become ineffective in our spiritual walk with Christ. To add emphasis to this command, Peter uses a strong expression in combining two Greek words which convey the idea of urgency and quickness to exert energy.[6] In other words, he urges us to hurry up with passionate zeal and start making an effort to increase in godly character. This verb choice is a far cry from the passive "let go and let God" quietism of the Keswick view of sanctification.

---

6. Peter combines the phrase "to make every effort" with "with diligent haste," both in the aorist imperative, which gives the command an urgency.

"MICROWAVE MAGIC" SANCTIFICATION?

My family went to Disneyland twice for vacation. Both times, we had the privilege of taking advantage of the convenient Fast Pass which makes standing in long lines a thing of the past. I hate standing in lines—any lines. We see this impatience all around us in our culture—from fad diets and high-speed internet to overnight express mail and apps for your smartphone. We live in a microwave magic world. We get impatient when we have to watch a television program in real time instead of fast forwarding through the commercials once we have recorded it on our DVR. Our culture demands instant pleasure. We want things yesterday! How does this translate into the area of growing in godliness? The Victorious Life doctrine of pursuing holiness claims that sanctification is instant, and victory is complete over all known sin. Through the use of techniques such as "letting go and letting God" or "ceasing from striving" or "absolutely surrendering," a believer can experience a higher level of spirituality. A person struggling with the sin of pornography, for instance, through a crisis of belief and a moment of surrender can be instantaneously free from this sin and achieve complete victory. One of the key early proponents of the Keswick view said, "A victory gained . . . by a gradual conquest over evil, getting one sin after another out of our life, is *counterfeit* victory."[7] If Christians struggle over a long period to kill indwelling sin (which we will explore in the next chapter) instead of defeating it through an immediate surrender, that victory proves inauthentic.

Does the Bible teach instantaneous and complete victory over all known sin in this life? Can we through a simple process of "letting go and letting God" never have to struggle with sin again? My wife and I enjoy hiking in our home state of Colorado. A few years ago, we decided to face a challenge we had wanted to do for a while—climb a 14er! For those not from Colorado, that means a mountain that is over 14,000 feet above sea level. So early one Saturday morning, we began the trek up Grey's Peak which others told us was a relatively easy climb. After four hours of stopping to catch our breath every fifteen feet, wincing in pain, and seeing all of these twentysomethings pass us by, we quickly reinterpreted the term "mountaintop experience." Our hike up the mountain was a visual allegory for the Christian's journey through life. There are peaks and valleys, twists and turns, rocks and hills, cliffs and flat meadows, but in the end, it is all uphill. There is no instantaneous arrival at the top of the mountain

---

7. Trumbull, *Victory in Christ*, 36.

unless you fly in by helicopter. The Christian life is not a casual helicopter flight with immediate results, but as John Bunyan has so vividly captured, it's a pilgrim's progress. We are on a lifelong journey full of adventure, struggles, heartache, doubt, and at times victory, on our way to heaven. J. C. Ryle said, "The theory of a sudden, mysterious transition of a believer into a state of blessedness and entire consecration, at one mighty bound, I cannot receive. It appears to me to be a man-made invention, and I do not see a single plain text to prove it in Scripture."[8] B. B. Warfield also warns against the expectation of instantaneous sanctification promised in the victorious life teaching by saying, "Its glowing and 'romantic' overtures that offer life on a higher plane are ultimately offers of victory to the impatient."[9]

INSTANT VICTORY OR CONSTANT WARFARE?

We find Scripture's emphasis on the reality of indwelling sin sprinkled throughout the New Testament. The apostle John addresses this issue in his First Epistle when he writes, "If we say we have no sin, we deceive ourselves, and the truth is not in us. If we confess our sins, he is faithful and just to forgive us our sins and to cleanse us from all unrighteousness. If we say we have not sinned, we make him a liar, and his word is not in us" (1 John 1:8–10). We can never get to the point where we can say that we are somehow without sin. John does not espouse the idea that we can be instantaneously free of all known sin. He tells us that when we confess our sin, God is faithful and just in his forgiveness and cleansing. The life of a believer is one of continual confessing of sins because we will always have sin in our lives. As we progress in holiness the sin in our lives will become less frequent and grievous.

In reality, the Victorious Life method confuses the historic Protestant distinctions between law and gospel. Our holy God demands absolute obedience to his moral law. We see these throughout the Scriptures as the moral imperatives codified in the Ten Commandments in the Old Testament and the ethical axioms in the New Testament. The law exists to show guilty sinners that we can in no way please God perfectly and that we have fallen short of God's standard. The gospel breaks in as the good news which announces to us that Christ lived the perfect life that

---

8. Ryle, *Holiness*, xxv.
9. Warfield, *Works of Benjamin B. Warfield, vol. 8*, 464.

none of us could live and obeyed every single command of God entirely in thought, word, and deed. Through his victorious life (not ours), his sacrificial death on the cross, and his triumphant resurrection, we trust in him, and he imputes his perfect record of righteousness to us. As a result, we stand not only forgiven before the Father, but also clothed in the positive righteousness of Christ. The grounds for our acceptance with God comes from both the life of Christ in keeping the law for us and the death and resurrection of Christ in purchasing us as his people.

This "higher life" theology has subtly shifted the emphasis on the law as God's standard of holiness and moved it to surrender as God's standard. The problem with this is that the Scriptures clearly state God's laws so that there is no confusion. The Bible gives us an objective standard of what God requires in his law. This concept of surrender, on the other hand, is such a nebulous term that it becomes difficult even to define or quantify. What exactly does it look like, practically, to surrender? How much surrendering do we need to do in order to please God fully? These questions become difficult to answer in comparison to the Bible's clear teaching concerning God's moral law. Michael Horton says this, "No longer did God require absolute perfection, but 'absolute surrender.' It was not external works of obedience that God required, but 'complete consecration' and 'yieldedness.' Those, however, who attempt to 'yield', 'surrender', and 'love' as God commands soon realize that this is even more difficult than conforming outwardly to divine commandments."[10]

INTROSPECTIVE FRUSTRATION

Ultimately, the Keswick or higher life movement leads to an unhealthy introspection where believers continuously wonder if they have surrendered or yielded themselves enough to God. This, in turn, leads to frustration when the struggle with sin continues. Christians who have tender consciences often wonder why they still struggle with sin even after many attempts to "let go and let God." They wonder if maybe they haven't let go enough. Also, how does one know how much to let go? How does one know if he or she has surrendered enough? What is the basis for this consecration? Is it external obedience to the revealed law of God, or is it some internal and subjective prompting or impression? Moreover, why are we in the driver's seat in this process? Why do we have to let go before

---

10. Horton, *In the Face of God*, 167.

we allow a sovereign, all-powerful God to do his work in our lives? Frustrated believers begin to question their faith and wonder if something is genuinely wrong with them. Did they do the technique of "letting go and letting God" correctly? Was it consistent enough? Were they truly serious about it? Frustration leads to despair as they begin to compare themselves to others who have reached this so-called higher plane of victorious spirituality. The spiritual haves tell the spiritual have-nots to stop striving and start letting go to truly arrive at this crisis of surrender so that they can achieve a quick victory. Instead of practicing gospel repentance in truly killing sin (which we will address in the next chapter), the defeated Christian falls into the trap of endless trips to the altar for a time of reconsecration. Frustrated with guilt, they rededicate their lives to the Lord for the thousandth time hoping that this time it truly sticks and that they have yielded enough to have victory. They wait for that moment of emotional crisis to yield to God so that they can subsequently be filled with the Spirit. However, what if that crisis never comes? What if every day we live in a state of warfare as the normal part of being a Christian? Michael Horton writes,

> War with sin and doubt, guilt and depression, are not signs of defeat, but proof of Christ's victory. After all, those who are not baptized into Christ by the Spirit are at peace with sin and unbelief. The absence of war within is true only of people in one of two states: unregenerate or glorified. The believer is presently neither. Such conflict is not the evidence that one is a "carnal Christian" but is the genuine experience of every true believer throughout the course of this life.[11]

If you continue to struggle with sin and have not experienced this immediate victory, do not think of yourself as a second-class Christian, but as a pilgrim on the long and winding road to heaven. Be encouraged that what God has begun in you he will sovereignly complete (Phil 1:6). In your frustration and desire to see growth in the battle with sin, find hope in the fact that our great Savior will bring you to completion in his perfect timing. In the end, the Keswick teachings on sanctification leave believers with an inadequate answer to help them in their quest to kill sin. Instead of passively surrendering to Christ through a fuzzy technique called "letting go and letting God," Paul gives us a different instruction. He writes in 1 Timothy 1:18 to "wage the good warfare." In the next chapter, we will explore how to fight the good fight through the process of killing sin.

11. Horton, *In the Face of God*, 193.

9

Killing Sin

"Be killing sin, or it will be killing you."
JOHN OWEN[1]

IN BETWEEN A ROCK *and a Hard Place* is the fitting title of a book by a mountain climber named Aron Ralston. In May 2003, while hiking in Utah, he was pinned between the canyon wall and an 800-pound boulder which crushed his right forearm. After five days of dehydration, delirium and a desperate attempt to dislodge the boulder, he used a dull utility knife to cut off his arm. Amputation was a drastic measure for Ralston to survive. This story eerily captures the powerful words of Jesus in Mark 9:43 where he says, "And if your hand causes you to sin, cut it off. It is better for you to enter life crippled than with two hands to go to hell, to the unquenchable fire." Jesus sounds very violent in this passage! How are we to take his emphatic words that command us to be brutal with our sin? While Jesus uses exaggeration and hyperbole here to show us the severity of sin, in the words of John Owen, we must be killing sin, or it will be killing us. We must deal forcefully with our sin because it is such a powerful force with which we must reckon.

---

1. Owen, *Mortification of Sin*, 28.

FLESH FOR FANTASY

In the past two chapters, we explored both the deception of indwelling sin and the constant struggle between the flesh and Spirit. But we have not answered the ten-million-dollar question: How do we kill sin? Romans 8:13 answers this question: "For if you live according to the flesh you will die, but if by the Spirit you put to death the deeds of the body, you will live." As we explore this text, we need to ask four specific questions concerning this practice of killing sin. First of all, what does it mean to live according to the flesh? Second, what are the deeds of the body? Third, what does it look like to kill sin? Fourth, what role do we play in killing sin and what role does the Holy Spirit play?

Let us answer the first question. Paul tells us that if we live according to the flesh, we will die. Spiritual death occurs when a person lives ultimately to feed the flesh. The key to understanding what it means to live according to the flesh comes in the tense of the verb. Paul uses the present active indicative, which denotes continuous action. In other words, if an individual habitually succumbs to sinful desires as the comprehensive characterization of his or her lifestyle, the result will be spiritual death. I believe Paul is describing an unregenerate person whom God has never made alive in Christ and given a new nature. John Owen provides this illustration[2] which describes what it means to live according to the flesh. Living according to the flesh is like a man who sets out on a journey determined to reach his destination. He obsesses over getting there as fast as he can. On his way, he gets caught in a menacing thunderstorm and tries to find immediate shelter. He goes into a house and temporarily waits for the storm to pass. He is impatient because this storm has ruined his plans, but he also knows that standing out in the pouring rain would not only be miserable but could result in being struck by lightning. Once the storm has passed, he immediately gets right back out on the road to continue his journey. This attitude characterizes people who are in bondage to sin and live according to the flesh. They are on this path of pursuing their lusts and enjoying sin. When they hear the gospel, or they hear about hell, or the thunder and lightning of the reality of eternal judgment, they get foxhole religion for a season. They turn temporarily for shelter from the horrors of their sin, but nothing has indeed changed. Once the storm passes, they are right back out on the path to sin again.

---

2. Owen, *Works of John Owen*, 6:317–18.

There has been no real transformation. Their entire course in life fixates on pursuing the path of sin by living according to the flesh.

As those who have a new identity in the Trinity, we have new desires and affections that intensely long to worship, obey, and follow Jesus. The entire course of a believer's life is one of actively pursuing holiness. On the other hand, evidence that a person has not experienced the miracle of the new birth shows itself in a lifestyle of slavery to sin and an ongoing pursuit of fleshly desires. Those who received the indwelling Spirit of Christ through the new birth do not live according to the flesh. That is no longer our nature. Our nature before salvation was enslavement to our flesh whereby our minds were hostile to God, and we could not submit to his law. Since God liberated us from this bondage to sin, we can freely submit to his law through the ministry of the Holy Spirit who has been poured out richly into our hearts.

But there is a clear warning here. Just because sin no longer enslaves us does not mean that it is no longer an active influence in our lives. We still retain the vestiges of our flesh and will never be completely sin free until the day we step foot into heaven. Only in our final glorification will we be free of the remnants of sin once and for all. For the believer, sin as a power and dominion no longer has its grip on us, and thus we are no longer under its rule. In our new-found freedom as God's regenerated and justified children, we can resist temptation and walk in obedience.

DEEDS OF THE BODY

The second question in our understanding of this passage comes in what Paul means by the "deeds of the body." We may initially think that Paul only addresses those sins that we commit with our body parts such as our eyes, ears, and hands. But within the context of Paul's argument throughout Romans 6–8, the deeds of the body can also be synonymous with the flesh. In other words, the deeds of the body can also be internal sins of the heart such as lust, greed, impatience, or an unforgiving spirit. They can also be external sins committed with our bodies such as sexual immorality, theft, or lying. In Colossians 3:5–8, we find a parallel passage which commands us to put sin to death:

> Put to death therefore what is earthly in you: sexual immorality, impurity, passion, evil desire, and covetousness, which is idolatry. On account of these, the wrath of God is coming. In these

you too once walked, when you were living in them. But now you must put them all away: anger, wrath, malice, slander, and obscene talk from your mouth.

From Paul's list, we see we must put both internal and external sins to death. Impurity of the heart may lie deep within the soul, while sexual immorality is an external sin committed with the body. Evil desire is also an internal sin which could lead to covetousness and subsequent thievery. In the same manner, anger is a secret sin we can express externally through slander or obscene talk. The list Paul uses here could be a summary of specific sins that he mentions in Romans 8:13 as "deeds of the body." We see many similarities between these two passages. In both cases, Paul commands us to kill sin and warns us of impending death if we live by the flesh. In Colossians 3:6 Paul describes it as God's coming wrath, while in Romans 8:13 he states it as death. Spiritual death in hell becomes the final ramification for those who die in their sins and have not experienced the miracles of regeneration, justification, and union with Christ in this new identity.

MORTIFICATION

The third question we must understand is this: What does it look like to kill sin? How do we put these deeds of the body to death? The King James Version uses the word "mortify," which no longer has much meaning in our contemporary culture. When people say that they are mortified, it usually means that they are embarrassed beyond all measure and want to slink away in shame. The Puritans of old called this process of killing sin "mortification." The word Paul uses here in Romans 8:13 for this act of killing sin was often used to describe an execution. Paul again uses the present active indicative verb choice to illustrate that this killing is not just a one-time action. Putting sin to death involves an ongoing, continual, brutal, endless lifestyle of mortification.

We have already seen how deceitful, tenacious, and corrupting indwelling sin truly is. Sin is a foe that will never back down. Sin does not take a halftime break in the locker room to catch its breath. Sin does not retreat to the beach for a day of relaxation. Sin does not fall asleep at the wheel because it has grown so tired after hours of dogging us. John Owen claims, "Sin will not only be striving, acting, rebelling, troubling, disquieting, but if left alone, if not continually mortified, it will bring forth great, cursed, scandalous, soul-destroying sins."[3] Sin does not take a break, so neither should we when it comes to this battle. We can never sleep. What did Jesus remind his disciples just hours before his betrayal in Matthew 26:40–41: "And he came to the disciples and found them sleeping. And he said to Peter, 'So, could you not watch with me one hour? Watch and pray that you may not enter into temptation. The spirit indeed is willing, but the flesh is weak.'" J. C. Ryle says, "Sin admits of no breathing time, no armistice, no truce."[4]

Randy Gardner holds the world record for going the longest time without any sleep—eleven days! In 1964, as a high school student in San Diego, California, he underwent a scientific study with a researcher from Stanford University to see how many days a person could go without sleep not using stimulants of any kind. Eventually, the human body shuts down and has to give in to the innate need for rest. We cannot physically stay awake forever. In stark contradiction to this, sin never sleeps. It remains awake. Because sin never sleeps, continually pursues us, and desires nothing but a hostile takeover of our souls, we need to adopt the same attitude. We need to kill sin actively, consistently, and fervently. John Calvin comments on this passage in Romans 8:13 by saying that Paul "bids us to make every exertion to subdue sin's lusts."[5] John Owen defines mortification this way: "To kill a man, or any other living thing, is to take away the principle of all his strength, vigour, and power, so that he cannot act or exert, or put forth any proper actings of his own."[6]

I need to issue a caution before we go any further. Ultimate mortification or total death of sin will never occur in this life. We will never totally kill all sin. This complete victory over sin should never be an expected part of our progressive sanctification. Our aim should be to mortify or kill all sin, but in reality, this will never happen this side of heaven. We may experience seasons of incredible success and victory against sin, but we will never get to the point where we no longer have to practice the grueling process of mortification. The moment we get to the point where we think that sin no longer can deceive us or manipulate us or that it somehow lies dormant within us becomes that exact moment that we are the most vulnerable. The apostle John tells us in 1 John 1:8 that "If

---

3. Owen, *Mortification of Sin*, 32.
4. Ryle, *Holiness*, 54.
5. Calvin, *Acts-Romans*, 294.
6. Ferguson, *John Owen*, 146.

we say we have no sin, we deceive ourselves, and the truth is not in us." Therefore, we must make it our constant duty to kill sin whenever it rears its ugly head.

What Mortification is NOT

Before we describe this process of mortification, it would be helpful for us to delineate what mortification is not. *First of all, mortification is not just a cosmetic makeover of our sin.* What is meant by this? The Bible often speaks of root sins and fruit sins. Root sins are those profoundly ingrained sins that lie way beneath the surface, such as pride, lust, selfishness, and idolatry. Fruit sins are those outward expressions of sin that we often equate with the Ten Commandments, such as lying, murder, theft, and adultery. Many attempts to manage sin only deal with the fruit sins instead of getting down to the root sins. It is nothing more than a makeover with window dressing to cover the problem without getting down to the depths of the real issue. For example, Gary struggles with pornography and stays up late filling his mind with illicit images while his unsuspecting wife is asleep. To deal with this problem, Gary tackles the issue of pornography and may use legalistic measures to somehow stop him from surfing the internet. He may slap his hand every time he wants to click on a porn site. His fruit problem is pornography, but his root problem is lust. He may eventually get over the pornography problem, but since he has not killed evil desire at the root, it may manifest itself in another outward fruit such as adultery or visiting massage parlors while on a business trip. Diverting sin is not enough. Covering it up is not enough. Mortification involves killing the sin at its root.

Second, ignoring sin and hoping that it goes away does not accurately describe the process of mortification. John Owen illustrates the problem with ignoring sin by saying, "Such a one never thinks his lust dead because it is quiet; but labors still to give it new wounds, new blows every day."[7] We must never get to the point where we think sin is inert within us just because we may not be experiencing a particular struggle for a season. Sin deceitfully lies dormant, but like a cobra, it springs forth with a venomous attack and will seek to destroy us when we least expect it.

Third, occasional attempts will not successfully work in this process of mortification. We can neither be haphazard nor inconsistent. We may

---

7. Owen, *Mortification of Sin*, 72.

be diligent for a period in killing sin and then let up in the fight and just coast. When we get in this posture of relaxation, we tend to drift toward apathy in our response to sin. As a result, we get lulled into a sinister sleep, and we may only practice mortification in a hit-and-miss fashion. John Owen again reminds us: "But now let the heart be cleansed by mortification; the weeds of lust constantly and daily rooted up, as they spring daily, nature being their proper soil; let room be made for grace to thrive and flourish; how will every grace act its part, and be ready for every use and purpose!"[8]

Five Aspects of Mortification

What then is true mortification of sin? Sinclair Ferguson defines it this way: "It is the constant battle against sin which we fight daily—the refusal to allow the eye to wander, the mind to contemplate, the affection to run after anything that will draw us from Christ. It is the deliberate rejection of any sinful thought, suggestion, desire, aspiration, deed, circumstance or provocation at the moment we become conscious of its existence."[9] Let me suggest five key aspects that will help us understand what it means to put sin to death.

First of all, we must have a seething hatred for sin as the destructive enemy it truly is. John Stott makes this assertion: "It (mortification) is rather a clear-sighted recognition of evil as evil, leading to such a decisive and radical repudiation of it that no imagery can do justice except 'putting to death.'"[10] Romans 12:9 says, "Abhor what is evil; hold fast to what is good." Thomas Brooks, in speaking of this word "abhor," says "it signifies to hate it (sin) as hell itself, to hate it with horror."[11]

Second, we need to think about the guilt and corruption of sin. We need to look sin in the face and see it for all its ugliness. Our flesh darkens our minds so that we do not see the true corrupting nature of sin and how it causes us to excuse or justify our sin. We must understand how condemning sin is. Thomas Brooks has given great insight into alerting ourselves to the corruption of sin. He writes, "Sin is but a bittersweet. That seeming sweet that is in sin will quickly vanish, and the lasting

---

8. Owen, *Mortification of Sin*, 56.
9. Ferguson, *Christian Life*, 162.
10. Stott, *Message of Romans*, 228.
11. Brooks, *Precious Remedies against Satan's Devices*, 30.

shame, sorrow, horror, and terror will come in the room thereof."[12] In Job 20:12–14, he mediates on the corruption of sin: "Though evil is sweet in his mouth, though he hides it under his tongue, though he is loath to let it go and holds it in his mouth, yet his food is turned in his stomach; it is the venom of cobras within him." Instead of focusing on the sweetness of sin, we must see it in all its corrupting guilt. Brooks also warns us with these words: "Alas! saith Satan, it is but a very little sin that you stick so at. You may commit it without any danger to your soul. It is but a little one; you may commit it, and yet your soul shall live."[13] There is no such thing as an innocent little sin. All sin is offensive to God, and little sins lead to more grievous sins. In 1 Corinthians 5:6, Paul rebukes the church by saying, "Your boasting is not good. Do you not know that a little leaven leavens the whole lump?"

Third, mortification involves examining the shock and utter danger of sin. We need to remind ourselves of how sinful sin truly is. We need to remind ourselves of how we gave in to sinful desires in past experiences of weakness. We need a healthy dose of how sin brings danger and destruction. We need to think clearly about how it damaged us in the past when we did not kill it. In turn, we must think about the devastating consequences of what might happen if we plunge headlong into sin. Thomas Brooks again gives wise counsel with these warnings:

> Ah, souls, often remember how frequently you have been overcome by sin, when you have boldly gone upon the occasion of sin; look back, souls, to the day of your vanity, wherein you have been easily conquered as tempted, vanquished as assaulted, when you have played with occasions of sin. As you would for the future be kept from the acting of sin, and be made victorious over sin, oh! flee from the occasion of sin.[14]

Martyn Lloyd-Jones illumines this concept of exposing the guilt of sin by saying, "We have to pull it (sin) out, look at it, denounce it, hate it for what it is; then you have really dealt with it."[15]

Fourth, we must be intimate with our particular areas of weakness and subsequently avoid areas or situations where we would be vulnerable.

---

12. Brooks, *Precious Remedies against Satan's Devices*, 32.
13. Brooks, *Precious Remedies against Satan's Devices*, 38.
14. Brooks, *Precious Remedies against Satan's Devices*, 68.
15. Lloyd-Jones, in Stott, *Message of Romans*, 143.

We see this very clearly illustrated in Proverbs 5:3–8 in the description of the enticing prostitute:

> For the lips of a forbidden woman drip honey, and her speech is smoother than oil, but in the end she is bitter as wormwood, sharp as a two-edged sword. Her feet go down to death; her steps follow the path to Sheol; she does not ponder the path of life; her ways wander, and she does not know it. And now, O sons, listen to me, and do not depart from the words of my mouth. Keep your way far from her, and do not go near the door of her house.

Notice how Solomon warns the young man not to even go near the door of her house. He must take every precaution to keep the maximum distance from her in order not to be seduced. In the same way, mortification of sin involves actively avoiding areas and situations that will cause us to stumble. First Thessalonians 5:22 tells us to "Abstain from every form of evil."

Fifth, we also need to expose the lie behind the sin and by faith believe the truth of God's word. We need to understand the exceeding deceitfulness of sin and not buy into the myth that sin brings pleasure. We must expose wrongdoing for what it is—a fleeting pleasure that leads to unfulfilled promises and destruction. Ultimately, we can summarize mortification with the word "repentance." When we begin to consistently hate sin with a holy passion, seriously contemplate its guilt and corruption, remain in a state of shock over its devastating effects, and continuously expose it in all its deception and destruction, we are in fact repenting. Through repentance, we are then weakening sin in our lives. Slowly, through this painful process of mortification, we begin to see the progress we are making in godliness as sin gets weaker and weaker. Indwelling sin never entirely goes away, but through persistent mortification, we can see a slow transformation in holiness.

Let us consider a situation between two women who are prone to gossip. Carol salivates over finding out about all of the juicy stories concerning everyone in the office. She is the ultimate cubical detective who always tries to dig up skeletons in everyone else's closet so that she can gleefully feel secure about her shortcomings. She sends Mary an enticing e-mail with some damaging information about their co-worker. The moment Mary sees the e-mail she faces a choice. Does she engage in the sin of gossip and indulge the flesh, or does she ruthlessly kill this sin on the spot? Since she has saturated herself in the word of God (see next chapter) and understands her true identity in the Trinity, she then exposes this sin for what it is. She brings gossip out into the open, clearly recognizes it, calls it sin, and then allows the law of God to condemn it as a violation of his will. She remembers in Romans 1:29 that Paul identifies gossip as an ungodly transgression deserving death. She hates gossip and thinks about all the devastating consequences that she has experienced in her own life because of this sin. She brings this sin under the just condemnation of God's word and recognizes it for the lie that it truly is. She sees that gossip deceives her into thinking she will find fulfillment in making fun of others and slandering their character. By faith, she rejects the lie as a temporary pleasure that cannot make good on its empty promise. In a moment of repentance, she violently deals with sin and immediately kills it. She deletes the e-mail and fills her mind with the devastating horrors of gossip and how this violates God's law. The more she begins to identify the sin, expose it for its sinfulness, and then subsequently kill it, the more she weakens gossip in her life. She may never be entirely free of gossip, but she can lessen it through repeated and sustained mortification.

SPIRIT-EMPOWERED KILLING

At this point, we need to be very careful that we do not fall into an error of legalistic works-based performance where mortification becomes a sheer act of the will without the transforming power of the Holy Spirit. The fourth question we must ask about mortification manifests itself in the role we play along with the part of the Holy Spirit in killing sin. In Romans 8:13, Paul says that we are to kill sin "by the Spirit." This work of killing sin is both monergistic and synergistic. By monergistic, we mean that the Holy Spirit alone does the job of killing sin. All the credit for spiritual transformation or growth in grace comes from the sovereign Spirit of God. He alone produces the spiritual fruit and causes the increase in progressive sanctification. John Owen again says this about the Holy Spirit: "He is the fire which burns up the very root of lust."[16] Again, Owen also gives this sober reminder: "Mortification from a self-strength, carried on by ways of self-invention, unto the end of a self-righteousness, is the soul and substance of all false religion in the world."[17] We must

---

16. Owen, *Mortification of Sin*, 47.
17. Owen, *John Owen*, 145.

implore the help of the great Helper himself and continuously ask the Holy Spirit to come to our rescue in this grueling battle to kill sin.

Romans 8:13 also commands us to be active in this process of killing sin. Mortification is synergistic in that we also participate and cooperate with the Spirit. If we look closely at this passage, it does not say that the Holy Spirit will put to death the deeds of the body, but that we are responsible for putting them to death. We do this by the power of the Holy Spirit in our lives. John Owen gives a compelling case for this by saying, "The Holy Ghost works in us and upon us, as we are fit to be wrought in and upon; that is, so as to preserve our own liberty and free obedience. He works upon our understandings, wills, consciences, and affections, agreeably to their own natures: he works in us and with us, not against us or without us." Since we are regenerated, indwelt, and sanctified by the Holy Spirit, he works with our renewed hearts and compels us to obey. But he does not obey for us. He works in us, but not without us. We are still morally responsible agents who must take the command seriously to kill sin. When genuine transformation occurs in our growth in godliness, we humbly thank the Spirit who has wrought this work in us and granted us the grace to obey. He alone deserves the credit for killing sin, but we are still responsible for our part in this process.

Through the sanctifying power of the Holy Spirit, he grants us the grace to personally take responsibility to kill the deeds of the body. If we do not take an active part in this process of mortification, we can fall prey to the error mentioned in the previous chapter about the quietism of the victorious Christian life. We will passively let go and let God, and not see that the ruthless nature of killing involves active participation on our part to fight the good fight and kill sin. Jerry Bridges comments on his personal experience with this type of thinking: "I misconstrued dependence on the Holy Spirit to mean I was to make no effort, that I had no responsibility. I mistakenly thought if I turned it all over to the Lord, he would make my choices for me and would choose obedience over disobedience."[18] J. C. Ryle reminds us, "He that pretends to condemn 'fighting' and teaches that we ought to sit still and 'yield ourselves to God', appears to me to misunderstand his Bible, and to make a great mistake."[19]

---

18. Bridges, *Pursuit of Holiness*, 79.
19. Ryle, *Holiness*, 53.

AUTOTOMY

Autotomy is a scientific term describing the act of self-amputation whereby a lizard severs its appendages as a self-defense mechanism to evade the clutches of an oncoming predator. Amazingly, the appendage may actually regenerate itself and grow back. For example, geckos and salamanders will shed part of their tail structure when captured in an attempt to escape. In a spiritual sense, Jesus calls us to perform autotomy on our sin. We must amputate or kill the deeds of the flesh whenever we fear being captured by its devious grasp. In similar fashion to the regeneration of the gecko's tail, our sin will always come back in full force. We will never entirely kill sin in this life, but we can be persistent, brutal, and ruthless in this pursuit of mortification.

Remember Jesus' words at the beginning of this chapter about cutting off your hand if it causes you to sin? Many times, we focus so much on the hyperbole of Jesus' statement and try to overexplain what it does not mean, that we fail to see what these powerful words do mean. Sin is a ruthless enemy that never sleeps, continually attacks us, and manipulates us with deception. Hear the words of Jesus again and instead of trying to explain away the outlandish demands of our Lord, receive them in the shocking manner in which he meant us to receive them. Jesus expects us to stand up in shock at such exaggerated autotomy because the stakes are so high. Jesus said in Mark 9:34: "And if your hand causes you to sin, cut it off. It is better for you to enter life crippled than with two hands to go to hell, to the unquenchable fire." The ultimate destination for one who is entrenched in unrepentant, chronic, and persistent sin is the lake of unquenchable fire. There is no time to trifle with the allurements and amusements that sin has to offer when our eternal destinies are on the line. As regenerated and justified believers, we hear these words not as threatening demands of condemnation from a Judge, but as warnings from a heavenly Father who loves us too much to allow us to stay in a state of apathy when it comes to killing sin. We must be killing sin, or it will be killing us. This chapter has focused primarily on how we negatively deal with sin by putting it to death. The next chapter will introduce us to the positive aspect of growing in our identity in the Trinity by taking advantage of God's ordinary means of grace.

10

The Authoritative Word

"The church must proclaim—clearly, urgently, persuasively—the Word of God without confusion, without change, without compromise—as its first order of business."

GREGG ALLISON[1]

IN THE PREVIOUS THREE chapters, we saw how indwelling sin proves a constant enemy that we must kill through the process of mortification. Mortification is the negative process by which we advance in obedience. The LORD has also given us some very positive practices that are instrumental to our gospel identity and growth in holiness. Listen to the encouragement from Martin Luther: "So when the sinful nature rages, the only thing to do is to take up the sword of the Spirit, which is the truth of salvation, and fight."[2] God saves us by grace in our initial salvation, but we continue to need his sustaining grace in our daily walk. God has appointed for us to use the means of grace to help strengthen our faith in him. What does this term "means of grace" describe? These are practices that God uses as ways to strengthen you, feed you, provide for you, and grow you. You are responsible for taking advantage of these means and putting forth the effort to do them, but through them the Holy Spirit will

---

1. Allison, *Sojourners and Strangers*, 435.
2. Luther, *Galatians*, 274.

empower you to walk in holiness. Acts 2:42–47 demonstrates how the early church made these practices a crucial part of their lives together in community:

> And they devoted themselves to the apostles' teaching and the fellowship, to the breaking of bread and the prayers. And awe came upon every soul, and many wonders and signs were being done through the apostles. And all who believed were together and had all things in common. And they were selling their possessions and belongings and distributing the proceeds to all, as any had need. And day by day, attending the temple together and breaking bread in their homes, they received their food with glad and generous hearts, praising God and having favor with all the people. And the Lord added to their number day by day those who were being saved.

We see five overarching practices here: (1) Bible intake or Scripture saturation, (2) prayer, (3) fellowship, (4) the Lord's Supper, and (5) evangelism. Richard Barcellos defines the means of grace as "delivery systems God has instituted to bring grace—that is, spiritual power, spiritual change, spiritual help, spiritual fortitude, spiritual blessings—to needy souls on earth."[3] Question 88 of the *Westminster Shorter Catechism* asks,

> *"What are the outward means whereby Christ communicates to us the benefits of redemption?"* Answer: The outward and ordinary means whereby Christ communicates to us the benefits of redemption are his ordinances, especially the Word, sacraments, and prayer; all of which are made effectual to the elect for salvation.

> Question 89: *How is the word made effectual to salvation?* Answer: The Spirit of God maketh the reading, but especially the preaching of the word, an effectual means of convincing and converting sinners, and of building them up in holiness and comfort through faith unto salvation.[4]

Louis Berkhof adds, "God has appointed them as the ordinary means through which he works his grace in the hearts of sinners, and their willful neglect can only result in spiritual loss."[5] We must not become

---

3. Barcellos, *Lord's Supper*, 23.

4. http://www.westminsterconfession.org/confessional-standards/the-westminster-shorter-catechism.php.

5. Berkhof, *Systematic Theology*, 608.

legalistic about these practices and think that by doing them, we win favor with God or improve our standing. As justified believers, we rest in a permanent position of acceptance before God on account of the imputed righteousness of Christ. In our sanctification, God does command us to put forth effort by his grace to grow in godliness. Neglecting these means of grace will not only hamper your spiritual growth, but may prove in the long run that you were never saved in the first place. Over the next few chapters, we will explore these more in depth, and I encourage you to take advantage of these—not begrudgingly as a burden to earn God's approval, but joyfully in thankfulness for how God has chosen to advance you spiritually in your gospel identity. Historically we can delineate the means of grace in two categories: the public means of grace and the private means of grace. Before we explore how to take advantage of these, we must understand the fundamental nature of God's word itself.

THE GOD-BREATHED WORD

In Paul's Second Epistle to Timothy, he gives some of the most explicit instructions about the nature of God's word as well as how that word should be preached with authority in the church. Second Timothy 3:15–17 reads:

> How from childhood you have been acquainted with the sacred writings, which are able to make you wise for salvation through faith in Christ Jesus. All Scripture is breathed out by God and profitable for teaching, for reproof, for correction, and for training in righteousness, that the man of God may be complete, equipped for every good work.

This passage brings up a few questions about the nature of Scripture itself. First of all, what is meant by the terms "sacred writings" and "Scripture?" These refer to the written word of God—in particular, the Old Testament here because the New Testament was still in the process of being written. Secondly, when Paul uses "all," it means the totality of the written word of God. The Greek preposition "all" (*pas*) means the totality of Scripture down to the very last written word. Third, what does it mean that the written word is "breathed out by God?" This is a compound word in the Greek language, *theopneustos*, combining *Theos* (God) with *pneuma* (breath). It means that God has breathed out his very word into the minds and hearts of the writers of Scripture so that what they wrote down is the literal word of God down to the very last detail. B. B. Warfield is very helpful when he writes, "What is *theopneustos* is 'God-breathed,' produced by the creative breath of the Almighty . . . What it affirms is that the Scriptures owe their origin to an activity of God the Holy Spirit and are in the highest and truest sense his creation. It is the foundation of divine origin that all the high attributes of Scripture are built."[6]

Some translations use the word "inspired" or "given by inspiration," which I think is confusing. When we think of inspired or inspiring we can think of a poet like Shakespeare who got inspired to write *Romeo and Juliet*, or we can say our favorite athlete was inspired to win the championship, or our favorite musical artist was inspired to write the latest chart-topping song. This word "God-breathed" does not mean that the Scriptures are "inspiring" in that they motivate you to follow Christ—even though the Bible does do this. It doesn't mean that when you read the Bible, you feel some inspiration. It does not mean that somehow the authors of the Bible had this personal inspiration that moved them to write something deeply spiritual. The Scriptures are the direct breathed-out word of God in their entirety. The final product—the whole of the written Scripture—is the very breathed-out word of God.

We don't know exactly how God did this. The Bible does not describe how he breathed out his word into the hearts and minds of the writers, but that the final product—the written Scripture—is inherently and fundamentally God-breathed. Peter gives us some insight into this process in 2 Peter 1:20–21: "knowing this first of all, that no prophecy of Scripture comes from someone's own interpretation. For no prophecy was ever produced by the will of man, but men spoke from God as they were carried along by the Holy Spirit." The Holy Spirit powerfully and supernaturally guided the human authors to write the Scriptures. Somehow God worked in their hearts and minds to record precisely what he wanted them to write down. God did not bypass their personalities in some mechanical way like a stenographer typing what is being dictated in a courtroom or like a little parrot mimicking words. We can trust that what we have as the written Scripture is the breathed-out word of God and is not the product of men, but has its ultimate origin in God himself.

---

6. Warfield, *Works of Benjamin B. Warfield*, 1:280.

PREACHING AS THE PUBLIC MEANS OF GRACE

Paul continues this instruction on the nature of the God-breathed word in relation to preaching in 2 Timothy 4:1–3:

> I charge you in the presence of God and of Christ Jesus, who is to judge the living and the dead, and by his appearing and his kingdom: preach the word; be ready in season and out of season; reprove, rebuke, and exhort, with complete patience and teaching. For the time is coming when people will not endure sound teaching, but having itching ears they will accumulate for themselves teachers to suit their own passions, and will turn away from listening to the truth and wander off into myths.

Paul charges Timothy to preach "the word," which contextually links back to 2 Timothy 3:16 as the God-breathed written Scriptures. John MacArthur claims, "The God-ordained means to save, sanctify, and strengthen his church is preaching."[7] Do you honestly believe this? Do you believe in the power of the preached word to strengthen you? To grow you in Christ? To help you live out your gospel identity?

Many times, pastors may become tempted to rely on other means or sources besides the sufficiency of Scripture to motivate and lead the church to spiritual growth. As such, he may preach personal opinion, trite stories, political speeches, motivational talks, or casual conversations, which unfortunately serve as the main diet of many evangelical pulpits. Instead, the content of expository preaching must include the bold proclamation and clear explanation of the sacred text of Scripture. Since our chief aim is to glorify God in our gospel identity, we as Christ-honoring churches should not be driven by pragmatism, popular opinion, or fads, but instead we should be motivated by what brings the most honor and glory to the Lord. What do I mean by pragmatism? John MacArthur defines it this way:

> It is a philosophy that says that results determine meaning, truth, and value—what will work becomes a more critical question than what is true. As Christians, we are called to trust what the Lord says, preach that message to others, and leave the results to him. But many have set that aside. Seeking relevancy and success, they have welcomed the pragmatic approach and have received the proverbial Trojan horse.[8]

---

7. MacArthur, "Preaching," 204.
8. MacArthur, "What's Inside the Trojan Horse?" para. 2.

A church that is driven by pragmatism always does what gets the best results by any means necessary through human ingenuity. In contrast, a church motivated by God's glory remains faithful to the Bible and trusts him for the results that he can only accomplish through his supernatural power. A. W. Tozer said,

> In my opinion, the great single need of the moment is that light-hearted superficial religionists be struck down with a vision of God high and lifted up, with his train filling the temple. The holy art of worship seems to have passed away like the Shekinah glory from the tabernacle. As a result, we are left to our own devices and forced to make up the lack of spontaneous worship by bringing in countless cheap and tawdry activities to hold the attention of the church people"[9]

Fads or popular opinion should not be what drive preachers of God's truth. The LORD does not call them to preach what people necessarily want to hear, but what they may need to hear. They shouldn't preach to win a popularity contest, but to proclaim the truth and let the Spirit sovereignly work on hearts. Pastors ought to do this with compassion and sensitivity, but it does nobody any good if they don't preach the whole counsel of God's word—even the controversial and harsh portions that make people uncomfortable. Leonard Ravenhill prophetically claimed:

> The New Testament church did not depend on a moral majority, but rather on a holy minority. The church right now has more fashion than passion, is more pathetic than prophetic, is more superficial than supernatural. The church that the apostles ministered in was a suffering church; today we have a sufficient church. Events in the Spirit-controlled church were amazing; in this day the church is often just amusing. The New Testament church was identified with persecutions, prisons, and poverty; today many of us are identified with prosperity, popularity, and personalities.[10]

We don't need the greatest technology. We don't need the most excellent techniques and programming. We don't need the most dynamic personalities in leadership. We don't need a marketing plan or a church-growth scheme. We don't need opinion after opinion after opinion. What we desperately need is the solid-rock promise that God speaks to his people

---

9. Tozer, *Keys to the Deeper Life*, 87–88.
10. Ravenhill, *Revival God's* Way, 57.

through the authoritative preaching of his word. Where else are we going to hear from the Lord if not through the preaching of the word? On a daily basis, we are bombarded with multiple voices that vie for our attention: the talking heads on your favorite news channel, the internet, social media, satellite radio, YouTube, podcasts, video games, and any other media you can think of! We have no shortage of voices, opinions, prognosticators, experts, and people who think they know everything. They speak with such authority, and some of what they say may be true, but we desperately need more. We need to hear a word from the Lord himself. God speaks to his people through the faithful preaching of the word. *The Second Helvetic Confession* teaches, "The preaching of the Word of God is the Word of God. Wherefore when this Word of God is now preached in the church by preachers lawfully called, we believe that the very Word of God is proclaimed."[11] When you listen to biblical preaching, the pastor better have a word from the Lord, or you've been short-changed. You don't need to hear his opinions. In my study, I have on my wall next to my computer a quote by Vance Havner: "God is on the lookout today for a man who will be quiet enough to get a message to him, brave enough to preach it, and honest enough to live it."

LIVING UNDER THE AUTHORITY OF GOD'S WORD

When you sit under the authoritative preaching of God's word, the Spirit graciously works faith and repentance deep into your soul. The Bible is shaping you, instead of the world. A lack of authoritative expository preaching inevitably leads to the congregation's lack of obedience. Walt Kaiser asks, "Where has the prophetic note in preaching gone? Where is the sense of authority and mission previously associated with the biblical Word? One of the most depressing spectacles in the Church today is her lack of power . . . At the heart of this problem is an impotent pulpit."[12] Unbiblical theology and practices may creep into the fabric of the church's ethos when congregations do not live under the authority of God's word. For example, churches can elevate their sacred traditions above the clear teachings of Scripture. Unbiblical core values embedded in the life of a congregation lead to toxicity and division. For example, the church in Corinth displayed an unhealthy fascination with their spiritual leaders,

---

11. "Second Helvetic Confession," 157.
12. Kaiser, *Toward an Exegetical Theology*, 20, 235–36.

causing Paul to address their divisions and factions. First Corinthians 3:1–4 reads,

> But I, brothers, could not address you as spiritual people, but as people of the flesh, as infants in Christ. I fed you with milk, not solid food, for you were not ready for it. And even now you are not yet ready, for you are still of the flesh. For while there is jealousy and strife among you, are you not of the flesh and behaving only in a human way? For when one says, 'I follow Paul,' and another, 'I follow Apollos,' are you not being merely human?

The ethos of leader worship had crept into the Corinthian church, demonstrating that they had forgotten the centrality of the gospel as well as the authority of the Scriptures. As their shepherd, Paul addressed these problems by appealing to their spiritual immaturity and their failure to live under the influence of the solid food of the Scriptures. A church can be tempted to adopt man-centered pragmatic techniques instead of relying on biblical principles to foster church growth. This lack of authoritative expository leadership can also result in biblical illiteracy—or even more hazardous—an abandonment of trust in the inerrancy and inspiration of Scripture. Albert Mohler claims, "In all true expository preaching, there is a note of authority. That is because the preacher dares to speak on behalf of God. He stands in the pulpit as a steward of the mysteries of God, declaring the truth of God's Word, proclaiming the power of that Word, and applying that Word to life."[13]

When pastors practice expository preaching that remains faithful to the written text, the Scripture inherently provides propositional truth along with the living and active ability to penetrate the souls of the hearers. Hebrews 4:12 says, "For the word of God is living and active, sharper than any two-edged sword, piercing to the division of soul and of spirit, of joints and of marrow, and discerning the thoughts and intentions of the heart." The key for the preacher is to remain as faithful to the text as possible as he preaches expositionally to unleash the Bible's inherent authority and potency. Isaiah 55:10–11 vividly explains the Scriptures' authority and power: "For as the rain and the snow come down from heaven and do not return there but water the earth, making it bring forth and sprout, giving seed to the sower and bread to the eater, so shall my word be that goes out from my mouth; it shall not return to me empty,

---

13. Mohler, *He Is Not Silent*, 71.

but it shall accomplish that which I purpose, and shall succeed in the thing for which I sent it."

God has mandated to the church the highest responsibility of proclaiming the truth of God without compromise. Through his expository preaching, the pastor sets the pace for the church's commitment to the authority of the Scripture to form their life together as a fellowship. Mohler asserts,

> Without a total commitment to the trustworthiness and truthfulness of the Bible, the church is left without its definite authority, lacking confidence in its ability to hear God's voice. Preachers will lack confidence in the power and truthfulness of the very word they are commissioned to preach and teach. This is not an issue of homiletical theory but a life-and-death question of whether the preacher has a distinctive and authoritative word to preach to people desperately in need of direction and guidance.[14]

THE IMPORTANCE OF INERRANCY

A robust belief in inerrancy impacts your attitude toward submitting to God's authoritative word. How do we define inerrancy? Paul Feinberg provides a helpful explanation: "Inerrancy means that when all facts are known, the Scriptures in their original autographs and properly interpreted will be shown to be wholly true in everything they affirm, whether that has to do with doctrine or morality or with social, physical, or life sciences."[15] Timothy Ward expands upon this definition: "To say that the Bible is inerrant is to make the claim that it does not assert any errors of fact; whether the Bible refers to events in the life of Christ, or to other details of history or geography, what it asserts is true."[16] Why is the inerrancy of Scripture essential to your growth in Christ as you listen to sermons? Sitting under expository preaching consistently exposes you to God's authoritative voice in the text, and not the selfish whims or authority of the pastor. Faithfulness to the Scriptures demonstrates the inherent power of the Bible, not the pseudoauthority of the pastor's opinions. Thus, the pastor's primary responsibility is to ensure that the people

---

14. Mohler, "When the Bible Speaks," 31.
15. Feinberg, "Meaning of Inerrancy," 294.
16. Ward, *Words of Life*, 130.

hear God's voice, not his own voice, which he accomplishes through expository preaching. Pastors who faithfully and systematically expose their people to God's word demonstrate the biblical basis for many of the values expressed, ministries adopted, and decisions made in the church. The rationale for the mission, vision, and values come from the Scriptures' authority, not from personal opinion or preference. This type of expository leadership guards the church against relying on man-centered traditions and selfish agendas to establish the foundation for the church's identity and ministries.

The word becomes what shapes and motivates the church to fulfill its mission when pastors affirm inerrancy and inspiration by preaching the authoritative Scripture with clarity and conviction. Expository preaching liberates the pastor to lead the church from the inherent authority of the Scriptures. In doing so, he can boldly challenge, confront, and correct the deficiencies and sins in his flock. When a pastor leads his people through expository preaching to live under the authority of the word, he becomes supernaturally empowered to proclaim like a herald, energized to teach like a sage, emboldened to plead like a father, and enabled to exhort like a shepherd. The pastor's spiritual leadership authority is not innate, but derives from the authority which resides in the text of Scripture. His task becomes the consistent preaching of that text to expose his people to God's voice as a means to lead them to obedience in fulfilling their mission.

PREACHING RESULTS IN GOSPEL TRANSFORMATION

The goal in preaching is not merely for the church to acquire information, but to undergo authentic change. Some biblical texts drive you to tears in the confession of sin, as other texts expose hidden transgressions like a dagger in the soul, while other texts comfort and console. Do you believe that God speaks to the depths of your heart through preaching and produces lasting gospel transformation? When you gather for worship, do you anticipate the preached word impacting and helping you grow in your identity in the Trinity? Do you come to church expecting a pep talk from a motivational speaker, or do you wait for God to show up in power and confront you in your sin, comfort you in your weakness, and equip you in your insufficiency? Craig Larson says, "God's full strength comes to bear when the Word of God is preached in the power of the Holy Spirit. When our purpose is to reshape people into the image of Jesus Christ—not merely helping them feel better or providing inspiration—nothing has greater potency than biblical preaching."[17]

When you listen to God's word preached faithfully, you should desire to act upon it with repentance, faith, and obedience. *The Westminster Longer Catechism* provides a helpful explanation in Question 160 of the responsibility of those who sit under expository preaching by asking,

> What is required of those who hear the word preached? Answer: It is required that they attend upon it with diligence, preparation and prayer . . . receive the truth with faith, meekness, and readiness of mind, as the word of God; meditate and hide it in their hearts and bring forth fruit of it in their lives.[18]

Expository preaching centers upon promoting true life change because the pastor has exposed the church to the word of God through faithful preaching. The Holy Spirit has so worked in the hearts of the people that they demonstrate authentic gospel transformation. Tim Chester says, "The measure of good preaching is not what people hear, but what people do as a result. It means that what counts is not so much good Bible teaching, as good Bible living."[19] I implore you to commit to submitting yourself under the authority of God's inerrant word as the Holy Spirit works mightily to transform you deeper into your identity in the Trinity through preaching.

SCRIPTURE SATURATION AS THE PRIVATE MEANS OF GRACE

Sitting under authoritative expository preaching in corporate worship is vital to your health as a believer and growth in grace. This is the primary public means of grace God has given for your holiness and repentance. In addition, the private means of grace involve personal Bible reading, study, and devotion. I call this Scripture saturation. To grow in our identity in the Trinity, the Lord calls us to *saturate* ourselves in the Scripture. What images does the word "saturate" evoke in your imagination? What

---

17. Larson, "What Gives Preaching its Power?" https://www.christianitytoday.com/pastors/2004/spring/2.30.html

18. "Westminster Larger Catechism," 232.

19. Chester and Honeycutt, *Gospel Centered Preaching*, 20.

is Scripture saturation? It involves five key activities:[20] (1) Reading the Scripture, (2) studying the Scripture, (3) memorizing the Scripture, (4) meditating on the Scripture, and (5) obeying the Scripture.

Reading the Scripture

Before we read the Scripture, we need to pray that the Holy Spirit will open our hearts and minds to the truth. I pray this Psalm often before I begin to read the Bible: Psalm 119:18 says, "Open my eyes, that I may behold wondrous things out of your law." Also, the Holy Spirit plays a powerful role in illuminating the Scriptures by guiding us in all truth. In John 16:13–14, Jesus says, "When the Spirit of truth comes, he will guide you into all the truth, for he will not speak on his own authority, but whatever he hears he will speak, and he will declare to you the things that are to come. He will glorify me, for he will take what is mine and declare it to you." The role of the Holy Spirit in our lives is to turn the light bulb on in our hearts and minds so that we can see and understand what we are reading in Scripture. John Calvin articulates this concept well:

> For God alone can properly bear witness to his own words, so these words will not obtain full credit in the hearts of men, until they are sealed by the inward testimony of the Spirit. The same Spirit, therefore, who spoke by the mouth of the prophets, must penetrate our hearts, in order to convince us that they faithfully delivered the message with which they were divinely entrusted.[21]

Read the Scriptures prayerfully, carefully, and repeatedly. Take time to focus while you read instead of merely skimming over the passage. If possible, use multiple solid translations to help you better understand what you're reading. I also encourage you to read the Scripture out loud so that you can feel the weight and majesty of the sacred text.

---

20. I am indebted to Don Whitney who discusses these practices at length in *Spiritual Disciplines for the Christian Life*, 41–64. His list includes hearing God's word, studying God's word, memorizing God's word, meditating on God's word, and applying God's word.

21. Calvin, *Institutes of the Christian Religion*, 72.

Studying the Scripture

To saturate ourselves in the Scripture, we need to do more than just read it. We need to study it. We need to dive into what the text means. There are two activities we do in this process. The first is *observation*, which asks the questions, "What is going on in the text? What is the context? What is being said to the original hearers/readers?" Many times, we want to jump straight to how the passage personally applies to ourselves instead of taking the time to understand what it meant to the original audience. Let me suggest an exercise that will help you immensely in this process of observation. I encourage you to either copy and paste your selected passage to a blank document and print it out, or hand write the text you're studying on a piece of paper. Then circle the key words. What are the main verbs in the passage? What are the repeated phrases? How do the sentences join together? What jumps out at you in the text? What has you baffled or leads you to ask more questions? Spend time marking up your paper with observations that will help you see what is going on in the text. Howard Hendricks's book *Living by the Book* serves as a helpful resource for this discipline.

The second activity involved in studying the Bible is *interpretation*, which asks the questions, "What does the passage mean? What did the unchanging text mean in its original context?" An often overlooked but critical component of interpreting the Bible comes in understanding the particular genre of the book, which we call the literary context. For example, you will read the Law portions in Leviticus differently than you would read the book of Revelation. The Synoptic Gospels (Matthew, Mark, and Luke) are very different than the Gospel of John. Hebrew narratives such as Genesis and Joshua differ from poetry such as the Psalms. The book of Proverbs reads differently than a Pauline Epistle. One of the best resources for biblical interpretation is *How to Read the Bible for All Its Worth* by Gordon Fee and Douglas Stuart.[22] Also, a good study Bible helps immensely. If you want to spend some extra money, you may want to invest in an excellent commentary series[23] or Bible software. You do not need to be proficient in the original languages of Greek and Hebrew

---

22. Other helpful books include Duvall and Hayes, *Grasping God's Words*; Fee and Stuart, *How to Read the Bible Book by Book*; Plummer, *40 Questions about Interpreting the Bible*; and Bickel and Jantz, *Knowing the Bible 101*.

23. www.bestcommentaries.com is an excellent resource that categorizes commentaries by "scholarly," "practical," and "devotional" for each book of the Bible.

to do effective Bible study. All you need is a good translation, a few commentaries, Bible software, and most importantly, the illuminating power of the Holy Spirit. You will be surprised how much the gracious Spirit will guide you into the truth when you take the time and effort to dig deep into the depths of the word.

Memorizing the Scripture

We grow in Christ by storing his word in our hearts or by memorizing Scripture. Psalm 119:9–11 reads, "How can a young man keep his way pure? By guarding it according to your word. With my whole heart I seek you; let me not wander from your commandments! I have stored up your word in my heart, that I might not sin against you." For many, memorization can become difficult. Think about how many songs you know where you can sing along perfectly to the lyrics. Think about sports statistics that you have memorized. Think about locker combinations or passwords or any other bits of information you have locked away in your brain. We need to read the word, study the word, and then begin to memorize the word. I refer you to an excellent resource for Scripture memorization by Andy Davis that will significantly help you in this process.[24]

Meditating on the Scripture

Before leading the Israelites to cross the Jordan River into the promised land, the LORD commanded Joshua regarding the importance of his word. Joshua 1:8 reads, "This Book of the Law shall not depart from your mouth, but you shall meditate on it day and night, so that you may be careful to do according to all that is written in it. For then you will make your way prosperous, and then you will have good success." Psalm 1:1–2 echoes this idea of meditating: "Blessed is the man who walks not in the counsel of the wicked, nor stands in the way of sinners, nor sits in the seat of scoffers; but his delight is in the law of the Lord, and on his law he meditates day and night." Psalm 119:99 says, "I have more understanding than all my teachers, for your testimonies are my meditation." The Hebrew word for meditate used in these verses means "to groan" or "to speak out loud." This concept of silent reading is a modern convention,

---

24. Davis, *Approach to Extended Memory*.

but in biblical times they read out loud. They heard the word vocally so that they could truly understand its meaning.

Living in the dry plains of Northeastern Colorado, we pray regularly for rain for the farmers and ranchers. We don't want hailstorms that destroy the crops or a quick thundershower that washes away the soil. Farmer and ranchers here pray for a long, steady drip of rain over many days that saturates the earth. Meditating is like letting your mind become saturated over time with God's word. Meditating can be analogous to taking chicken or beef and letting it marinate in a sauce before you cook it. Meditation involves allowing the word to soak in your heart and soul—to think about it, ponder it, and to let it takes its full effect in your life. Spurgeon gave this metaphor: "Try to get saturated with the gospel. I always find that I can preach best when I can manage to lie asoak in my text . . . after I have bathed in it, I delight to lie down in it, and let it soak into me."[25] What is the purpose of a bath? You take the time to relax, enjoy it, and to soak in hot water. When was the last time you took a bath with the Bible—not literally, that would not be a good idea, but figuratively?

In Philippians 4:8, Paul gives us a command related to how we think or meditate on God's truth. He writes, "Finally, brothers, whatever is true, whatever is honorable, whatever is just, whatever is pure, whatever is lovely, whatever is commendable, if there is any excellence, if there is anything worthy of praise, think about these things." The word for "think" means to reckon, credit, calculate, dwell upon, consider strongly, or deliberate on. The present-tense verb carries the idea of taking the time and energy needed to scrutinize and examine on a continual basis. Thinking deeply about God's word should be part of our lifestyle. Meditating on Scripture involves focusing your mind on the truths of Scripture, so you can not only understand what it says, but more importantly, obey what it says in all aspects of your daily life. I have found that journaling, while not prescribed in the Bible as a mandatory practice, is helpful in this process of meditation. I usually take a smaller portion of Scripture and write out my thoughts, questions, and personal application in a journal and then use these insights to inform my praying. I usually pray back the truths I have just read so that I can internalize them and think more deeply about them through the day. My advice is: Don't rush—take time! It is better to read a small amount of Scripture and meditate on it than to read an

---

25. Spurgeon, in Stott, *Between Two Worlds*, 220.

extensive section without meditation. Walter Marshall claims, "And the end of our meditation must not be mere speculation and knowledge of the truth, but rather the vigorous pressing it upon our consciences, and the stirring up our hearts and affections to the practice of it."[26] Meditation excites our hearts to worship and also fuels our obedience.

Obeying the Scripture

The book of James reads like the Old Testament book of Proverbs in that it contains pithy statements that aim straight for practical application and obedience. James 1:22–25 reads,

> But be doers of the word, and not hearers only, deceiving yourselves. For if anyone is a hearer of the word and not a doer, he is like a man who looks intently at his natural face in a mirror. For he looks at himself and goes away and at once forgets what he was like. But the one who looks into the perfect law, the law of liberty, and perseveres, being no hearer who forgets but a doer who acts, he will be blessed in his doing.

If we don't obey what we have heard, read, meditated upon or memorized, then James says that we are living a lie. This word "look" means to bend over and carefully examine something from the clearest possible view. As we look deeply into God's word and then obey it joyfully, this process brings freedom, not bondage.

THE BENEFITS OF SCRIPTURE SATURATION

In Psalm 19:7–9, David provides four wonderful benefits we receive from reading, studying, memorizing, meditating on, and obeying God's word:

> The law of the Lord is perfect, reviving the soul; the testimony of the Lord is sure, making wise the simple; the precepts of the Lord are right, rejoicing the heart; the commandment of the Lord is pure, enlightening the eyes; the fear of the Lord is clean, enduring forever; the rules of the Lord are true, and righteous altogether. More to be desired are they than gold, even much fine gold; sweeter also than honey and drippings of the honeycomb.

---

26. Marshall, *Gospel Mystery of Sanctification*, 194.

First of all, God's word "revives or converts the soul" which connotes that God's word restores from disorder or decay. The truth of God's word not only brings about our conversion to Christ, but it also revives us. It sinks deep down within our hearts and gives us refreshing and encouragement. Second, it makes wise the simple. This does not address mere intelligence, but speaks about moral judgments. When the Bible, especially the book of Proverbs, speaks about the simple and wise, it addresses areas of moral living. The Bible gives us instruction on how to remain morally pure. It shows us how to live holy lives. Titus 2:11–12 reminds us, "For the grace of God has appeared, bringing salvation for all people, training us to renounce ungodliness and worldly passions, and to live self-controlled, upright, and godly lives in the present age." The means of grace God uses to say "no" to worldly passions come through reading, studying, memorizing, meditating upon, and obeying the Scriptures.

Third, obedience to the Bible makes the heart rejoice. It is not drudgery to obey God's word, but a joy. It is not a duty, but a delight. First John 5:2–4 reads, "By this we know that we love the children of God, when we love God and obey his commandments. For this is the love of God, that we keep his commandments. And his commandments are not burdensome. For everyone who has been born of God overcomes the world. And this is the victory that has overcome the world—our faith."

Fourth, it enlightens our eyes. It opens our eyes to the truth. David shows us how God's word is righteous and true and worth obeying. He also shows how longing for, desiring, and following God's word is similar to the joy of discovering gold and eating honey. There is a play on words used here by David when he says that God's word is more to be "desired." That word, "desired," is the same word used of the fruit in the garden of Eden in Genesis 3:6: "So when the woman saw that the tree was good for food, and that it was a delight to the eyes, and that the tree was to be *desired* to make one wise, she took of its fruit and ate, and she also gave some to her husband who was with her, and he ate." How desirable the fruit looked instead of obeying God's word. How much do we truly desire God's word?

RENEWED MINDS

In Romans 12:1–2, Paul instructs us on how Scripture saturation leads to a lifestyle of obedience: "I appeal to you therefore, brothers, by the mercies of God, to present your bodies as a living sacrifice, holy and acceptable to God, which is your spiritual worship. Do not be conformed to this world, but be transformed by the renewal of your mind, that by testing you may discern what is the will of God, what is good and acceptable and perfect." Paul doesn't start with our obedience, but focuses on the mercies of God as the foundation of our identity. In light of all that God has done for us in making us this new creation in Christ, God calls us to present our bodies as living sacrifices in lives of worship back to him. The only way we can obey is because of grace in the gospel and through the power of the Holy Spirit.

Paul appeals to us to present our bodies as a living sacrifice. Now, why does he refer to our physical bodies? Why doesn't Paul say, "Present our hearts or present our souls or present our emotions?" God intends that we follow his commands in practical obedience. We can say we love him all we want, and we can think that we love him all we want, and we can feel that we love him all we want, but we haven't demonstrated that we love Jesus until we obey him in our bodies. John Stott says this, "No worship is pleasing to God which is purely inward, abstract, and mystical; it must express itself in concrete acts of service performed by our bodies."[27] As a pastor, I can't tell you how many times I've confronted a person who was living in sin or having an affair, and they told me that God providentially brought their lover to them. People have even said to me that through this adultery they have actually connected with God on a deeper spiritual level. In cheating on their spouse, they thought that God blessed them with this other person as his gift at just the right time. This confusion exists because people have disconnected the relationship between the body and mind. We have not fully obeyed Jesus until the totality of our lives (soul and body) demonstrates practical holiness that adheres to Scripture.

Paul uses the word "reasonable" or "fitting" to describe our lives of spiritual worship. When we offer our bodies as a living sacrifice, this lifestyle of worship becomes an appropriate response of obedience because of our identity in Christ. In other words, it just makes sense. When we realize how much God loves us as a new creation in Christ, we want to obey him with a lifestyle of sacrificial worship. Because of God's mercies in giving us this new identity, it makes sense, it is reasonable, it is only fitting and appropriate to respond to him with a life of obedience.

---

27. Stott, *Message of Romans*, 322.

Paul not only focuses on the body, but the mind as well. There is a strong correlation between the mind and body. Our thoughts usually dictate how we will respond in concrete action. In verse 2, Paul gives two commands—one negative and the other positive. First of all, in the negative, he commands us not to be conformed to this world, which is this present evil age over which Satan holds sway and where the power of sin is paramount. First John 2:15–17 reaffirms this truth, "Do not love the world or the things in the world. If anyone loves the world, the love of the Father is not in him. For all that is in the world—the desires of the flesh and the desires of the eyes and pride of life—is not from the Father but is from the world. And the world is passing away along with its desires, but whoever does the will of God abides forever."

Second, in the positive, Paul commands us to continue being transformed by the renewal of our minds. The Holy Spirit works in us to become more and more like Jesus. As such, we cannot control our spiritual transformation, but we can sure put ourselves in positions and a posture where he can renew our minds. If we focus on conformity to this present evil age, we will fill our minds with the things of this world. When we spend time in the word by meditating on Christ and filling our time with things that glorify Jesus, we place ourselves in a position for the Holy Spirit to do this work of transformation. The Kaiser Family Foundation recently conducted a study called "Generation M2: Media in the Lives of 8- to 18-Year Olds"[28] on how technology impacts the lives of teenagers. Here are some of its findings: "Eight-to-eighteen-year-olds spend more time with media than in any other activity besides (maybe) sleeping—an average of more than 7 1/2 hours a day, seven days a week." The report goes on to say that due to multitasking, the average child actually consumes eleven hours of media in that 7.5–hour time frame. We must realize how much this present evil age consumes our minds as compared to how much we consistently take in God's holy word.

Paul tells us that as our minds are being renewed in this process of transformation, we will begin to discern God's will. A renewed mind leads to a better understanding of God's will which leads to a better understanding of how we are to obey. Do you see the process? We place ourselves in a position of filling our minds with the things of God through Scripture saturation so that the Holy Spirit can transform us and renew our minds. In this process, we see more clearly the beauty of Jesus as we

---

28. Rideout et al., "Generation M2."

find him as our absolute treasure. Since we value him so highly and make it our ambition to glorify him, we express this love for Christ in obedience to the Bible.

Through reading and studying the commands in Scripture, we discover the will of God, and then our entire lives reorient around the supremacy of Christ. We come to realize through experience that God's ways and his will are good, acceptable, and perfect. We desire to obey Jesus out of a deep love for what he has done for us in the gospel. Because of his great mercies in giving us this new identity, and in the power of the Holy Spirit renewing our minds, we begin to look more and more like Jesus. This reality most clearly expresses itself in outward obedience to him in a lifestyle of sacrificial worship. In other words, being (identity) comes before doing (obedience).

THE TRUTH WILL SET YOU FREE

We can read, study, meditate and memorize the Bible diligently, but if it does not translate into active obedience, then we are not becoming what God has intended us to become. Our identity in the Trinity should motivate us to obey. In John 8:31–32, Jesus addresses this issue of Scripture saturation: "If you abide in my word, you are truly my disciples, and you will know the truth, and the truth will set you free." Notice the "if . . . then" construction of Jesus' statement. If you abide in my word, then you are truly my disciples. The grammatical construction proves vital to understanding this statement in which the verb "abide" is in a mood that means probability. In other words, if you abide in Jesus' words, there is a high probability that you are indeed a disciple. And the converse is also true. If you do not abide in his words, then there is a high probability that you may not be a disciple. The word "abide" means to remain, continue, hold onto, live in his word, hold fast, and commit to his word.

Colossians 3:16 addresses this issue of abiding and holding fast to God's word: "Let the word of Christ dwell in you richly, teaching and admonishing one another in all wisdom, singing psalms and hymns and spiritual songs, with thankfulness in your hearts to God." Are you letting the word of Christ dwell in you richly? Fundamentally, here's what it means to abide in Jesus' word: it means that you delight and enjoy reading, studying, meditating, memorizing, and ultimately obeying God's word in every area of your life. Does this passion for God's word describe you? Or are you bored with God's word? Do you have a daily time alone with God where you read his word?

The context of Jesus' teaching here in John chapters 7–8 centers on the Feast of Tabernacles where the truth has everything to do with his identity as the Messiah. Jesus is the real source of living water and the light of the world. He clearly says that if you don't follow him, you will die in your sins. Do you know the truth of who Jesus is? Have you come to grips with the fact that he is more than just a good teacher or a moral example or a traveling miracle worker? Do you realize that he is God in the flesh, the eternal Son, and the Sovereign Lord? Knowing this truth about Jesus as revealed in his written word will set you free! This truth prevents you from being swayed by falsehoods. This truth produces sound theology and helps you to be discerning. This truth guards you against heresy. Paul instructs us in Ephesians 4:14–16:

> So that we may no longer be children, tossed to and fro by the waves and carried about by every wind of doctrine, by human cunning, by craftiness in deceitful schemes. Rather, speaking the truth in love, we are to grow up in every way into him who is the head, into Christ, from whom the whole body, joined and held together by every joint with which it is equipped, when each part is working properly, makes the body grow so that it builds itself up in love.

Over a decade ago, my wife and I spent a week in Cancun for a time of relaxation and fun. One day as we were swimming in the ocean, the waves got very choppy, and the sea almost swept her away. Afterward, she was pretty shaken up. Ominous riptides and undertow can carry you out to sea, without you even knowing it. The internet, social media, and much of Christian broadcasting contains so much falsehood, that if you're not careful, they can toss you to and fro like waves by every wind of doctrine that comes down the pike. Are you growing in your knowledge of the truth? First Timothy 4:1 warns, "Now the Spirit expressly says that in later times some will depart from the faith by devoting themselves to deceitful spirits and teachings of demons." Abiding in Christ's word will greatly help you from this deception. Hebrews 5:14 reads, "But solid food is for the mature, for those who have their powers of discernment trained by constant practice to distinguish good from evil." Are you able to distinguish good from evil and truth from error by regularly practicing discernment?

There is a direct correlation between abiding in the word and growing in the knowledge of the truth. The more you abide in the word, the more you know the truth and false teaching does not easily influence you. Now does this mean that as a true Christian you are always one hundred percent correct in every area of doctrine and can never get influenced or swayed? Does this mean that you don't get tripped up from time to time? This may happen at times and shows the importance of connecting yourself to the church and being under the leadership of godly elders who know sound doctrine. The writer of Hebrews urges the church to submit to the godly leadership of their pastors. Hebrews 13:17 reads, "Obey your leaders and submit to them, for they are keeping watch over your souls, as those who will have to give an account. Let them do this with joy and not with groaning, for that would be of no advantage to you." He expresses the gravity and eternal consequences of pastoral leadership in that shepherds will stand before God on the day of judgment and give an account of how they cared for the souls entrusted to their care. Strauch says, "Spiritual leaders must always be keenly alert, conscientious, and diligent. Watchfulness demands tireless effort, self-discipline, and selfless concern for the safety of others."[29] A congregation's response to pastoral leadership does not rest in blind obedience; instead, obedience to pastors must come in conformity to the Scriptures they faithfully preach and the godly lives they exemplify. As those who will give an account, pastors must remember that this authority is a derived authority in that it only comes from their faithfulness to the Scriptures and not their selfish agendas.

Jude 3 says, "Beloved, although I was very eager to write to you about our common salvation, I found it necessary to write appealing to you to contend for the faith that was once for all delivered to the saints." In his high priestly prayer in John 17:17, Jesus prays, "Sanctify them in the truth; your word is truth." Notice how Jesus says that God's word is "truth." He doesn't say that God's word is "true," which would not be inaccurate, but by saying "the" truth, Jesus asserts that there is no hint of ambiguity. God's word is the authoritative, inspired word of truth without any mixture of error. Saturating yourself in the word of truth is God's primary means of growing you to look more like his Son Jesus. The Lord has delivered to us his written, inspired, and inerrant word once and for all as the means by which we mature in our identity in the Trinity. He

---

29. Strauch, *Biblical Eldership*, 270.

has graciously given us the public means of grace through the powerful preaching of his word to help us grow in grace and godliness. He has also prescribed for us the private means of grace through personal Scripture saturation. Are you taking advantage of these practices? Are you actively involved in a church family that values the expository preaching of God's truth? Are you spending daily time in private devotion where you read, study, memorize, meditate, and obey God's word? J. C. Ryle gives this warning:

> One thing essential to growth in grace is diligence in the use of private means of grace. Here are the roots of true Christianity ... Wrong here, a man is wrong all the way through! Here is the whole reason why many professing Christians never seem to get on. They are careless and lazy about their private prayers. They read their Bibles but little, and with very little heartiness of spirit. They give themselves no time for self-inquiry and quiet thought about the state of their souls.[30]

---

30. Ryle, *Holiness*, 89.

11

The Intimacy in Prayer

"Prayer is awe, intimacy, struggle—yet the way to reality. There is nothing more important, or harder, or richer, or more life-altering. There is absolutely nothing so great as prayer."

TIM KELLER[1]

THE PREVIOUS CHAPTER INTRODUCED us to the means of grace as practices God has mercifully given us to help us grow in holiness. The first means of grace was Scripture saturation through the public preaching of God's word and your own private Bible intake. The second means of grace is prayer. Eric Alexander claims,

> God is not only sovereign and gracious, but he also delights to be entreated by his children, and had decreed certain means by which his grace is brought to us ... Prayer is a means of God's grace. If we really believed that, and took it seriously, then prayer would become fundamental, instead of supplemental, in all our thinking about Christian work and service.[2]

In Acts 2:42–47, the early church not only devoted themselves to the apostles' teaching (Scripture saturation), but they also had a passion for prayer. Devoting themselves to prayer meant that they persevered,

1. Keller, *Prayer*, 32.
2. Alexander, *Prayer*, 13–14.

persisted, and remained strong in crying out to the Lord. They didn't give up. They stuck to it. They worked hard in prayer. It wasn't just a token prayer here or there, but they were serious about gathering for extended times of intercession. Prayer was one of the early church's highest priorities, and it should be one of the highest priorities in your life as well. Samuel Chadwick said, "The one concern of the devil is to keep Christians from praying. He fears nothing from prayerless studies, prayerless work and prayerless religion. He laughs at our toil, mocks at our wisdom, but trembles when we pray."

FOUR FOUNDATIONS FOR PRAYER

First of all, we must be honest that we all struggle with prayer and need to learn to pray. Jesus had a powerfully dynamic prayer life because in Luke 11:1–2 his disciples ask him a critical question: "Now Jesus was praying in a certain place, and when he finished, one of his disciples said to him, 'Lord, teach us to pray, as John taught his disciples.'" It's interesting what they don't ask Jesus. In the Gospels, we never see any of his disciples asking, "Jesus, teach us to do evangelism. Jesus, teach us to use our spiritual gifts. Jesus, teach us to perform miracles. Jesus, teach us to do more effective Bible study. Jesus, teach us how to do children's ministry. Jesus, teach us how to run a youth group." Now we don't know if the disciples didn't ask those questions, but the inspired Scripture records their specific request: Lord, teach us to pray!

Do you pray as often as you should? Do you genuinely know *how* to pray? Why is prayer such hard work? Here's the reality: prayer does not come easy. It is not glamorous and exciting like attending a concert or hearing your favorite preacher. Prayer takes time, energy, and focus. Yet there is nothing more important than prayer. Martin Luther said that prayer "is the hardest work of all . . . a labor above all labors, since he who prays must wage a mighty warfare against the doubt and murmuring excited by the faintheartedness and unworthiness, we feel within us . . . There is no greater work than praying."[3] Colossians 4:2 says, "Continue steadfastly in prayer, being watchful in it with thanksgiving." Eric Alexander asserts, "The truth is that prayer is the real work, and apart from it all other work is in vain . . . There are endless lists of things that men and women can do: we can intellectually convince people, we

---

3. Luther, in Beeke and Najapfour, *Taking Hold of God*, 9.

can emotionally move them, and we can materially improve them. But only God can spiritually resurrect them out of spiritual death into life in Christ."[4]

Second, prayer is a response to God as he has first spoken to us in the written Scriptures. Perhaps you think that prayer is a two-way conversation between you and God. Is this an accurate statement? In prayer, we speak to God, but does he speak to us? We need to make sure that if we are going to use this terminology, we understand that God speaks primarily through his written word. We need to be very careful how we define our terms concerning prayer. We must be suspicious of people who say things like "God told me" or "God spoke to me," and then make decisions that directly contradict the Bible. God does speak, but he speaks now through the Bible. God speaks to us first in his word, and then in response, we talk back to him in prayer. That is why meditating on Scripture should almost always precede prayer. Martin Luther said, "We must first hear the Word, and then afterward the Holy Spirit works in our hearts; he works in the hearts of whom he will, and how he will, but never without the Word."[5] The more we grasp who God is as revealed in the Scripture, the more our prayers will be shaped accordingly. Tim Keller says, "Without immersion in God's words, our prayers may not be merely limited and shallow, but untethered from reality. We may be responding not to the real God but to what we wish God and life to be like."[6]

Third, prayer is the lifeblood of all true believers. John Calvin defines prayer as "communication between God and us whereby we expound to him our desires, our joys, our sighs, in a word, all the thoughts of our hearts."[7] Joel Beeke says, "Prayer is the outpouring of the soul, the deepest root of piety, the bedrock of assurance. Prayer is the most important part of the Christian life; it is the lifeblood of every true believer."[8] When you think of lifeblood what comes to your mind? We can't exist without blood and oxygen pumping through our veins. When we say something is our lifeblood, it means that we can't live without it. It is vital to our lives. Prayer is essential to our spiritual lives, and we will not survive long without it.

4. Alexander, *Prayer*, 39–40.
5. Luther, in Keller, *Prayer*, 57.
6. Keller, *Prayer*, 62.
7. Calvin, *Instruction in Faith*, 57.
8. Beeke and Najapfour, *Taking Hold of God*, 29.

The LORD commands us throughout the Bible to pray as our Christian duty. Ephesians 6:18 tells us to "pray at all times in the Spirit, with all prayer and supplication. To that end keep alert with all perseverance, making supplication for all the saints." Philippians 4:6–7 also admonishes us "do not be anxious about anything, but in everything by prayer and supplication with thanksgiving let your requests be made known to God. And the peace of God, which surpasses all understanding, will guard your hearts and your minds in Christ Jesus." First Thessalonians 5:17 makes this obligation to pray very clear: "pray without ceasing."

The Bible not only commands us to pray as our duty, but prayer is also an incredible privilege. Think about what prayer truly is. You have permission to enter the very throne room of Almighty God and worship him, ask him for things, and pour your heart out to him. The psalmists give us great insight into how desperate we should be for Christ as we cry out to him in prayer. Psalm 73:25–26: "Whom have I in heaven but you? And there is nothing on earth that I desire besides you. My flesh and my heart may fail, but God is the strength of my heart and my portion forever." Psalm 86:11–12: "Teach me your way, O Lord, that I may walk in your truth; unite my heart to fear your name. I give thanks to you, O Lord my God, with my whole heart, and I will glorify your name forever." Martyn Lloyd-Jones asserts, "Prayer is beyond any question the highest activity of the human soul. Man is at his greatest and highest when, upon his knees, he comes face-to-face with God."[9]

Fourth, all great movements of God have begun when God's people take prayer seriously. Revival and spiritual awakening are a sovereign work of God who sometimes chooses to break into a church or a people and do something uniquely great for his glory. We cannot force God to do this. We can't manufacture these results or manipulate God to bring revival. But we can pray for God to move. When you trace the history of spiritual awakenings that have happened throughout history all over the world, one common denominator emerges: revival came after a period of intense and strategic prayers by God's people. Spurgeon said, "I have no confidence at all in polished speech or brilliant literary effort to bring about a revival, but I have all the confidence in the world in the poor saint who would weep her eyes out because people are living in sin."[10]

---

9. Lloyd-Jones, *Studies in the Sermon on the Mount*, 322.
10. Spurgeon, in Comfort, *Hell's Best Kept Secret*, 171.

The United States experienced a period of upheaval in that late 1850s as the Civil War loomed on the horizon. In 1857, the Supreme Court handed down the Dred Scott case, which said that African-American slaves could not be U.S. citizens. That same year there was a massive banking crisis in New York, Boston, Philadelphia, and Chicago, which caused the stock market to crash. In the midst of these uncertain times, a businessman named Jeremiah Lamphier believed that God would bring revival to America, so he began noon businessmen prayer meetings in New York City on Fulton Street. On the first day, nobody showed up. On the second day, six men showed up and then by March of 1858, over 10,000 businessmen were praying daily from noon to one for revival in America. Historians tell us that there has never been a point in United States history where revival was so widespread, unity among denominations so healthy, and the gospel zeal for overseas missions so powerful. Historians called it the "Great Revival" or the "Fulton Street Revival." This awakening all started with a businessman, not a preacher or a missionary, who desired to see a powerful movement of God, so he led people to pray like crazy for an outpouring of God's Spirit on America. Jonathan Edwards claimed, "It is a very suitable thing, and well-pleasing to God, for many people, in different parts of the world, by express agreement, to come into visible union in extraordinary, speedy, fervent, and constant prayer, for the great outpouring of the Holy Spirit, which shall bring on that advancement of Christ's church and kingdom."[11]

THE LORD'S PRAYER: AN INTRODUCTION

In Matthew 6:7–13, Jesus provides for us a concise, yet profound prayer which has traditionally been called the model or Lord's Prayer. Learning to incorporate the Lord's Prayer into your private worship is one of the best ways to grow in your identity in the Trinity.

> And when you pray, do not heap up empty phrases as the Gentiles do, for they think that they will be heard for their many words. Do not be like them, for your Father knows what you need before you ask him. Pray then like this: "Our Father in heaven, hallowed be your name. Your kingdom come, your will be done, on earth as it is in heaven. Give us this day our daily bread, and forgive us our debts, as we also have forgiven our

---

11. Edwards, *Works of Jonathan Edwards*, 2:320.

debtors. And lead us not into temptation, but deliver us from evil. For yours is the kingdom, and the power, and the glory, forever. Amen."

Before we explore the Lord's Prayer, in more detail, let us consider two main observations.

First of all, the prayer's brevity is surprising. The effectiveness of our praying is not in how long we pray, but in how earnestly and passionately we pray. We can use a lot of filler words that don't mean anything. Think about how you may pray at times. Do you find yourself praying phrases like, "Lord, um, Father, bless so and so? Lord, um, just be with so and so. We thank you, Lord, um, just be with us." We can use a lot of words that don't mean much, and thereby, not pray effectively. Solomon warns us in Ecclesiastes 5:2: "Be not rash with your mouth, nor let your heart be hasty to utter a word before God, for God is in heaven and you are on earth. Therefore let your words be few." We can often spout off Christian clichés and use theological jargon to impress others when we pray publicly.

Second, this is not a passionless prayer you recite mechanically. Jesus says, "Pray *like* this or in *this manner.*" He doesn't say, "Pray this exact prayer by memory without any passion or meaning." The Lord's Prayer serves as a blueprint for how we should pray. We don't merely recite this prayer in a rote manner where we say the words but don't mean them. You can recite this prayer word-by-word and never really pray, as if you can do it in a way that is mechanical and lifeless. Jesus gives us this model prayer so that we will pause before we pray and think about both *how* we are praying and for *what* we are praying, so that we will consider that there is a certain attitude we must have when praying. There is a specific order to our praying. There are particular requests we should be asking. We must not rush into prayer without thinking through why and how we are praying. This prayer is a template that helps guide our hearts and minds with purpose, direction, and strategy so that our praying is not mindless, ineffective, and empty. Thomas Brooks gives this encouragement: "God looks not at the elegancy of your prayers to see how neat they are; nor the geometry of your prayers to see how long they are . . . but at the sincerity of your prayers, how hearty they are . . . as God loves a broken and contrite heart."[12]

---

12. Brooks, *Works of Thomas Brooks,* 2:256.

THE ADDRESS TO OUR FATHER

Jesus tells us to pray "in this way" or "this manner" and begins by addressing our Father in heaven. This address to the Father comes before we ask for anything and proves vitally important in understanding how to pray biblically. Almost every recorded prayer in the Bible starts with an address to the sovereign God. Here are a few examples:

> "You are the Lord, you alone. You have made heaven, the heaven of heavens, with all their host, the earth and all that is on it, the seas and all that is in them; and you preserve all of them; and the host of heaven worships you." (Neh 9:6)

> "I prayed to the Lord my God and made confession, saying, "O Lord, the great and awesome God, who keeps covenant and steadfast love with those who love him and keep his commandments." (Dan 9:4)

> "And when they heard it, they lifted their voices together to God and said, "Sovereign Lord, who made the heaven and the earth and the sea and everything in them." (Acts 4:24)

Why does Jesus begin the prayer with an address to the Father? Let us explore three truths that encourage us to start our prayers in this manner.

First, because of Christ's work on the cross, we can boldly approach the Father's throne of grace as adopted children. You can tell a lot about a person's theology in how they address God. Do they address him only as "God" or as "Father?" There's nothing wrong with calling him God, but when we call him Father, it means we can express joy in our intimate relationship with him as an adopted child through the merits of Christ. Addressing God as our Father means that we recognize his goodness and steadfast love as his children who can approach him with boldness. Hebrews 4:16 exhorts us: "Let us then with confidence draw near to the throne of grace, that we may receive mercy and find grace to help in time of need." Not everyone can call God our Father except those he has adopted into his family through faith in Christ. This is a privilege reserved just for those who are "in Christ" as John 1:12 says, "But to all who did receive him, who believed in his name, he gave the right to become children of God." (See chapter four on our identity in adoption).

The fact that we can call God our Father denotes intimacy, nearness, and confidence in his goodness. It means that we can come to him as dependent children with open hands ready to receive from a kind and generous Father. "Father" in Aramaic is *Abba*, which conveys intimacy where we can approach our God with confidence, not fear. Paul reminds us in Romans 8:15–16: "For you did not receive the spirit of slavery to fall back into fear, but you have received the Spirit of adoption as sons, by whom we cry, 'Abba! Father!' The Spirit himself bears witness with our spirit that we are children of God." Thomas Boston said, "There is no child so unnatural as to be still in his father's presence, and never to converse with him."[13]

Many people have a hard time relating to God as their Father because they have not had the greatest earthly fathers. Maybe your father abused you. Maybe your father was distant. Maybe your father was cruel. Maybe your father was absent. This whole concept of God being a Father is either foreign or perhaps even unsettling to you. When you come to faith in Christ, God adopts you into his family and grants you a new identity, and he is a perfect Father. He loves you, cares for you, will never abandon you, will always be there for you, is not distant, and is not absent. He loves to give gifts to his children. He has abundant blessings for you. You are cherished in his eyes because of Christ (see chapter four). The beauty of praying to our Father is that we can experience the nearness of God. He is close. James 4:8 implores us: "Draw near to God, and he will draw near to you." Martin Luther said, "Prayer is not overcoming God's reluctance, but laying hold of his willingness."[14] Our Father is not reluctant to hear our prayers but stands ready, willing, and able to grant us grace in our time of need.

Second, as our majestic Sovereign in heaven, we must humbly approach the Father's throne of grace with awe and reverence. In Exodus 3:5, God appeared to Moses in the burning bush and said, "Do not come near; take your sandals off your feet, for the place on which you are standing is holy ground." When we draw near to God with confidence, we know that he is our good Father who cares for us, but we are also standing on holy ground. We are in the presence of a holy, majestic, and sovereign God. We are in the presence of God Almighty. The prophet Isaiah experienced the transcendent LORD in the temple when he saw the Lord in all his majesty. In Isaiah 6:3–5, the flying creatures called to another and said: "'Holy, holy, holy is the Lord of hosts; the whole earth is full of his glory!' And the foundations of the thresholds shook at the

---

13. Boston, *Complete Works of Thomas Boston*, 11:43.
14. Luther, in Pink, *Sovereignty of God*, 169.

voice of him who called, and the house was filled with smoke. And I said: 'Woe is me! For I am lost; for I am a man of unclean lips, and I dwell in the midst of a people of unclean lips; for my eyes have seen the King, the Lord of hosts!'"

Our Father is imminent and near, but we should not express a flippant attitude when we address him in prayer. Let us remember that we have the confidence to enter into his holy presence, but yet we must come with reverence, awe, and humility. We must not barge into God's presence with a careless attitude that he is somehow obligated to hear us. We should never "command" God to answer our prayers. We should always approach the Lord from a position of humility, awe, and reverence, yet through Christ we can approach his throne of grace boldly. God is our good Father who stands ready to hear us on account of Christ. But let us also remember that he is Almighty God in heaven, who rules and reigns in absolute sovereignty as the Creator of all things.

Third, because we address God as our Father, we must be unified in our prayers as members of the same family. We can often pray in a very selfish manner by only thinking of ourselves and our individual needs. We have become so privatized in our Christian lives that we don't see ourselves as brothers and sisters whom Christ has bought with his blood and adopted into God's family. Jesus does not tell us to pray "my Father," which in and of itself is not necessarily bad. God is your personal Father. He draws near to you personally. He listens to you specifically. He cares for you intimately. He loves you deeply. But Jesus draws our attention to the corporate or unifying nature of the prayer by addressing God as "our Father." When you pray, are you thinking about your church family and brothers and sisters in Christ? Or are you simply praying very individualistically? If we're not careful, we can give in to this privatized, consumeristic, individualistic me-centered version of Christianity that so permeates American evangelicalism. When we pray to our Father, it demonstrates that we are brothers and sisters who are interconnected in unity in Christ. We have a corporate identity in the Trinity as God's collective people who jointly offer our prayers to him as a family of faith.

Fourth, our praying must be thoroughly Trinitarian. Remember the foundational definition of our identity in the Trinity. We are chosen, adopted, and loved by the Father; we are purchased, forgiven, and righteous in the Son; and we are regenerated, indwelt, and sanctified by the Spirit. The nature of God as Trinity affects not only our gospel identity, but how we should pray. We pray to the Father in the name of Jesus through the power of the Holy Spirit. We have access to the Father and can approach his throne of grace. But the only way we can access and pray to the Father is through the merits and work of Christ who is our one mediator, as 1 Timothy 2:5–6 says: "For there is one God, and there is one mediator between God and men, the man Christ Jesus, who gave himself as a ransom for all, which is the testimony given at the proper time." By his death, burial, and resurrection, Jesus has granted us access to the Father, so we pray in his name. John Calvin reminds us: "Let us learn to wash our prayers with the blood of our Lord, Jesus Christ."[15] Jesus tells us in John 16:23 that "whatever you ask of the Father in my name, he will give it to you." But we also are weak and helpless at times when we pray and don't often know what to pray for, so we need the power of the Holy Spirit to intervene. Romans 8:26 says, "Likewise the Spirit helps us in our weakness. For we do not know what to pray for as we ought, but the Spirit himself intercedes for us with groanings too deep for words."

In summary, we address our prayers to our Father in heaven in the name of the one mediator, Christ, by the power of the Spirit who intercedes for us in our weakness. John Calvin articulates the Trinitarian nature of prayer: "To know the Father as the sovereign disposer of all good . . . that whatever is defective in us is supplied in our Lord Jesus Christ that we may draw as from an inexhaustible fountain . . . by faith, the Spirit of adoption, who seals the witness of the gospel in our hearts, raises our spirits to show forth to God our desires and confidently cry, 'Abba! Father!'"[16]

Allow me to model how I usually start my prayers when I do my private devotion. I often say something like this: "Father, I am so thankful to come into your presence right now and I can only approach your throne of grace on account of Christ, so I come to you in his name and by his work for me on the cross. And Holy Spirit, I desperately need your help to pray. So would you empower my praying? Dear Lord, the one true God, maker of heaven and earth, Father, Son, and Holy Spirit, I worship you today."

---

15. Calvin, *Sermons on Election and Reprobation*, 210.
16. Calvin, *Institutes of the Christian Religion*, 146.

REQUEST NUMBER ONE: HALLOWED BE THY NAME

Jesus purposely begins the Lord's Prayer with three specific requests which are thoroughly God-centered. These requests in the original language denote urgency, passion, and an eagerness for God to answer. We can translate the first request as "we ask that your Name be hallowed." This is not a declaration of worship where we acknowledge God's holiness, but an actual request that we revere his name as holy. Why does Jesus tell us to focus on God's Name? Why didn't Jesus say, "Let God be hallowed?" Why the focus on the name of God? God's name represents his character and the very essence of who he is. As finite creatures belonging to an infinite God, we can never even begin to fully comprehend him in all of his majesty, glory, and holiness. One of the amazing ways he's chosen to reveal himself to us is through providing us his specific names.

In Genesis 1:1, we see God's name as *Elohim*, which serves as the basic word for God in the Old Testament whereby it describes his transcendence and power. God also revealed his name as YHWH or the LORD, which is a derivative of "I AM" (see chapter one). God also revealed himself as *El-Shaddai* or God Almighty, which conveys power and sovereignty, but most importantly it means that God is faithful to fulfill his covenant promises to his people. Throughout the Old Testament, God provides many names that elaborate on his infinite character:

- *Adonai*: "Master"
- *El Roi*: "The God Who Sees"
- *Jehovah-Jireh*: "The LORD who provides."
- *Jehovah-Rophe*: "The LORD who heals."
- *Jehovah Sabaoth*: "The LORD of hosts."
- *Jehovah-Nissi*: "The LORD is my banner."

When Jesus teaches us to ask that God's name be hallowed, this first request goes to the very essence of God's character. What does it mean to ask for God's name to be hallowed? The word means "holy," "revered," "worshipped," "glorified," "magnified," or "set apart." To ask for God's name to be hallowed is nothing less than a consuming passion that the entire world honor, glorify, and recognize that Almighty God is holy, sovereign, and worthy of worship. The Psalms instruct us on this type of praying:

> Sing praises to the Lord, O you his saints, and give thanks to his holy name (Ps 30:4).
>
> Oh, magnify the Lord with me, and let us exalt his name together (Ps 34:3)!
>
> Bless the Lord, O my soul, and all that is within me, bless his holy name (Ps 103:1)!
>
> He sent redemption to his people; he has commanded his covenant forever. Holy and awesome is his name (Ps 111:9)!

A. W. Pink states, "We cannot pray aright unless the honor of God be dominant in our hearts. If we cherish a desire for the honoring of God's name, we must not ask for anything which it would be against the Divine holiness to bestow."[17] If God is inherently holy, majestic and awesome, then why would he need us to pray and request that his name be holy? We don't add anything to God that he doesn't somehow already have when we pray. We are not praying to increase the holiness of God's name. By this request, we express a heartfelt desire that the entire world would recognize God as holy and that people would not blaspheme or dishonor his name. Is that your supreme desire when you enter into God's presence in prayer? Is that what you are genuinely requesting when you begin praying to the Father? Is your desire to see God's name as holy in your personal life and then for the entire world to see the glory of God? The following verses illustrate what it means to request that God's name be hallowed in all the earth:

> Blessed be his glorious name forever; may the whole earth be filled with his glory! Amen and Amen (Ps 72:19)!
>
> Not to us, O Lord, not to us, but to your name give glory, for the sake of your steadfast love and your faithfulness (Ps 115:1)!
>
> And one called to another and said: "Holy, holy, holy is the Lord of hosts; the whole earth is full of his glory (Isa 6:3)!"
>
> For the earth will be filled with the knowledge of the glory of the Lord as the waters cover the sea (Hab 2:14).

Joel Beeke urges, "Though self-centered prayers seem to address our needs, in reality they do not satisfy, for our greatest need is to know God and to show his glory to the world. To aim our prayers at anything less is

---

17. Pink, *Exposition of the Sermon on the Mount*, 162.

to exchange our high calling as God's image-bearers and children for the role of mere clients in search of a service provider. It asks for mud instead of gold."[18]

REQUEST NUMBER TWO: THY KINGDOM COME!

This second request for God's kingdom to come flows logically from the first request of desiring God's name to be hallowed in the earth. Why isn't God's name hallowed, revered and glorified? Why is God's name blasphemed throughout the world? Here's the answer: sinners are in bondage to the kingdom of darkness. Satan holds them captive, blinds them to the truth, and enslaves them to sin, which is why they don't glorify God and revere his name. Paul tells us in 2 Corinthians 4:3–4: "And even if our gospel is veiled, it is veiled to those who are perishing. In their case the god of this world has blinded the minds of the unbelievers, to keep them from seeing the light of the gospel of the glory of Christ, who is the image of God." Colossians 1:13–14 also portrays the gravity of this enslavement to darkness as Jesus rescues us from the domain of darkness and transfers us to the kingdom of light.

The second request is a passionate and urgent desire for God's kingdom to come quickly, which brings up another question: What exactly is the kingdom of God? In John 18:36 when Pilate interrogated Jesus, he answered, "My kingdom is not of this world. If my kingdom were of this world, my servants would have been fighting, that I might not be delivered over to the Jews. But my kingdom is not from the world." The kingdom of God consists of his rule and reign as King over the entire universe. It does not specify a geographic area, but a spiritual reality. The Bible speaks of three aspects of the kingdom of God. First of all, the kingdom of God has already come in the first coming of Christ in his life, death, and resurrection, as evidenced in Matthew 4:17: "From that time Jesus began to preach, saying, 'Repent, for the kingdom of heaven is at hand.'" Second, the kingdom of God is also a present reality in the hearts of believers who submit to Christ's rule and reign as King and Savior. Hebrews 12:28 urges us, "Therefore let us be grateful for receiving a kingdom that cannot be shaken, and thus let us offer to God acceptable worship, with reverence and awe." Third, the kingdom of God is a future hope when Christ at his second coming will establish his ultimate and final kingdom and rule

---

18. Beeke, "Hallowing God's Name," 41.

over all the earth. Revelation 11:15 gives us this hope: "The kingdom of the world has become the kingdom of our Lord and his Christ, and he shall reign forever and ever." In light of these three realities concerning the kingdom of God, we should have a burning passion for seeing the rule and reign of Christ and his gospel break into the lives of lost people trapped in spiritual slavery. We should cry out in prayer for nonbelievers to trust in Christ alone and surrender to his kingship.

In other words, this request for God's kingdom to come is a missionary prayer in that we desire the powerful advancement of the gospel. Ultimately, we pray for non-Christians to repent and believe in Jesus as their King so that they can submit to his rule and reign in their lives. Are you praying this way? Are you passionate to see lost sinners come to faith in Christ so that they can surrender to his kingship? Are you praying for the advancement of the gospel, especially to unreached people groups? Are you urgently asking God to bring his kingdom to rule and reign in the hearts of unsaved people dwelling in darkness?

REQUEST NUMBER THREE: THY WILL BE DONE!

This request can be confusing if we don't fully understand what Jesus means by God's will. If the Father is sovereign and he is going to accomplish his purpose, then why pray for his will to be done? Does this mean that God's will is somehow not going to be done? Does it mean that God is not sovereign and that something can thwart his will? We need to understand how the Bible distinguishes between the two types of wills of God. The first type is what we call the secret or sovereign will of God, which he infallibly accomplishes by his power. We sometimes don't ever see how God orchestrates events behind the scenes through his providence. Deuteronomy 29:29 informs us, "The secret things belong to the Lord our God, but the things that are revealed belong to us and to our children forever, that we may do all the words of this law."

Do our prayers somehow change God's mind? Is God dependent on our prayers to work out the counsel of his will? Absolutely not! What then is the purpose of prayer? Is the purpose of prayer to change God's mind? Or is the purpose growing in closer intimacy and fellowship with our great God? John Calvin gives great insight, "It is very important for us to call upon him: First, that our hearts may be fired with a zealous and burning desire ever to seek, love, and serve him, while we become accustomed in every need to flee to him as to our sacred anchor."[19] We call upon God because we desperately need him as our sacred anchor. We don't pray to change his mind, manipulate, or control him. Instead, we pray to seek his face in intimacy, fellowship, and show our utter dependence upon him. R. C. Sproul writes,

> Does prayer change God's mind? No! Does prayer change things? Of course! The very reason we pray is because of God's sovereignty because we believe that God has it within his power to order things according to his purpose. That is what sovereignty is all about—ordering things according to God's purpose. What prayer most often changes is the wickedness and the hardness of our own hearts. That alone would be reason enough to pray, even if none of the other reasons were valid or true.[20]

The Bible affirms that God is absolutely and meticulously sovereign over all things:

> The counsel of the LORD stands forever, the plans of his heart to all generations (Ps 33:11).

> Whatever the LORD pleases, he does, in heaven and on earth, in the seas and all deeps (Ps 135:6).

> I perceived that whatever God does endures forever; nothing can be added to it, nor anything taken from it. God has done it, so that people fear before him (Eccl 3:14).

> Remember the former things of old; for I am God, and there is no other; I am God, and there is none like me, declaring the end from the beginning and from ancient times things not yet done, saying, "My counsel shall stand, and I will accomplish all my purpose (Isa 46:9–10)."

> I know that you can do all things, and that no purpose of yours can be thwarted (Job 42:2).

> In him we have obtained an inheritance, having been predestined according to the purpose of him who works all things according to the counsel of his will (Eph 1:11).

The Bible also speaks of God's will of command, which he reveals in his moral law summarized in the Ten Commandments. God's written word

---

19. Calvin, *Institutes of the Christian Religion*, 147.
20. Sproul, "Why Pray?," 5–8.

informs us of what the LORD requires from his creatures. Sinful people often reject and disobey God's moral will. When Jesus teaches us to ask for God's will to be done on earth, I believe he is referring to the second type of will—the will of command. The angels in heaven perfectly honor God's name, obey him, and submit to his kingdom rule. On the other hand, currently on planet earth, people reject, break, and disobey God's revealed will in the Bible all the time. Why? Non-Christians steeped in depravity don't properly honor God's name. They don't submit to him as King as they flagrantly reject his commands in Scripture on a daily basis.

But what about you as a follower of Christ? Do you desire to obey everything he has commanded in the Bible? Do you heed the words of Deuteronomy 26:16: "This day the Lord your God commands you to do these statutes and rules. You shall therefore be careful to do them with all your heart and with all your soul." Does your heart reflect Psalm 119:9–1: "How can a young man keep his way pure? By guarding it according to your word. With my whole heart I seek you; let me not wander from your commandments! I have stored up your word in my heart, that I might not sin against you?" Do you confidently ask for God's will to be done in your life through obedience to his word? First John 5:14–15 says, "And this is the confidence that we have toward him, that if we ask anything according to his will he hears us. And if we know that he hears us in whatever we ask, we know that we have the requests that we have asked of him." John Calvin comments on this request, "By this prayer we are taught to deny ourselves, that God may rule us according to his pleasure; to wish nothing of ourselves, but have our hearts governed by his Spirit that we may learn to love those things which please him and hate those things which displease him. Hence we must desire that he would nullify and suppress all affections which are repugnant to his will."[21]

REQUEST NUMBER FOUR:
FATHER, PLEASE HELP ME BE DEPENDENT

Jesus teaches us to ask the Father for daily bread, which addresses our physical needs. This request reminds us of how God provided daily manna for the Israelites while they were in the wilderness (Exod 16:4). According to Matthew 6:8, your Father knows what you need before you ask him. So then, why pray? Why ask God to meet our daily needs if

---

21. Calvin, *Institutes of the Christian Religion*, 191.

he already knows what we need? Why pray if God knows everything? Are we somehow telling him something he doesn't know? Is he surprised by our prayers? Do they catch him off guard? Asking for daily bread in prayer shows our utter dependence upon a gracious and sovereign God. We pray to cultivate deep fellowship with him. We pray to rely on him in humble dependence as the lifeblood of who we are in our identity in the Trinity.

We have a significant problem in America that affects our prayer life—affluence. We have numerous daily comforts that make us self-sufficient. The Pew Research Center did a study on how affluent Americans compare to the rest of the world.[22] The study included 111 countries that account for almost 90 percent of the world's population. The middle-class in the world as a whole has an annual income of around $21,000 a year for a family of four. The United States is way ahead of the rest of the world. Fifty-six percent of Americans are high income by global standards. Another 32 percent are upper-middle class, as 9 in 10 Americans have a standard of living that is considerably higher than most of the world. Even for those who are considered as living at or below the poverty level, their standard of living is still higher than the rest of the world. In 2011, the official poverty line in the U.S. was $23,021 for a family of four. This means that many Americans who live in poverty by U.S. standards would be middle income by global standards. Here's the real kicker: 71 percent of the world lives on $10 or less a day. That means that most of the world lives on around $4,000 a year.

In our self-dependence, we pray when tragedy strikes, or when we face tough times, but do we ask God to meet our daily needs? The reason we often don't pray this prayer is that we don't think we need daily bread. We usually trust in our ability and resources until things get really bad. When things are going well, we don't pray for daily bread because we are not dependent, but self-sufficient. Kevin DeYoung said this: "Prayerlessness is an expression of our meager confidence in God's ability to provide and of our strong confidence in our ability to take care of ourselves without God's help."[23] God knows our deepest needs. He knows when a sparrow falls out of a tree (Matt 10:29) and he knows the number of hairs on our heads (Matt 10:30). He is intimately acquainted with every minute detail of our lives and knows what we need even before we have

---

22. Kochhar, "How Americans Compare."
23. DeYoung, *Good News We Almost Forgot*, 232.

a clue. In this request, Jesus teaches us to ask our good Father for what we need in a way that is not pretentious or selfish. We are to come to our Father with a child-like faith that shows a total dependence upon him to meet our daily needs. James 1:17 tells us that "every good gift and every perfect gift is from above, coming down from the Father of lights with whom there is no variation or shadow due to change." Are you thankful for the good gifts your heavenly Father showers you with or are you an ungrateful child who only complains about what you don't have? Bryan Chapell gives some good encouragement on the difference between childish praying and mature praying:

> Children pray, "Lord, give me what I want;" the mature pray, "Lord, conform me to what you want." Children pray for the fulfillment of their desires; the mature pray for the fulfillment of the Savior's purposes. Children pray for things they can see; the mature pray that God will be seen. Children pray, "My will be done"; the mature pray, "Thy will be done."[24]

Why pray for *daily* bread? Think about it this way. If the Father were to give you all of his blessings and provisions in one lump sum how would you treat him? You would probably fritter it away or enjoy it all at once and forget about him. God knows what he's doing by only giving you what you need each day. Millions of people in our nation put their hopes in winning the lottery to make millions of dollars. Three significant universities conducted a study recently on whether winning the jackpot would lead to permanent financial improvement. They examined 35,000 winners in the Florida Lottery over a nine-year span and discovered that 7 in 10 lottery winners squandered their earnings and filed for bankruptcy after only a few years.[25] The research overwhelmingly shows that those who take the lump sum are more prone to wasting their money than those who elected to have their winnings in monthly installments.

Are you dependent for daily bread? Are you humble for God's daily supply of resources? Or are you self-sufficient and trusting in your abilities to produce results? Are you praying for what you need, or what you selfishly want? Jonathan Edwards said, "With respect to God, prayer is but a sensible acknowledgment of our dependence on him to his glory... Our prayer to God may excite in us a suitable sense and consideration of our dependence on God for the mercy we ask, and a suitable exercise of faith

---

24. Chapell, *Praying Backwards*, 26–27.
25. Wiles, "Winner's Guide to Managing," para. 9.

in God's sufficiency, so that we may be prepared to glorify his name when the mercy is received."[26]

REQUEST NUMBER FIVE: FATHER, PLEASE HELP ME BE REPENTANT

Jesus teaches us to ask God to forgive our debts as we also have forgiven our debtors. This request at first can sound confusing because it almost seems like Jesus is saying that God won't forgive unless you forgive others. What exactly is Jesus saying here? Does this request nullify salvation by grace alone and promote works-based righteousness? I want you to consider a few truths. First of all, God saves us by grace alone through faith alone in Christ alone, and once we trust him for salvation, he forgives all our sins past, present, and future. Colossians 2:13–14 reminds us that "you, who were dead in your trespasses and the uncircumcision of your flesh, God made alive together with him, having forgiven us all our trespasses, by canceling the record of debt that stood against us with its legal demands. This he set aside, nailing it to the cross." Because God imputes Christ's righteousness to us by faith, we stand in a permanent position of forgiveness before the Father. Your status as a forgiven sinner does not change (see chapter five)! In our justification, the Lord canceled the penalty of sin that stood against us and counted us righteous in Christ. In our regeneration, God broke the power of sin and made us alive in Christ. Through the new birth, God forever rescued us from the dominion of sin as our master (see chapter six).

As believers, we continue to transgress his law and God must cleanse us from the polluting effects of sin's presence in our lives. Our remaining corruption is still an offense to a holy God. We still grieve the Holy Spirit (Eph 4:30) when we sin. This indwelling sin pollutes us by its darkness and affects our fellowship with our Savior. My son and I are in a permanent relationship by birth as father and son. We have a great relationship and love each other deeply. But what would happen if he becomes rebellious, disowns me, and never wants to see me again? Would my relationship with him as his father change? Absolutely not. I'm still his father no matter what choices he makes to offend or hurt me. But would the intimacy between us be dramatically affected? Absolutely. We would be estranged in fellowship even though our relationship would

---

26. Edwards, *Works of Jonathan Edwards*, vol. 2, 116.

always be permanent as father and son. This analogy is similar to how God the Father relates to his children. Once he adopted us into his family through salvation in Christ alone, we are permanently his children in that our relationship never changes. But when we sin, we lose that closeness, fellowship, and the broken intimacy needs to be restored. It doesn't mean that we have lost our salvation or somehow God kicked us out of the family, but it does mean that we need to ask for forgiveness, draw close, and seek to restore that severed fellowship. First John 1:9 instructs us in this reality: "If we confess our sins, he is faithful and just to forgive us our sins and to cleanse us from all unrighteousness."

This request to forgive our debts means we should have a soft heart toward God by keeping short accounts of sin so that its presence in our lives will not pollute us. A careful look at Jesus' wording in this request reveals that he does not say that we will be forgiven "if," "because," or "on account of" forgiving others. He says "*as* we have also forgiven our debtors." Evidence or proof that God has genuinely forgiven you in salvation means that you are quick to forgive others. Because God has extravagantly forgiven you by grace, you are ready to forgive others out of the overflow of God's mercy shown to you. Do you pray with this attitude of repentance? Do you pray with a heart toward forgiving others who have wronged you? Are you thankful for God's tremendous patience toward you in his forgiveness?

REQUEST NUMBER SIX: FATHER, PLEASE HELP ME BE VIGILANT

In this final request, Jesus instructs us to pray that we will not be led into temptation, but delivered from evil. We need to be careful here with the wording about temptation because God does not tempt us to do evil as evidenced in James 1:13-14: "Let no one say when he is tempted, 'I am being tempted by God,' for God cannot be tempted with evil, and he himself tempts no one. But each person is tempted when he is lured and enticed by his own desire." This request focuses on protection against evil in all forms—Satan, our flesh, or the temptations of the world—that will lead us to fall into future sin. The previous request addressed the need to be forgiven of sins we already committed, but this request relies upon God to help us be vigilant so that we don't succumb to committing future sins. We tend to have overconfidence in our ability to fight temptation and to wage spiritual warfare. The unholy trinity of the world, the flesh, and the devil never sleep and always attack us, so we should never sleep either, but be ever more vigilant to resist temptation (see chapter 7 on sin).

Conductor William Rockefeller made the news a few years ago when his train barreled down the tracks in the Bronx at 82mph, killing four passengers and injuring seventy-five. Why did the train crash? Rockefeller fell asleep on the job and lost control. We can trace some of the world's worst disasters back to someone who fell asleep on the job. The nuclear explosion in Chernobyl, Ukraine, occurred because operators working thirteen hours straight fell asleep on the job. The Three Mile Island incident, in Pennsylvania, in 1979, also resulted from workers falling asleep on the job. Some reports have linked the Space Shuttle Challenger explosion in 1986 to NASA officials coming to work sleep deprived that day. The third mate fell asleep at the wheel, causing the Exxon Valdez oil spill in 1989. Falling asleep at the wheel or on the job can lead to disasters. In the same way, falling asleep in this battle with sin and temptation can also lead to spiritual failure. Jesus warned his disciples in Mark 14:38: "Watch and pray that you may not enter into temptation. The spirit indeed is willing, but the flesh is weak."

Let us retrace our steps so far in the Lord's Prayer. We started with a passionate desire for God's name to be honored and glorified. Then we moved to ask God for his kingdom to come and the gospel to advance so that he would liberate sinners by bringing them into his family through salvation. Then we prayed that we would be obedient to his will as revealed in the Bible. Then we asked God to help us be dependent as we trust in him for our daily bread. Then we asked God to help us be repentant in that we would be quick to confess sins. Through this entire prayer, we are cultivating intimacy and fellowship with the Father as we draw closer to him and enjoy his presence in our lives. While we don't lose our salvation when we sin, that sin does interrupt the sweet fellowship we have with God. This sin makes us not want to pray, and the last thing we want to do is draw near to God. This final request is a passionate desire to keep that sweet communion with God a reality by not sinning. In this request, we plead with God for help so that we don't give into temptation. We don't want to succumb to the snares of the devil, give into the passions of our flesh, or fall prey to the allurements of the world. Instead, we long to walk in holiness and purity by avoiding sin and temptation at all costs. This is a prayer against a false sense of security in our ability to handle temptation. Paul encourages us in 1 Corinthians 10:12–13: "Therefore let anyone who thinks that he stands take heed lest he fall. No temptation has overtaken you that is not common to man. God is faithful, and he will not let you be tempted beyond your ability, but with the temptation he will also provide the way of escape, that you may be able to endure it." We must acknowledge that in our flesh we are weak and susceptible to temptation. We need God's power to protect us and to keep us vigilant. Our prayer should echo James 4:7: "Submit yourselves therefore to God. Resist the devil, and he will flee from you."

THE DOXOLOGY

Many modern translations do not include the ending of praise to the Father: "Yours is the kingdom, the power, and the glory, forever Amen!" You will find a footnote in your Bible that tells you that the most reliable and earliest manuscripts do not contain this doxology. Even though this is not in the most reliable manuscripts, I still think it is an appropriate way to end the prayer because we see an example of it in the Old Testament. This concluding praise resembles 1 Chronicles 29:11: "Yours, O Lord, is the greatness and the power and the glory and the victory and the majesty, for all that is in the heavens and in the earth is yours. Yours is the kingdom, O Lord, and you are exalted as head above all." Honoring God's glory and power is a fitting way to end the prayer because it focuses us back on being God-centered instead of self-centered. It reminds us of God's glory, God's kingdom, and God's power to answer these requests. This doxology reveals our utter dependence upon him by showing that we should end our prayers in worship, adoration, and confidence in God's sovereignty. Jonathan Edwards wrote, "While believers are praying, he gives them sweet views of his glorious grace, purity, sufficiency, and sovereignty; and enables them with great quietness, to rest in him, to leave themselves and their prayers with him, submitting to his will, and trusting in his grace and faithfulness."[27]

Let's recap the Lord's Prayer and again ask the simple question: Is this how you pray?

The address: Do you intimately address God as your Father who is accessible and good, but yet at the same time who is sovereign and ruling in heaven? Do you also approach him with awe and reverence?

---

27. Edwards, *Works of Jonathan Edwards*, vol. 2, 114.

The first three requests: Are your prayers thoroughly God-centered or self-centered? Do you earnestly pray for his name to be hallowed? Do you intensely pray for his kingdom to come? Do you passionately pray for his will to be done?

The last three requests: Do you intensely pray for him to help you be dependent? Do you pray for him to help you be repentant? Do you humbly pray for him to help you be vigilant?

The doxology: Do you end your prayer bringing it back around to God's glory, kingdom, and power? John Bunyan wrote, "You can do more than pray, after you have prayed, but you cannot do more than pray until you have prayed."[28]

Do you need Jesus to teach you to pray? Is your prayer life weak, dry, and lifeless? Do you need some significant encouragement in how you should pray? The Lord's Prayer is a powerful model that Jesus has given us as a means of grace to grow in our identity in the Trinity. Can you genuinely say that prayer is your lifeblood? Scottish preacher Robert Murray M'Cheyne said this, "What a man is on his knees before God, that he is, and nothing more."

---

28. Bunyan, *Works of John Bunyan*, 1:65.

12

The Celebration of the Ordinances

"Christ is the only food for our soul, and therefore, our heavenly Father invites us to him, that, refreshed by communion with Christ, we may have experience new strength and grace until we reach heaven."[1]

JOHN CALVIN

ON A SUNDAY NIGHT in 1979, as an eight-year old boy, I came under strong conviction of my sin against a holy God. I asked my parents to come to my room and comfort me, and they shared the gospel with me with a compassion and earnestness I will never forget. That evening, I repented of my sins and placed all of my trust in Jesus Christ alone as Lord and Savior. The following Sunday, I was baptized by immersion as a public testimony of how God had inwardly saved me by grace. I am a Baptist by conviction and have been one my entire life. I believe that the differences surrounding the mode and meaning of baptism are secondary doctrinal issues that should not divide the body of Christ. Nonetheless, the following position in this chapter advocates an unapologetic baptistic understanding of the two ordinances of baptism and the Lord's Supper.

---

1. Calvin, *Institutes of the Christian Religion*, 557.

In Acts 2:41, we see what happened as a result of Peter's Spirit-empowered sermon on the day of Pentecost: "So those who received his word were baptized, and there were added that day about three thousand souls." In the verses immediately following, Luke describes how these three thousand new believers functioned as a church family in that they devoted themselves to the apostles teaching, prayer, fellowship, and the breaking of bread or the Lord's Supper. In the previous two chapters, we explored Scripture saturation and prayer as a means of grace for our growth in godliness. In addition to these, God has also given the church two ordinances—baptism and the Lord's Supper—as effective ways to nurture our faith and confirm our gospel identity in Christ. Some church traditions view these two ordinances as merely outward symbols, yet baptism and the Lord's Supper are a means of grace. John Calvin noted that these were "outward signs by which the Lord seals on our consciences the promises of his good will toward us to sustain the weakness of our faith, and we, in turn, attest our piety toward him in the presence of the Lord and of his angels and before men."[2] The Holy Spirit strengthens our weak faith and grants us a fuller understanding of our gospel identity in the Trinity when the church baptizes new believers and regularly observes the Lord's Supper.

FOUR ASPECTS OF BAPTISM

Mark 1:9–11 reveals that Jesus himself was baptized to fulfill all righteousness: "In those days Jesus came from Nazareth of Galilee and was baptized by John in the Jordan. And when he came up out of the water, immediately he saw the heavens being torn open and the Spirit descending on him like a dove. And a voice came from heaven, 'you are my beloved Son; with you I am well pleased.'" Also, in the Great Commission, Jesus commanded us to baptize new believers in "Go therefore and make disciples of all nations, baptizing them in the name of the Father and of the Son and of the Holy Spirit" (Matt 28:19). Furthermore, the early church in Acts faithfully practiced the baptism of new believers into the church. In Acts 8:35–39, Philip baptized the Ethiopian eunuch, and in Acts 16:30–33 Paul baptized the Philippian jailer and his family, to name a few examples. The New Testament provides for us four primary aspects concerning the practice of baptism as a means of grace.

---

2. Calvin, *Institutes of the Christian Religion*, 491.

First, baptism is the immersion of a believer in water in the name of the Father, the Son, and the Holy Spirit

The word "baptism" comes from the Greek term *baptizo*, which means to plunge, dip, or immerse under the water. In Jesus' baptism in Mark 1:10, and the Ethiopian's baptism in Acts 8:39, the Scripture uses the terminology that each "came up out of the water," which signifies immersion under the water. Baptism is the initiating oath sign of the new covenant whereby a new believer formally submits to the Triune God in obedience to Jesus' command to be baptized. Also, we are baptized into the name (singular) of the Father, Son, and Holy Spirit, which undergirds our identity in the Trinity. Edmund Clowney gives excellent insight into this, "Christian baptism is a naming ceremony. The baptized person is given a name, not the name on a baptismal certificate, but the name of the triune God . . . Baptism gives Christians their family name, the name they bear as those called the children of God."[3] As a believer in Christ, you are chosen, adopted, and accepted in the Father; purchased, forgiven, and righteous in the Son; and regenerated, indwelt, and sanctified by the Spirit. In sovereign grace, the Triune God has done this amazing work in transforming your spiritual identity. Baptism in the name of the Father, Son, and Spirit further celebrates and reinforces this identity in the Trinity. Don Whitney says,

> Baptism in the name of the Father and the Son and the Holy Spirit confesses your belief that each member of the Trinity is involved in your salvation and that you are brought into a relationship with each. God the Father chose you before the foundation of the world. God the Son died a bloody, painful death to make you right with the Father. God, the Holy Spirit, opened your eyes, enabling you to see your need to be reconciled to God and believe in the work of Jesus Christ.[4]

The outward symbol of baptism as not only involving immersion under the water, but also receiving a new name in the Trinity, helps you understand more fully your gospel identity as a new creation in Christ.

Our being (identity) comes before doing (obedience). As a result of our Trinitarian identity, baptism becomes the first act of obedience that a new believer does after coming to faith in Christ. Once you have

---

3. Clowney, *Church*, 278.
4. Whitney, *Spiritual Disciplines Within the Church*, 35–36.

repented of your sins and trusted in Christ alone to save you, you follow both Jesus' example of being baptized himself and his command to be baptized. In baptism, you are submitting yourself to the Trinity—Father, Son, and Spirit—as an overflow of your new gospel identity.

Second, baptism is a public profession of repentance and faith

Baptism does not save anyone, but instead shows visually and verbally that God has saved him or her by his free grace alone. Baptism serves as a public expression that lets everyone know what has happened to you on the inside. Think about what happens at a wedding ceremony. A man and woman stand before family and friends, and repeat covenant vows in which they publicly pledge their love for one another. In the exchanging of vows, God does a mysteriously incredible act. He spiritually joins the two people together as one flesh. The couple also exchanges rings which are outward tokens or symbols of that love and commitment. The rings don't make the couple married, but they do symbolize or signify publicly for all to see that they are married—even to those who were not at the wedding ceremony. In the same way, baptism is like the wedding ring. Baptism doesn't make you saved—only God saves you by his grace alone—baptism is an outward profession or visible token that God has already saved you.

The act of plunging a believer under the water signifies a confession of repentance and faith. The image of immersion in the water and then coming back up symbolizes our cleansing from sin. Mark Dever writes, "The submission of a believer to the water of baptism represents his or her humble request to God for a conscience cleared of guilt because of Christ's atoning blood. Baptism is an act of confession and utter dependence."[5] We are born into this world as sinners who have inherited the pollution of Adam, and thus we are totally depraved from head to toe. Sin stains the entirety of our being with rebellion and corruption. While baptism does not rid us of this original sin, it does visually paint a picture for us of the reality that Christ has cleansed us by grace from head to toe in salvation.

---

5. Dever, *Church*, 36.

Third, baptism is an act of obedience symbolizing the believer's faith in Christ's death, burial, and resurrection

Think about the visual image that baptism presents. When you stand in the water, you symbolize Christ lifted up to die on the cross. When you go under the water, you visualize the burial of Christ in the tomb. When you come up out of the water, you portray the resurrection of Christ. Baptism is a visual picture of the gospel where you identify with Jesus in his death, burial, and resurrection by publicly proclaiming that you believe in him. Paul stresses the connection between baptism and Christ's death and resurrection in Romans 6:3–4: "Do you not know that all of us who have been baptized into Christ Jesus were baptized into his death? We were buried therefore with him by baptism into death, so that, just as Christ was raised from the dead by the glory of the Father, we too might walk in newness of life." Not only do we identify with the historical reality of the death, burial, and resurrection of Christ when we undergo baptism by immersion, but we also portray the spiritual reality of dying to our old life of sin and rising to a brand-new identity. In salvation, God took our former selves, steeped in depravity, and raised us to new life by grace alone. Through the gospel, we are now new creations in Christ who have this beautiful identity in the Trinity. Baptism represents a death to sin, the world, and the devil that dominated our old lives, and reflects the reality of the newness of life in Christ. I can think of no other symbol that so graphically and beautifully depicts the riches of the gospel than baptism. Colossians 2:12 also emphasizes this connection: "Having been buried with him in baptism, in which you were also raised with him through faith in the powerful working of God, who raised him from the dead." Baptism is a sign of the believer's death to sin, the burial of the old life, and the resurrection to walk in newness of life in Christ Jesus.

Fourth, baptism signifies that you belong to God's family, the church

To baptize a new believer is to add him or her to the church family. In Acts 2:41, Luke could have simply stated that a significant number were baptized after Peter's sermon and just stopped there with no other explanation or qualification. Instead, he gave the specific number—3,000—and said that they were added that day. Added to what? In the context of

Acts, those baptized were added to the church in Jerusalem. Before they were saved and baptized, these 3,000 people were not part of the church. After their salvation and baptism, they had undergone the initiation oath and public profession of faith and then were added to the church. We must assume that they did not self-baptize without any connection to a local body of believers, but were immediately incorporated into the life of the early church. While baptism is a personal act of obedience, it is never private. In baptism, we celebrate our individual identity in the Trinity as those saved by sovereign grace. As a unified body, we also celebrate our corporate identity in the Trinity as God's people called to live out that identity together as the visible church. John Hammett provides this summary about the importance of baptism:

> Baptism is a powerful means of worship. The very act pictures the transforming power of the gospel to put to death an old life and grant a new life and may communicate in a more vivid way than words alone. For the one being baptized, it should be a memorable day like a wedding, the day of public commitment to a life of love and union with the Lord. For the baptizing community, it should be an occasion as joyous as a birth of a new child into the family, with the solemn dedication to the task of caring for this new member of the family.[6]

Baptism becomes not only a means of grace for the individual baptized, but also strengthens the faith of the congregation who views the baptism performed in a worship service. The Holy Spirit works through the baptismal ceremony to not only bless the person baptized, but also to stir up and encourage the faith of those who watch. Every time a new believer gets baptized, God ministers strengthening grace to both the individual participant as well as the entire church family who get reminded all over again of the riches of God's grace in the gospel and the blessing of their identity in the Trinity. If you have repented of your sin and trusted in Christ alone for salvation but have yet to follow the Lord in obedience through baptism, I encourage you to discuss this with your pastor or seek out a local church that can assist you in this. Every time a new believer gets baptized, I encourage you to celebrate God's mercy anew as a means of grace he uses to stimulate and excite your faith!

---

6. Hammett, *Biblical Foundations for Baptist Churches*, 276.

THE LORD'S SUPPER

The Lord's Supper uniquely depicts continuing fellowship with God as a repeated act whereby the believer remembers the Lord's death and renews his commitment to Christ and participation in his church. This is also a means of grace as Herman Bavinck describes: "Of primary importance in the Lord's Supper is what God does, not what we do. The Lord's Supper is above all a gift of God, a benefit of Christ, a means of communicating grace."[7] Bobby Jamieson explains, "The Lord's Supper pictures the priority, sufficiency, and efficacy of God's grace by presenting to us a salvation that Christ has unilaterally accomplished. This salvation is always and only appropriated by faith, which we picture and profess as we partake."[8] Let us explore four aspects of the Lord's Supper that help us understand this ordinance as a means of grace, as well as a way to strengthen us in our gospel identity.

First, the old covenant Passover impacts our understanding of the new covenant Lord's Supper

The LORD gave instructions for the Israelites to celebrate the Passover in Exodus 12 on the evening before they left Egypt and passed through the Red Sea. Exodus 12:24–27 reads,

> "You shall observe this rite as a statute for you and for your sons forever. And when you come to the land that the Lord will give you, as he has promised, you shall keep this service. And when your children say to you, 'What do you mean by this service?' you shall say, 'It is the sacrifice of the Lord's Passover, for he passed over the houses of the people of Israel in Egypt when he struck the Egyptians but spared our houses.'" And the people bowed their heads and worshipped.

The Passover meal involved slaughtering a spotless lamb and then smearing its blood over one's doorposts to avert God's wrath in the killing of their firstborn sons. When the Destroyer or Angel of Death "passed over" the Israelites' houses and saw the blood, that house experienced God's salvation due to the blood of the Lamb. The New Testament often refers to Jesus as the Passover Lamb who was slain to appease God's wrath

---

7. Bavinck, *Reformed Dogmatics*, 4:567.
8. Jamieson, *Going Public*, 117.

against our sin and obtain our salvation. John the Baptist called Jesus, "The Lamb of God who takes away the sins of the world" (John 1:29). In 1 Corinthians 5:7, Paul identifies Christ as our Passover Lamb who was sacrificed. Peter uses the same terminology to describe Jesus redeeming us with his blood as a lamb without blemish or spot (1 Pet 1:19).

On the night he was betrayed, Jesus used the images and motifs from the old covenant Passover ceremony and transformed them when he instituted the Lord's Supper. Jesus has come as the ultimate Passover Lamb who shed his blood on the cross so that all who trust in him would not experience eternal death in hell. The ordinance of the Lord's Supper pictures this reality in Matthew 26:26–28: "Now as they were eating, Jesus took bread, and after blessing it broke it and gave it to the disciples, and said, 'Take, eat; this is my body.' And he took a cup, and when he had given thanks he gave it to them, saying, 'Drink of it, all of you, for this is my blood of the covenant, which is poured out for many for the forgiveness of sins.'" When we partake of the Lord's Supper, we eat a covenant meal instituted by the Lamb of God whose blood inaugurated the new covenant. Just as the Israelites bowed and worshipped the LORD after receiving instructions on the Passover, we as new covenant believers also bow and worship our great God when we partake of the Lord's Supper because it symbolizes all the benefits Christ won for us in the new covenant. Jeremiah 31:33–34 gives us the new covenant promise:

> For this is the covenant that I will make with the house of Israel after those days, declares the Lord: I will put my law within them, and I will write it on their hearts. And I will be their God, and they shall be my people. And no longer shall each one teach his neighbor and each his brother, saying, "Know the Lord," for they shall all know me, from the least of them to the greatest, declares the Lord. For I will forgive their iniquity, and I will remember their sin no more.

What are these new covenant promises that we celebrate at the Lord's Table? When the LORD says, "I will be their God and they shall be my people," he speaks of adoption—that glorious truth where the Father brings us into his family permanently. In verse 34, the prophet says that we will all know the LORD, which conveys an intimate knowledge. Through Christ's shed blood on the cross for you, God grants you the privilege to experience dynamic union with him. Also, we receive the absolute forgiveness of all sins where he will remember them no more. Micah 7:19 reminds us, "He will again have compassion on us; he will tread our iniquities under foot. You will cast all our sins into the depths of the sea." In summary, we can describe the Lord's Supper as "looking up" in worship to our heavenly Father who sent Jesus to propitiate his righteous justice against our sin through grace alone.

Second, in the Lord's Supper, we both symbolize and remember the death of Christ

Paul provides the most explicit instructions on how we celebrate the Lord's Supper in 1 Corinthians 11:23–26:

> For I received from the Lord what I also delivered to you, that the Lord Jesus on the night when he was betrayed took bread, and when he had given thanks, he broke it, and said, "This is my body, which is for you. Do this in remembrance of me." In the same way also he took the cup, after supper, saying, "This cup is the new covenant in my blood. Do this, as often as you drink it, in remembrance of me. For as often as you eat this bread and drink the cup, you proclaim the Lord's death until he comes."

The Lord's Supper is symbolic in that the elements do not literally become bread and wine. When we partake of the elements, we look back to what Jesus accomplished for us on the cross in his sacrificial death. The supper becomes a memorial where we reflect on the horrors of the cross and meditate upon the atonement and our sin against a holy God. Through memorializing Christ's death, the Lord ministers to our hearts because we remember that it was our rebellion and depravity that nailed Jesus to the cross. As enemies of God, Christ reconciled us through his death and procured for us eternal salvation that can never be taken away. In summary, we can express the Lord's Supper as "looking back" at what Christ did for us in his sacrificial death.

Third, in the Lord's Supper, we picture the spiritual nourishment that Christ gives to our souls

Is communion more than merely a symbol or memorial where we look back to what Christ accomplished for us on the cross? Does Jesus deeply and spiritually minister to our souls in the present when we take the Lords' Supper? The historic Reformed Baptist stance on this question has been that the Lord's Supper is a means of grace through which Christ is present by his divine nature. When we come to the Lord's Table, the Holy Spirit nourishes our souls with the benefits won for us by Christ's death. Paul describes this real presence or spiritual participation with Christ in 1 Corinthians 10:16–17: "The cup of blessing that we bless, is it not a participation in the blood of Christ? The bread that we break, is it not a participation in the body of Christ? Because there is one bread, we who are many are one body, for we all partake of the one bread." In verse 16 we see the vertical aspect of the Lord's Supper as participation in the blood and body of Christ. The Greek word for "participation, communion, sharing" is *koinonia*. Since the verb is in the present tense, Paul describes the *real presence* of Christ in the Supper. It is a present communion with Christ in that we experience the benefits that his broken body and shed blood have won for us—namely, forgiveness of sins, a right standing before God, the indwelling Holy Spirit, and all the benefits of his finished work.

This participation means more than taking communion together as a unified body as a shared experience. Since we have union with Christ through the Holy Spirit living in us, we commune or share in Christ himself. Baptists throughout history have held this view, like Charles Spurgeon, who said, "At this table, Jesus feeds us with his body and blood."[9] In other words, the Lord's Supper does not redeem you like a sacrament that confers saving grace every time you take it, but instead the supper is God's way of continuing to sanctify and strengthen you by grace as one who has already experienced salvation.

One of the primary ways the Holy Spirit helps you continue to grow in your faith is through the Lord's Supper. Every time we take the Lord's Supper, not only do we remember what Christ did in the past, but in the present—at the moment we partake—we receive sustaining grace by the Holy Spirit who nourishes our souls with thankfulness, strength, and peace because of Christ's finished work. Have you ever wondered why communion is an ordinance that requires eating? Jesus could have told us to draw a picture, form a sculpture, watch a movie, or even hear a sermon about the Lord's Supper. Instead, he gave us an ordinance that involves taking bread and the cup into our mouths and swallowing as a way to show that we have tasted and seen that the Lord is good. While not explicitly addressing the Lord's Supper, in John 6, after the feeding of the 5,000, Jesus utilizes the imagery of eating and drinking to convey his identity as the Messiah. Jesus said to them in John 6:35, "I am the bread

---

9. Spurgeon, *Spurgeon's Sermons on the Death*, 94.

of life; whoever comes to me shall not hunger, and whoever believes in me shall never thirst." He continues to teach on this idea in John 6:53–57:

> Truly, truly, I say to you, unless you eat the flesh of the Son of Man and drink his blood, you have no life in you. Whoever feeds on my flesh and drinks my blood has eternal life, and I will raise him up on the last day. For my flesh is true food, and my blood is true drink. Whoever feeds on my flesh and drinks my blood abides in me, and I in him. As the living Father sent me, and I live because of the Father, so whoever feeds on me, he also will live because of me.

Jesus does not urge these people to eat his literal flesh and drink his literal blood. This description of eating and drinking is a metaphor for saving faith or coming to Christ. What does the metaphor depict? When we come to Jesus in faith, we have life, we abide in him, and he grants us a relationship with the Father. All the blessings and benefits of Jesus are ours since he unites us to himself in salvation. Louis Berkhof says, "It is the grace of an ever closer fellowship with Christ, of spiritual nourishment and quickening, and of an ever increasing assurance of salvation."

Have you ever thought about how partaking of communion increases your assurance of salvation? The Lord's Supper does not save you or confer redemptive grace upon you; God saved you by grace alone through faith alone in Christ alone. Yet, every time we eat the bread and drink the cup, we contemplate the Father's love for us in the cross of Christ. Through this experience, the Holy Spirit grants us the assurance that we are indeed God's adopted children. We should never come to the Lord's Table and approach the Father as a judge where we tremble in fear, wondering if we are worthy enough to partake. Instead, we come to the supper through the intimacy granted to us by Jesus who has ushered us into the presence of our loving Father. Communion should always be a means whereby the Triune God assures us of our salvation deep within our souls.

In the Lord's Supper, we must realize that Jesus is currently present in heaven seated at the right hand of the Father, but he has sent the Holy Spirit to live in us so that we can experience the fullness of Christ. Do you see the Trinitarian nature of communion? The Father has sent the Son to accomplish our redemption. Through his finished work on the cross, Jesus sits in heaven as our one mediator. The Son sent the Holy Spirit to indwell us and minister grace in our lives. In reality, the Lord's Supper pictures this spiritual life and nourishment we have in the fullness of the Triune God. Psalm 34:8 expresses this metaphor of spiritually tasting the Lord: "Oh, taste and see that the Lord is good! Blessed is the man who takes refuge in him!" When you partake of the Lord's Supper, you are experiencing the fullness of the goodness of God for you in Christ. After listening to a good sermon, you would have no problem with the idea that God's word fed you spiritually. You came away from hearing the preaching of God's truth with your soul fed as the Holy Spirit ministered to your heart. How did you receive the preached word? It came to you through your ears. The Lord's Supper is also God's means of nourishing you, but it comes to you through your mouths. Edmund Clowney summarizes this spiritual experience in communion: "We feed on him, draw life from him, and this vital connection appears in the eating and drinking of the Lord's Supper. The sacrament brings both assurance of the saving power of his death and joy in the renewal of his life."[10] The next time you celebrate the Lord's Supper, I encourage you to taste and see that the Lord is good!

Fourth, a unified church family celebrates the Lord's Supper together as we share in the benefits of Christ's death

In 1 Corinthians 10:17, we see the horizontal aspect of the Lord's Supper. Not only do we commune with Christ, but we commune or have fellowship with each other as a unified body. We are many, but we are all one body in Christ, and when we celebrate the Lord's Supper we are doing it together. It is not a private affair you practice alone in your house. This is a church ordinance that we are to celebrate together as a church family which publicly demonstrates our unity, fellowship, and oneness in Christ. Jonathan Edwards said, "The Lord's Supper was instituted as a solemn representation and seal of the holy and spiritual union Christ's people have with Christ and one another."[11]

Paul gives further instructions on how the Lord's Supper impacts our interaction together as a church family in 1 Corinthians 11:27–29: "Whoever, therefore, eats the bread or drinks the cup of the Lord in an unworthy manner will be guilty concerning the body and blood of the Lord. Let a person examine himself, then, and so eat of the bread and drink of the cup. For anyone who eats and drinks without discerning the

---

10. Clowney, *Church*, 287.
11. Edwards, *Sermons on the Lord's Supper*, 71–72.

body eats and drinks judgment on himself." What does Paul mean about discerning the body? The Corinthian church understood the symbolism of the bread and wine as the body and blood of Christ. Their problem was the selfish and disrespectful way they were treating each other in the church. They were breaking up into factions and divisions where the wealthier members were taking advantage of the less fortunate members. They were not understanding or discerning the "body," namely the body of Christ, the church as one unified body. They did not understand the unity, interdependence, and fellowship we have together as a church family. They were abusing or mistreating others in the body instead of looking out for the interests of others in the church. We can take the Lord's Supper in an unworthy manner when we have relational friction with others in the congregation or harbor bitterness and unforgiveness.

To deal with this problem, Paul urges a self-examination before taking communion. What exactly does this self-examination mean? Do we engage in morbid introspection and worry if we're holy and righteous enough to take the Lord's Supper? Have we measured up this week in our sanctification to be worthy enough for communion? When we rest in our gospel identity in the Trinity, we have the assurance that God accepts us, and if we confess our sins, he forgives and cleanses us of all unrighteousness. Our identity grants us the freedom to partake of the Lord's Supper with joy instead of remorse. Gregg Allison explains, "The self-examination is specifically for the purpose of detecting broken relationships, division-causing behavior, disrespect, and mistreatment of brothers and sisters in Christ."[12] This examination means that if you have any unrepentant sin in your life, you need to go to the Lord and confess it privately, but it may also suggest that you if you have any grievances, bitterness, or unforgiveness toward another person in the church, you need to get that right before you take the Lord's Supper. Jesus instructs us in Matthew 5:23–24: "So if you are offering your gift at the altar and there remember that your brother has something against you, leave your gift there before the altar and go. First be reconciled to your brother, and then come and offer your gift."

---

12. Allison, *Sojourners and Strangers*, 407.

THE UNIQUENESS OF COMMUNION

Celebrating the Lord's Supper gives us a worship experience like no other. It is different than prayer, or listening to preaching, or singing songs together in worship. There is something unique, extraordinary, and spiritual happening where we encounter the genuine presence of Jesus Christ when we take the Lord's Supper. We commune with Christ by faith through the Holy Spirit, who has bonded us together as a church family. When you participate in the Lord's Supper, you remember that Jesus died for you as you participate in the benefits of his death. You receive spiritual nourishment for your soul and God unites you with all other believers who take it together as a church family. This should be a cause for great thanksgiving, joy, and unity. In summary, we can explain the Lord's Supper as "looking outward" toward our brothers and sisters as we share this covenant meal.

The Lord's Supper is also an opportunity for you to publicly proclaim your need, trust, and hope in Christ alone, who has saved you. You would still be dead in your sins and under God's wrath without his sacrifice. Michael Horton argues,

> If baptism is a means of initiating grace, the Supper is a means of persevering grace—not because it gives us an additional ingredient, or a power not present in preaching or baptism, but because it is the perpetual ratification of God's peace treaty with his people. Faith is created by the preached gospel and confirmed and strengthened by the sacraments.[13]

In taking communion, we proclaim his death until he comes. What will happen when Jesus comes back? Revelation 19:9 gives us a beautiful glimpse into this future reality: "Blessed are those who are invited to the marriage supper of the Lamb." The Lord's Supper serves as a tremendous act of worship and joy where we anticipate the glory that awaits us at the final communion—the marriage supper of the Lamb, where all the redeemed of all the ages gather together with Jesus himself. It will no longer be a memorial where we look back at what he did. It will no longer be a spiritual presence given to us by the Holy Spirit. Instead, it will be a joyous meal shared personally with Jesus that we get to enjoy for eternity! The celebration of the Lord's Supper is a beautiful foretaste of that future reality.

---

13. Horton, *Better Way*, 119.

In summary, we can describe communion as a "look forward" to the glories of heaven. Edmund Clowney beautifully describes our future: "The unchanging Christ still gives the bread and the cup, sealing his presence until the day when the mission of the church is finished, and with that host from every family and nation we will see him whom we love, and he will eat with us again in resurrection glory." [14] The next time you celebrate the Lord's Supper, would you look up, look back, look outward, and look forward as you enjoy communion as a means of grace God has given to nourish your soul and strengthen your identity in the Trinity?

---

14. Clowney, *Church*, 290.

13

Practicing the Gospel "One Anothers"

> "The church lies at the very center of the eternal purpose of God. It is not a divine afterthought. It is not an accident of history . . . his purpose is not just to save isolated individuals and so perpetuate loneliness, but rather to build his church."
>
> JOHN STOTT[1]

THE PIXAR MOVIE *WALL-E* serves as a modern-day parable of an ancient problem. This film, set in 2805, shows Earth as an abandoned planet covered in trash due to the excess and consumerism brought about by a megacorporation called "Buy-n-Large." With no hope for restoring the earth, little trash compactor robots called Wall-Es are sent back to clean up the planet. Since the toxic environment on earth cannot sustain life, one Wall-E unit is left. He is lonely and longs for true love as his only friend is a cockroach. He ends up falling in love with E.V.E.—another robot—and they go on an adventure in a spaceship called Axiom back to where all the humans live as obese and selfish consumers. This film addresses the issues of loneliness, disconnectedness, the desire for real loving relationships, the tricky way we have to handle technology, and

---

1. Stott, *Living Church*, 19.

our consumer-driven culture of selfishness. The film's writer, Andrew Stanton, described its overall theme:

> We all fall into our habits, our routines, and our ruts, consciously or unconsciously to avoid living. To avoid having to do the messy part. To avoid having relationships with other people, of dealing with the person next to us. That's why we can all get on our cell phones and not have to deal with one another. I thought, "That's a perfect amplification of the whole point of the movie."[2]

As believers who have a gospel identity in the Trinity, can we avoid having relationships with other people? Can we avoid the messy parts of living life together as the body of Christ? In a culture obsessed with technology and plagued by isolation and loneliness, how do we as God's people handle these issues of relational disconnectedness? How does the gospel address a sincere desire for lasting friendships?

In the previous chapters, we explored how the early church devoted themselves to the apostles' teaching, prayer, and the ordinances of baptism and the Lord's Supper as means of grace to grow in Christlikeness. God has given the church a fourth practice to strengthen us in our spiritual journey—fellowship. Acts 2:42–45 reads:

> And they devoted themselves to the apostles' teaching and the *fellowship*, to the breaking of bread and the prayers. And awe came upon every soul, and many wonders and signs were being done through the apostles. And all who believed were together and had all things in common. And they were selling their possessions and belongings and distributing the proceeds to all, as any had need.

The word fellowship, or *koinonia*, means to share or to have a partnership as it carries the idea of having things in common. As Christians, we share a common Savior, theology, life, and mission. We may have diverse backgrounds, ethnicities, ages, and education levels, but all those differences broke down when God created his church. We not only have an individual identity in the Trinity but a corporate identity as well.

This passage describes fellowship with two particular details: (1) breaking bread together, and (2) taking care of each other's needs. In that ancient Jewish culture, eating a meal together signified a deep friendship and intimacy where they shared life around the table. Today, we often

---

2. McConnell, "Interview," para. 8.

relegate fellowship to something that happens in a fellowship hall with a quarterly potluck. Luke also describes the early church as selling their possessions and having everything in common. The sharing of possessions was a voluntary, spontaneous act of love that was not compulsory. This fellowship was a beautiful expression of gospel generosity. God prescribes for us to love one another in biblical fellowship, or what I call practicing the gospel "one anothers" as a means of grace to grow in Christ.

THREE RUTHLESS ENEMIES

Before delving into these practices, I want to address three ruthless enemies that stand against these gospel "one anothers" and which are so commonplace in our lives that we barely recognize them. These are *selfishness, busyness, and complacency*. Let's face it, we are selfish people that put *me* at the center of the universe. We don't even bat an eye at the fact that selfishness is a sin against God. Selfishness says, "I'm more important than everybody else; therefore, everyone else must serve me." We end up using other people for our gains whether we know it or not. Selfishness is an enemy to biblical fellowship and does not reflect our gospel identity. The second enemy is busyness, where we overplan, overcommit, and overextend ourselves so that there's no time to cultivate genuine relationships and friendships with others. Busyness says, "My life is too complicated; therefore, I will not invest in building relationships." This too stands in contradiction to our gospel identity. The third enemy to fellowship is complacency, where you don't want to make the effort to foster new relationships. You want to avoid the messiness of getting heavily involved in others' lives. You may silently want deeper relationships, but you make no effort to actually grow in this area. We face an uphill battle in light of our culture and the sinfulness within our soul that fights against practicing true biblical fellowship. J. I. Packer argues, "I believe that one of the reasons why great sections of the modern church are so often sluggish and feeble is that the secret of fellowship has been lost . . . A body in which the blood does not circulate properly is always below par, and fellowship corresponds to the circulation of the blood in the body of Christ. We gain strength through fellowship, and we lose strength without it."[3]

---

3. Packer, in Whitney, *Spiritual Disciplines Within the Church*, 153.

Paul writes in 1 Thessalonians 2:8–9: "So, being affectionately desirous of you, we were ready to share with you not only the gospel of God but also our own selves, because you had become very dear to us. For you remember, brothers, our labor and toil: we worked night and day, that we might not be a burden to any of you, while we proclaimed to you the gospel of God." Do you hear Paul's affection and love for other believers? Paul was not content to share the gospel with them, and then quickly move on to the next town on his missionary agenda. Instead, he also wanted to share his life generously with them. Are you marked by selfishness, busyness, and complacency? Do you possess a deep affection for other believers shaped by the gospel of grace where you share your life generously? Your identity in the Trinity is personal, but never private. Tim Chester and Steve Timmis argue, "My being in Christ means being in Christ with those others who are in Christ. This is my identity. This is our identity. To fail to live out our corporate identity in Christ is analogous to the act of adultery; we can be Christian and do it, but it is not what Christians should do."[4] We have a community identity as those joined together as brothers and sisters in Christ. As believers, we all are chosen, adopted, and accepted by the Father. We all are purchased, forgiven, and righteous in the Son. We all are regenerated, indwelt, and sanctified by the Spirit. While not a comprehensive list of all the gospel "one anothers," the following six practices are vital to our growth in godliness and in living out our identity in the Trinity. In the original language, every one of these activities (verbs) shows up in the present tense, which indicates that we should practice them on a continual basis as part of our everyday lifestyle.

LOVE ONE ANOTHER

First John 4:7–11 exhorts us with the obligation to love one another continually:

> Beloved, let us love one another, for love is from God, and whoever loves has been born of God and knows God. Anyone who does not love does not know God, because God is love. In this the love of God was made manifest among us, that God sent his only Son into the world, so that we might live through him. In this is love, not that we have loved God but that he loved us and

---

4. Chester and Timmis, *Total Church*, 41.

sent his Son to be the propitiation for our sins. Beloved, if God so loved us, we also ought to love one another.

John gives us a strong appeal that we have an obligation to love another. We owe a debt to love one another. It's nonnegotiable. Paul issues this command to love in Romans 13:8–10:

> Owe no one anything, except to love each other, for the one who loves another has fulfilled the law. The commandments, "You shall not commit adultery, you shall not murder, you shall not steal, you shall not covet," and any other commandment, are summed up in this word: "You shall love your neighbor as yourself." Love does no wrong to a neighbor; therefore love is the fulfilling of the law.

We don't love one another to earn God's favor in salvation. Salvation is a gift of grace from first to last. First John 4:10 says, "In this is love, not that we have loved God but that he loved us and sent his Son to be the propitiation for our sins." Once we have experienced God's love firsthand in Christ, we obey his commandments out of joy in pleasing him; not so that he will love us in return, but because he already loves us.

How does the Bible define this type of love? What does it look like in practice? Leviticus 19:18 summed up this type of love for Israel in the Old Testament: "You shall love your neighbor as yourself: I am the LORD." Jesus takes this commandment one step further in John 13:43, where he says, "A new commandment I give to you, that you love one another: just as I have loved you, you also are to love another." Why does Jesus call it a new commandment? Doesn't he simply repeat Leviticus to love your neighbor as yourself? Our Lord adds another essential element when he says, "*just as* I have loved you." That little phrase, "just as," radically changes the nature of this new commandment to love one another. It's fairly easy to love those who love us back. We have no problem loving our neighbors when they are nice, cooperative, and do helpful things for us. By using the phrase "just as," Jesus puts the gospel in perspective more clearly. Every religion on earth has a moral ethic similar to the Golden Rule. In Islam, Hinduism, Buddhism, and American secularism, there exists a general rule that we need to love one another. Notice how Jesus makes this love truly cross-centered and thoroughly Christian. He doesn't merely command us to love one another, but to love one another in the way that he has specifically loved us.

What kind of love did Christ demonstrate on our behalf? He loved us with a self-giving, self-denying, and sacrificial love that he most clearly expressed on the cross. Christ showed this unfathomable love to rebel sinners as evidenced in Romans 5:10: "For if while we were enemies we were reconciled to God by the death of his Son, much more, now that we are reconciled, shall we be saved by his life." Do any of us deserve Christ's love for us? There was nothing within us that moved him to die for us except for his sheer grace. Grace is the reality that although we rightfully deserve hell, Christ joyfully endured pain for us to purchase for himself a people. Is this the way we love each other? Do others deserve our love at times? What if people annoy us? What if we can't get along? What if we think they're weird? What if they sinned against me and I can't get past it? What if Jesus had that attitude toward us? The world does not understand this type of love. The world loves those who love them back or those who are lovable. But Jesus condemns this type of shallow love in Matthew 5:43–47 when he says

> You have heard that it was said, you shall love your neighbor and hate your enemy. But I say to you, Love your enemies and pray for those who persecute you, so that you may be sons of your Father who is in heaven. For he makes his sun rise on the evil and on the good, and sends rain on the just and on the unjust. For if you love those who love you, what reward do you have? Do not even the tax collectors do the same? And if you greet only your brothers, what more are you doing than others? Do not even the Gentiles do the same?

We cannot reproduce this type of love toward each other to the fullest extent because we are not the incarnate Christ who died a once-for-all death to obtain our eternal redemption (Heb 9:12). Jesus serves as our perfect model in showing us how to love one another with a self-giving, self-denying, and sacrificial kind of love.

The Power to Love

Demonstrating this Christlike love is a whole lot easier said than done. Why? Because we are selfish! We want everything to revolve around us. We want to be the receivers, not the givers. We want the attention, the accolades, the drama, and the spotlight. We want everything to come to a screeching halt at the flip of a switch so our wants can become paramount.

How can we, who are selfish, petty, and prideful, consistently show this type of sacrificial love? How do we receive the power to love? First John 4:7 says, "Whoever loves has been born of God and knows God." The phrase "born of God" clearly expresses the truth of regeneration (see chapter 6). When God saved you, he caused you to be born again and gave you a new identity. As an unregenerate sinner before God's sovereign grace invaded our lives, we lacked two fundamental resources. First of all, we lacked the *power* to obey God. No matter how hard we tried, we had no power because of our spiritual deadness and slavery to sin. We didn't have the Holy Spirit of grace living inside of us. And second, we lacked the *desire* to obey God. We looked at the commands of God and laughed at them. We no more wanted to obey God than to have our eyes gouged out! But once the Holy Spirit regenerated us, he gave us two things that we lacked. Now we have the power and the desire to obey. We can now love one another with this sacrificial type of love because we have been born again. The only way we can love one another is because of the new birth. Because we are regenerated, indwelt, and sanctified by the Spirit, we have the power to love. God makes those who were previously dead in their sins alive to him and gives them new hearts. He resurrects them to new life and implants his Spirit within them so that they can obey consistently. How can we ever begin to love one another "just as" Jesus loved us? We have a new identity in the Father, Son, and Spirit in which the power flows from the gospel. The Father first loved us and sent the Son to die for us. The Holy Spirit indwells us and provides the ability for us to love one another.

Second Peter 1:3-4 gives this wonderful encouragement: "His divine power has granted to us all things that pertain to life and godliness, through the knowledge of him who called us to his own glory and excellence, by which he has granted to us his precious and very great promises, so that through them you may become partakers of the divine nature, having escaped from the corruption that is in the world because of sinful desire." God's divine power—that power that created the universe, that power that raised Jesus from the dead—gives us everything we need for life and godliness. In your Trinitarian identity, you can never say "I can't do it! I can't possibly love that way!" You may say, "I don't want to love sacrificially," but we can never say "I can't do it." God gives us this incredible power to love. We can't love others the way Christ has called us in the flesh, because left to ourselves, we are weak, helpless, and selfish. But through the power of Christ, we can practice these gospel "one anothers" and fight against the stream of selfishness, busyness, and complacency.

WELCOME ONE ANOTHER

Paul instructs us in Romans 15:7: "Therefore welcome one another as Christ has welcomed you, for the glory of God." This word "welcome" means to accept or admit others into fellowship. Paul roots this command to receive one another in the example of how Christ has welcomed us in the gospel. How did our Savior welcome or receive us as rebel sinners? Did he wait for us to get our acts together before he died for us? Did Christ expect us to get rid of all of our depravity before he decided to come to earth and serve us? What if Christ had the attitude that he would only accept or welcome us if we were worthy or polished enough to earn God's love? If Christ adopted that attitude, none of us would ever be saved. At the end of the verse, Paul tells us the overarching aim of embracing one another—the glory of God. When we have a lifestyle of accepting and welcoming one another by showing love and concern, we model the love of Christ, which glorifies God. The opposite of embracing one another involves a plastic fakeness where we display attitudes of perfectionism, hypocrisy, and judgmentalism where there is no real communication or authenticity. That behavior does not glorify God.

So how do we welcome or accept one another as Jesus accepted us? Galatians 3:28 provides a helpful, practical model of how we should welcome one another as fellow believers. Paul writes, "There is neither Jew nor Greek, there is neither slave nor free, there is no male and female, for you are all one in Christ Jesus." Paul addresses three issues that our sinful culture abuses and distorts and which should have no place in the life of the church. Think about the questions or comments our culture asks: "What color is your skin? What language do you speak? How much money do you make? Why are you so poor? She's a stupid blond. He's a male chauvinist." These statements reflect a worldly attitude toward others instead of welcoming one another for the glory of God. First, there is neither Jew nor Greek, which represents the ethnic or racial barrier that prevents us from receiving one another. In that culture, Greek and Roman men regularly thanked the pagan gods that they were not born as barbarians, slaves, or women. Jewish men would ask rabbis to say a blessing of thanksgiving over them that they were not born a Gentile, slave, or woman as well. As baptized believers, we are all one in Christ as the children of God. He has adopted us into his family, and there should be no sinful divisions. We all share a unified gospel identity in the Trinity that binds us together. Christ eradicates all ethnic barriers in the church. Sadly, not understanding this unity can lead to the sin of racism. Racism is utterly sinful, and we should never mistreat, malign, or show prejudice against anybody who is of a different color or ethnicity than we are. In the church, we should fellowship and love one another across racial and ethnic barriers.

The second issue reflects the socioeconomic barrier of neither slave nor free in Christ. Our world naturally associates according to class and socioeconomic issues where the rich look down on the poor and the poor look down on the rich. We should fellowship across socioeconomic barriers. Sadly, this barrier often leads to materialism and oppression. The rich get richer by oppressing the poor. Or those less fortunate shun and resent the well-off. James 2:1–4 addresses this problem:

> My brothers, show no partiality as you hold the faith in our Lord Jesus Christ, the Lord of glory. For if a man wearing a gold ring and fine clothing comes into your assembly, and a poor man in shabby clothing also comes in, and if you pay attention to the one who wears the fine clothing and say, "You sit here in a good place," while you say to the poor man, "You stand over there," or, "Sit down at my feet," have you not then made distinctions among yourselves and become judges with evil thoughts?"

Paul's final description refers to the gender or sex barrier of neither male nor female in Christ. We need to be careful here because some have taken this verse to promote radical feminism and say that there are no gender distinctions in the home or the church. I hold to a complementarian theology which means that I believe that the Bible instructs that men should be the spiritual leaders in their homes and that wives should graciously submit to that leadership. Likewise, in the church, only males can be elders who teach and preach in positions of authority. This verse warns against the sin of chauvinism, sexism, or misogyny. Here's the bottom line: When God saved us from sin and baptized us into a church family, he freed us from the evil forces of racism, materialism, oppression, and sexism. Instead of acting like the world which abuses and distorts these categories and distinctions, we who have a gospel identity in the Trinity should live lives which are radically different from the culture around us.

BEAR THE BURDENS OF ONE ANOTHER

Paul addresses the ministry of restoration in Galatians 6:1–3: "Brothers, if anyone is caught in any transgression, you who are spiritual should restore him in a spirit of gentleness. Keep watch on yourself, lest you too be tempted. Bear one another's burdens, and so fulfill the law of Christ. For if anyone thinks he is something, when he is nothing, he deceives himself." The word "caught" can imply any sin, but in this context means that someone in the church family fell into a grievous sin that impacted a lot of people and had some very negative consequences. Those "who are spiritual" does not mean some class of super-spiritual or elite Christians who have arrived at a higher level of victorious living or sanctification. In the context of Galatians, it merely means those believers who are maturing in Christ by evidence of the fruit of the Spirit in their lives. In classical Greek, the word for "restore" meant to mend a broken bone or mend holes in a fishing net. Paul uses this word to show how to mend broken relationships and make them whole again. If a brother or sister sins, we should not treat him or her with disdain, gossip about them, or shun them. We don't say, "Serves him right!" or "Let her deal with the consequences, that will teach her a lesson!" Restoring one another also means that we don't just brush over sin by sweeping it under the carpet. We address their sin and confront our fellow Christian in a spirit of gentleness. Proverbs 27:6 says, "Faithful are the wounds of a friend; profuse are the kisses of an enemy." When people sin, there are two unhealthy ways you can treat them. You can isolate them as outcasts, or you can entirely cut them off and kick them out of the church without any due process.

Jesus gives us the steps for how to practice church discipline in Matthew 18:15–17:

> If your brother sins against you, go and tell him his fault, between you and him alone. If he listens to you, you have gained your brother. But if he does not listen, take one or two others along with you, that every charge may be established by the evidence of two or three witnesses. If he refuses to listen to them, tell it to the church. And if he refuses to listen even to the church, let him be to you as a Gentile and a tax collector.

We can be tempted to be vindictive when exercising church discipline. We may want to punish sinners out of malice, gossip, or a desire to teach them a lesson. That is why Paul is very clear that we should practice this restoration with a spirit of gentleness. We should never exercise church discipline in a self-righteous, legalistic, or prideful manner. If it were not for the restraining grace of God, we would be just as susceptible to plunging headlong into sin as the one who has fallen. Paul also instructs us in 2 Corinthians 13:11: "Finally, brothers, rejoice. Aim for restoration, comfort one another, agree with one another, live in peace; and the God of love and peace will be with you."

In Galatians 6:2, Paul exhorts us to bear one another's burdens. The word for "burden" means "a hefty weight or stone," in other words, something that is impossible to carry by yourself. Here's the reality: Every single one of us will have, at times, a burden that is too difficult to bear alone. This could be a physical ailment, a struggling marriage, a wayward child, a financial setback, a dire situation at work, a bout of depression, spiritual warfare, a family crisis, or anything you can think of that makes life very difficult to handle alone. Many of us struggle from a rugged individualism where we don't want to bother anybody else. We even say things like "I don't want to be a burden." We have a false idea that we can be self-sufficient, which is actually pride. This bearing each other's burdens cuts both ways. On the one hand, those who aren't struggling with a burden may look down on those who are as being incompetent and weak. In arrogance, you don't help because you think they should have it all together and you don't want to inconvenience yourself. On the other hand, those that truly struggle are too prideful and self-sufficient to admit weakness and the need for help, so they remain silent and try to endure it alone. After a while, they get bitter and frustrated because nobody helps them. Romans 15:1 urges us: "We who are strong have an obligation to bear with the failings of the weak, and not to please ourselves." Bearing one another's burdens fulfills the law of Christ which our Lord summarizes in the passage we saw earlier about loving one another: "A new commandment I give to you, that you love one another: just as I have loved you, you also are to love one another" (John 13:34).

FORGIVE ONE ANOTHER

A casual glance at social media and television will reveal how popular therapists or motivational speakers champion the power of forgiveness. Our world places a value on forgiving one another, but unfortunately, this practice leaves the gospel out of the equation entirely. Paul emphasizes this point in Ephesians 4:32: "Be kind to one another, tenderhearted, forgiving one another, as God in Christ forgave you." In Christ, we have complete forgiveness of our sins through his blood. God chose to wipe our slate clean even when we mistreated him, blasphemed his name, and rebelled against him time and time again.

Sometimes, while doing pastoral counseling, people will tell me that they struggle to forgive someone who has wounded them deeply. They will say things like this: "Well, I just don't feel like God has called me to forgive that person." In response, I gently tell them that they have no option. Forgiving one another is a command. It is not optional. We cannot choose whether or not we want to obey the Lord. Don't get me wrong. It is excruciatingly painful because many of us have some deep scars from people who have treated us horribly. When we think of the cross of Christ, we can rest securely in how Jesus forgave us as motivation for us to forgive others.

Corrie ten Boom, a woman of great faith, survived the Nazi concentration camps in Ravensbruck during WWII. After the war, she traveled around Germany sharing the gospel of God's grace in forgiveness. As she was sharing her testimony in a church in Munich, a balding, heavy-set man approached her after the service. As he moved toward her, she remembered the atrocities she endured at Ravensbruck at the hands of this ruthless and hardened man. Corrie's message that night was on God's forgiveness and how he casts our sins to the bottom of the ocean. As the man reached out his hand to her, she froze in fear, not knowing what to do as the terrifying memories came racing back to her at that moment. This former concentration camp guard had now become a Christian and experienced God's full forgiveness, but he also wanted to hear it from her mouth as well that she would forgive him. This was the most challenging thing Corrie could do, so she asked for the strength and the Lord provided her the grace to extend her hand in forgiveness. As tears welled up in her eyes, she said, "I forgive you, brother! With all my heart!" In our power, we can't possibly offer forgiveness to a person who has hurt us, but in Christ, we can. We look at the cross and see his extraordinary love for us. We have hurt him beyond measure with our sin, and yet he died for us while we were still sinners (Rom 5:8).

We sometimes do a lousy job of forgiving others biblically. For example, when we ask a person for forgiveness, often he or she says, "That's okay." Saying "That's okay" falls short of practicing gospel forgiveness. In reality, it's not "okay." If I have sinned against someone, I need to confess that sin and ask for forgiveness. If all the person says is "that's okay," then he or she has minimized my transgression by brushing it under the carpet. Instead, we need to say, "I know you've sinned against me and it hurt deeply, but in Christ, I accept your confession, and I forgive you just as Christ forgave me." In the cross, the Father did not just say to sinful humanity, "It's okay!" If our rebellion was simply "okay" then why did his perfect Son have to die a brutal death to pay for these sins? We committed actual transgressions against a holy God, and Jesus needed to offer himself as a definitive atonement to pay for these offenses. When we forgive one another, we need to make sure that we acknowledge sin instead of brushing it off. Then we must offer forgiveness to one another through the power of the gospel in our new identity as those forgiven in the Son.

ENCOURAGE ONE ANOTHER

In Hebrews 3:13, the writer urges us to "exhort one another every day, as long as it is called today." We often think of exhortation or the ministry of encouragement like that of a cheerleader who vapidly cheers from the sidelines with a perky smile. In our relationships with others, we often relegate the ministry of exhortation to cheering from a distance with plastic smiles. We offer casual platitudes and pat each other on the back while never attempting to go deeper into a true biblical exhortation. The word used here for "exhortation" means to come alongside other believers to motivate and strengthen them to grow in grace. Exhortation means that we get personally involved down in the trenches of another person's life. We walk alongside them in their pursuit of holiness by providing counsel, encouragement, and motivation. We must also notice that this ministry of exhortation happens on a daily basis. The Bible calls us to "exhort one another every day as long as it is called today."

Adoniram Judson was a missionary to Burma in the 1800s whose ministry reached thousands with the gospel. During a time of civil war between Burma and England, he was imprisoned in terrible conditions where captives were often hanged by their thumbs as a means of torture. Adoniram survived by daily words of encouragement from his wife, Ann. Day by day, she would enter the filthy prison cell, walk past the taunting guards and look her husband in the eye and say, "Don't give up, Adoniram. God will give us the victory." She would visit him almost every day with these loving words of encouragement until one day the visits stopped. He was eventually released from prison and went to look for her and found out that she was dying. He found her in a government-assigned tent that was almost as bad as the prison. She was lying on tattered blankets with her body shrunken by disease and malnutrition. He looked into her eyes, and she said to him one last time, "Do not give up, Adoniram. God will give us the victory." The Lord saved thousands of souls as a result of the missionary endeavors of Adoniram Judson. But we often do not hear of Ann, his wife. She could have abandoned her husband and headed back to America, but instead, she submitted ultimately to the will of Christ by supporting him. She is the hero of this story. Ann Judson was the spark of energy and exhortation that God used to send Adoniram forth in perseverance.

Hebrews 10:24–25 also challenges us: "And let us consider how to stir up one another to love and good works, not neglecting to meet together, as is the habit of some, but encouraging one another, and all the more as you see the Day drawing near." The writer urges us to "consider" one another, which means to notice, observe, understand, or pay attention to the welfare of one another. He gives us two particular areas in which we should stir or stimulate each other—in love and good works. First John 3:18 captures this truth: "Little children, let us not love in word or talk but in deed and in truth." In addition to these, the writer also admonishes us not to forsake meeting together. Some in the church didn't think they needed others and stayed home from worship on the Lord's Day. Their habit of forsaking worship demonstrated an apathy or indifference toward the things of God and the community of faith. Taking advantage of the public means of grace in corporate worship was not a priority for them anymore. They did not value how God grows us spiritually through sitting under sound preaching, engaging in corporate prayer, and celebrating the Lord's Supper. Those who gave up meeting together probably did so because of fear of persecution or identifying themselves publicly as Christians. This passage emphasizes the urgency of encouraging one another as it reminds us about the second coming of Christ. Since the day of his return is drawing near, we should support, motivate, and urge each other toward spiritual transformation so we will be ready for the Lord's return.

Paul also issues this command to encourage one another in light of the second coming of Christ in 1 Thessalonians 5:9–11: "For God has not destined us for wrath, but to obtain salvation through our Lord Jesus Christ, who died for us so that whether we are awake or asleep we might live with him. Therefore encourage one another and build one another up, just as you are doing." As believers in Christ, we will not experience the wrath of God on that great day. Our hope is in the death of Jesus as our sacrificial substitute who shed his blood and died in our place to save us from judgment. Our ultimate joy is that we will forever live with him. Paul urges us to never get over the death of Christ and his love for us in the gospel. In verse 11, he issues the command to encourage and build one another up. We should encourage one another to remain alert and to not live as children of darkness, but rather to walk in holiness in light of that day. What is going to sustain you as you wait for the second coming of Christ? What will sustain you is for other believers to continuously remind and encourage you of the beauty of the gospel. Romans 5:9 reminds us, "Since, therefore, we have now been justified by his blood, much more shall we be saved by him from the wrath of God." We need to regularly exhort each other that God has saved us from his coming wrath by reconciling us as his friends and showering us with forgiveness.

I want you to notice what Paul does not instruct us to do with respect to how to encourage one another. He doesn't say: "Hey Thessalonians, pull yourself up by your bootstraps and try hard to hunker down as you wait for Jesus to come back. Busy yourself with all kinds of activities, so you can wear yourself out trying to be religious, so maybe when Jesus comes back, you can have a fighting chance to make it to heaven somehow." No! What does he do? He tells us to encourage and build each other up in the gospel! As God's child, you're not destined for wrath. Jesus took that wrath on the cross in our place. We will be caught up to meet him in the air. We will live with Jesus forever. He's taken us out of the kingdom of darkness and placed us in the kingdom of light. We are saved by grace and loved by God! Encourage one another with these words!

PRAY FOR ONE ANOTHER

In chapter eleven, we learned that prayer is the lifeblood of all true believers. James 5:16 says, "Therefore, confess your sins to one another and pray for one another, that you may be healed. The prayer of a righteous person has great power as it is working." At first, we may think this passage teaches that when we pray God will promise physical healing to those who are sick. Of course, when we pray for a person who's ill or having an operation or is suffering from cancer, we want them to be healed physically. But is that all this passage means? Can there be such a thing as healing that is spiritual and emotional? Think about it this way—if we love one another, welcome one another, bear one another's burdens, forgive, and encourage one another, will our lives become more spiritually healthy? This healing does not mean that all of our problems will go away, but if we practice these gospel one anothers, God will produce a healthier environment in your life, family, marriage, and church. Here's where this passage gets controversial and risky. Many of us pray for one another, but do we confess our sins to one another? Do we live in a culture of repentance where we don't hide sin or brush it under the carpet, but we own it, and we confess it to each other? Do we have healthy relationships with others that allow for vulnerability and accountability in confessing sin?

Many of us often come up short in prayer as we say, "I'll be praying for you," and then what do we do? We walk off, forget about it, and never pray. Let me challenge you to pray for that person right there on the spot. This prayer doesn't have to be extended or wordy. It can be one sentence. It's not the length, but rather the heart that counts as you show genuine concern. James tells us there is great power in prayer. God guarantees us that he will listen to our prayers, answer our prayers, and promises to show up in power to give us exactly what we need. This healing or spiritual transformation can only come through the gospel. Why do we pray for God's power? We want to see broken lives healed. We long to see marriages restored. We desire to see families reunited. We pray for God to save people and to transform them by the power of the gospel. Can God supernaturally transform us or change our circumstances through an instantaneous sovereign work of grace? Absolutely! Yet as we pray for one another, God uses weak, feeble, and broken people like us to demonstrate his power.

Are you thankful for God's gift of fellowship as a means of grace to strengthen your faith? Dietrich Bonhoeffer said,

> If we do not give thanks daily for the Christian fellowship in which we have been placed, even when there is no great experience, no discoverable riches, but much weakness, small faith, and difficulty; if on the contrary, we only keep complaining to God that everything is so paltry and petty, so far from what we expected, then we hinder God from letting our fellowship grow according to the measure and riches which are there for us all in Jesus Christ.[5]

---

5. Bonhoeffer, *Life Together*, 29.

How often do we complain about other believers? How often do we criticize our church family because others have not bent over backward to meet our selfish needs? We often experience the harsh realities of community life together where we do not often see exponential growth but instead see the pain and sin of each other close up. We may have this idealized vision of what true fellowship should be in our lives, and when it falls short, we get discouraged. A thankless heart toward the beauty of fellowship creates a toxic environment where we may not experience the blessings of God to their fullest extent. Instead, we should praise the Lord for knitting us together in dynamic fellowship as the church of Jesus Christ. Hebrews 12:15 urges the entire church body to "see to it that no one fails to obtain the grace of God." It is the responsibility of every member of the congregation to pay careful attention to one another so that we are all growing spiritually. John Stott reminds us, "The church is supposed to be God's new society; the living embodiment of the gospel, a sign of the kingdom of God, a demonstration of what human community looks like when it comes under his gracious rule."[6] Are you consistently practicing the gospel one anothers as a means of grace to undergird your identity in the Trinity?

---

6. Stott, *Living Church*, 66.

14

Obeying the Great Commission

"Missions is not the ultimate goal of the church. Worship is. Missions exists because worship doesn't . . . Therefore, worship is the fuel and goal of missions."

JOHN PIPER[1]

THE FAMOUS DAY WAS July 20th, 1969, as astronauts Neil Armstrong and Buzz Aldrin became the first humans to ever walk on the moon, traversing the Sea of Tranquility. Just nine years earlier, President John F. Kennedy had a dream that by the end of the decade our nation would be the first to accomplish this amazing feat. The Apollo 11 mission was a significant victory for the U.S. in the space race against Russia. We can think of many famous missions in the history of the world, like D-Day, when Allied troops landed on the Normandy Coast in 1944, thus signaling the eventual end of World War II. Or we think of the mission of Lewis and Clark, who led the first expedition to the Pacific Coast in the early 1800s. Or that famous mission in 1492 when Columbus discovered a whole new world in the Western hemisphere. We resonate with the excitement and challenge of a mission. We want to be part of something bigger than

---

1. Piper, *Let the Nations Be Glad*, 17.

ourselves. We root for our favorite sports team to succeed in its mission to win the championship. You may have a mission at your workplace that you are trying to accomplish this year. Major corporations, school districts, community organizations, local churches, and even families all have mission statements. Jesus accomplished the most significant mission in the history of the world as he came to seek and save the lost. The Father sent him to leave the glories of heaven, come to earth, live as a man, and humble himself to death on a cross where he cried out, "It is finished!" Then he was buried, rose again, and now has ascended into heaven and is seated is at the right hand of the Father as the King of kings and Lord of lords, having faithfully accomplished his mission.

Acts 2:42–47 serves as our crucial text to demonstrate how the early church practiced the ordinary means of grace to grow in this identity in the Trinity: (1) Scripture saturation, (2) intimacy in prayer, (3) celebration of baptism and Lord's Supper, and (4) fellowship through practicing the gospel one anothers. What did God sovereignly accomplish through the church practicing these ordinary means of grace? Acts 2:46–47 reads, "And day by day, attending the temple together and breaking bread in their homes, they received their food with glad and generous hearts, praising God and having favor with all the people. And the Lord added to their number day by day those who were being saved." As the early church met regularly for worship, prayer, the ordinances, and fellowship to reflect the glory of God through their proclamation of the gospel, God called sinners to himself in salvation through their evangelism. Acts 2:47 demonstrates God's sovereign activity as he added to their number. He is still doing this today—through the church. Why do we gather as baptized, regenerated believers each week to practice the means of grace? As the church, we assemble to submit ourselves under the authoritative preaching of God's word, pray together fervently, fellowship, worship the Lord in awe, and express thanksgiving for his goodness and mercy in our lives. We do this as a corporate witness to a watching world to display the beauty of the gospel. As believers, we embody what it means to live together in our new identity in the Trinity. A significant part of our identity comes in understanding our mission.

WHAT IS THE MISSION?

Jesus gave the church a crystal-clear mission: he commands us to make disciples of all nations through the preaching of the gospel so that rebels will bow their knees to his lordship and worship him alone. The Father sent Jesus as our Redeemer on a rescue mission to seek and save the lost, and calls the church to embrace this mission for the ultimate goal of glorifying him. Kevin Deyoung and Greg Gilbert provide a helpful and succinct description of the mission of the church: "The mission of the church is to go into the world and make disciples by declaring the gospel of Jesus Christ in the power of the Spirit and gathering these disciples into churches, that they might worship the Lord and obey his commands now and in eternity to the glory of God the Father."[2] Jesus, as the living word, dictates and establishes the mission of the church. This mission revolves around being a distinctly holy people who purposely make disciples of all nations through the proclamation of the gospel for the glory of God. John Stott makes this surprising assertion,

> The highest of all missionary motives is neither obedience to the Great Commission (important as that is), nor love for sinners, who are alienated and perishing (strong as that incentive is), but rather zeal—burning and passionate zeal—for the glory of Jesus Christ . . . Before this supreme goal of the Christian mission, all unworthy motives wither and die.[3]

We exist first and foremost to display God's glory and the primary way we do this comes in declaring the gospel to a world in rebellion against the One who alone is worthy of all our allegiance.

Right before Jesus ascended to heaven to be with his Father, he defined for us the mission on five occasions. The first occurrence comes in Matthew 28:19–20, where he issued the Great Commission: "Go therefore and make disciples of all nations, baptizing them in the name of the Father and of the Son and the Holy Spirit, teaching them to observe all that I have commanded you. And behold, I am with you always, to the end of the age." The primary command in this passage is to make disciples, with three participles or descriptors explaining how this is to be done.[4] The

---

2. Deyoung and Gilbert, *What Is the Mission of the Church?*, 62.

3. Stott, *Message of Romans*, 53.

4. The verb "make disciples" is in the aorist imperative, denoting the main verb or command in the sentence followed by three modifying participles.

first participle involves the activity of "going" in the natural ebb and flow of life by interacting with unsaved people. The second consists of baptizing new believers and incorporating them into the life of the church (see chapter twelve on baptism). The final step in the disciple-making process is a never-ending one—teaching believers to observe all that Jesus commanded. Our Lord emphasized the importance of teaching, not just for information, but also for obedience. Craig Blomberg claims,

> The verb 'make disciples' also commands a kind of evangelism that does not stop after someone makes a profession of faith. The first of these (baptizing) will be a once-for-all, decisive initiation into Christian community. The second (teaching them obedience) proves a perennially incomplete, life-long task.[5]

Think about your identity in the Trinity that we've seen so far: you're chosen, adopted, and accepted by the Father; purchased, forgiven, and righteous in the Son; and regenerated, indwelt, and sanctified in the Spirit. When a sinner trusts Christ for salvation, he or she is baptized into this new Trinitarian identity. We baptize new believers in the name of the Father, Son, and Holy Spirit, which symbolizes that they have died to their former status as a rebel against God and have been raised to new life as his children. The process of making disciples involves showing new believers their glorious identity in the Trinity. Disciple-making focuses not on merely getting a sinner to say a prayer or walk an aisle, but instead salvation involves a radical transformation from the inside out that results in a new creation. Paul reminds us of this newness of life in 2 Corinthians 5:17: "If anyone is in Christ, he is a new creation. The old has passed away; behold, the new has come." Part of teaching believers to obey all that Jesus commanded involves helping them understand their new gospel identity so that they can rest securely in God's sovereign grace.

Mark 16:15 provides the second aspect of Christ's commission to the church: "Go into all the world and proclaim the gospel to the whole creation." While Matthew's version focuses more on making disciples, Mark's version emphasizes the universal scope of our mission to share the gospel all over the world. The evangelism mandate focuses on the key word "proclaiming" or "heralding" the gospel. In ancient Greek culture, the office of the herald was vital for both the political and cultural life of the empire. Entrusted with a message from his sovereign, a herald held

---

5. Blomberg, *Matthew*, 431.

no authority to deviate from the message but instead had to deliver it faithfully as the official spokesman for his superior.[6] Mark introduces Jesus by portraying him as a preacher. Mark 1:14–15 states, "Now after John was arrested, Jesus came into Galilee, proclaiming the gospel of God, and saying, 'The time is fulfilled, and the kingdom of God is at hand; repent and believe in the gospel.'" Jesus spoke of the urgency of his preaching mission in Mark 1:38–39: "'Let us go on to the next towns, that I may preach there also, for that is why I came out.' And he went throughout all Galilee, preaching in their synagogues and casting out demons." The disciples wanted to capitalize on his merely being a traveling miracle worker. As such, they tried to hinder him from his mission of preaching. Knowing that his Father had sent him with the expressed purpose to preach the gospel, Jesus remained focused on this mission. William Lane comments on the nature of Jesus' heralding a call to repentance:

> Jesus calls men to a radical decision . . . Jesus proclaims the kingdom not to give content but to convey a summons. He stands as God's final word of address to man in man's last hour. Either a man submits to the summons of God, or he chooses this world and its riches and honor . . . His purpose is to confront men with the demand for decision in the perspective of God's absolute claim upon their person.[7]

Luke 24:46–47 records the third occasion of Jesus' final instructions to his disciples concerning the mission of the church: "Thus it is written, that the Christ should suffer and on the third day rise from the dead, and that repentance for the forgiveness of sins should be proclaimed in his name to all nations, beginning from Jerusalem." Luke's version stresses the command for all people everywhere to repent of their sins to receive forgiveness. The Synoptic Gospels provide a more detailed description of Jesus' final words to the disciples regarding their mission in evangelism.

The Gospel of John, on the other hand, provides a brief yet significant insight into our commission to make disciples of all nations. In John 20:21, Jesus provides the fourth occasion of this mission by saying, "Peace be with you. As the Father has sent me, even so I am sending you." The Father has sent (perfect-tense verb) Jesus, which means the mission

---

6. Gerhard Friedrich says, "It demanded, then, that they deliver their message as it was given to them. The essential point about the report which they give is that it does not originate with them. Behind it stands a higher power. The herald does not express his own views. He is the spokesman for his master" (*Theological Dictionary*, 3:687–88).

7. Lane, *Gospel of Mark*, 66–82.

of Jesus still stands and continues to this day through his followers. We don't start a brand-new mission unrelated to his mission to seek and save the lost. We continue the mission of Jesus as those sent to share the gospel. Acts 1:8 provides the fifth and final occasion where Jesus commands us as his followers to this task of evangelism: "But you will receive power when the Holy Spirit has come upon you, and you will be my witnesses in Jerusalem and in all Judea and Samaria, and to the end of the earth." The mission of the church involves making disciples of all nations through the authoritative proclamation of the gospel in the power of the Holy Spirit whereby we call all people to repent and believe in Jesus for the forgiveness of sins.

So many methods of sharing Christ inundate our evangelical world that it is essential to provide a working definition of evangelism. J. I. Packer offers a helpful one: "To evangelize is to present Christ Jesus in the power of the Holy Spirit, that men shall come to put their trust in God through him, to accept him as their Savior, and to serve him as their King in the fellowship of his church."[8] John Cheeseman provides this definition: "To evangelize is to declare on the authority of God what he has done to save sinners, to warn men of their lost condition, to direct them to repent, and to believe in the Lord Jesus Christ."[9] Evangelism involves verbally telling sinners about the death, burial, and resurrection of Jesus Christ and then commanding them with urgency to repent and believe in him. As believers who have a new identity in the Trinity, how can we obey the Great Commission and practice evangelism for the glory of God?

EMPOWERED BY THE SPIRIT

After I finished my 8th grade year, our family moved from Texas to Colorado. One of my best friends was a Muslim boy from India who came over every day to play basketball. He was the smartest kid in school, and we had a friendly competition in who could read the most books and get the highest grades on our tests. He was a voracious reader. On the day before we moved as I was packing up my room, he came over to say goodbye. My Bible was laying open on my desk, and he picked it up and began reading. I froze in fear because I thought he would ask me a question I couldn't answer. So I grabbed the Bible out of his hand and

8. Packer, *Evangelism and the Sovereignty of God*, 37–38.
9. Cheeseman, *Saving Grace*, 113.

awkwardly suggested we go outside and play basketball. At that moment, I was paralyzed in fear to share my faith with a Muslim friend who could have been open to the gospel at that moment. I have lived with regret from that experience as it exposed what many of us often feel—fear of rejection and lack of power when it comes to sharing our faith.

In the Upper Room discourse in John 16, Jesus instructs us on the role of the Holy Spirit in empowering us to bear faithful witness to the gospel. John 15:26–27 reads: "But when the helper comes, whom I will send to you from the Father, the Spirit of truth, who proceeds from the Father, he will bear witness about me. And you also will bear witness, because you have been with me from the beginning." To bear faithful witness to Jesus Christ and his gospel, we desperately need the empowering of the Holy Spirit. Listen to how John Calvin describes our need for the empowering of the Holy Spirit: "When the world rages on all sides, our only protection is, that the truth of God, sealed by the Holy Spirit on our hearts, despises and defies all that is in the world; for, if it were subject to the opinions of men, our faith would be overwhelmed a hundred times in a day."[10] Jesus gave us the Spirit of truth to overturn and combat the lies that the world will throw at us. When we engage in sharing our faith with a hostile world, we immediately discover a fundamental problem with non-Christians that Paul describes in 1 Corinthians 2:14: "The natural person does not accept the things of the Spirit of God, for they are folly to him, and he is not able to understand them because they are spiritually discerned." The natural person is an unsaved person who is blind to the truth. Because of their darkened hearts, sinners believe Satan's lies and stand opposed to God's word. Notice how stark this lostness truly is. The non-Christian is *not able* to understand the gospel because they are dead in sin. They are hopeless, helpless, and hell-bound. When you share the gospel with the natural person, they think what you're saying about Jesus is foolishness. It is crazy talk! The message of the cross offends them. In essence, the Holy Spirit has to do a work in their hearts to give them understanding.

How does this happen? How does the Holy Spirit empower us to witness? How does the Holy Spirit sovereignly overcome this inability of sinners to comprehend spiritual truth and come to faith in Christ? Paul underscores the need for sinners to experience a new creation or

---

10. Calvin, *John 12–21 and Acts*, 130.

regeneration by providing an analogy of the first day of creation where God spoke light into darkness. In 2 Corinthians 4:3–6 he writes,

> And even if our gospel is veiled, it is veiled to those who are perishing. In their case the god of this world has blinded the minds of the unbelievers, to keep them from seeing the light of the gospel of the glory of Christ, who is the image of God. For what we proclaim is not ourselves, but Jesus Christ as Lord, with ourselves as your servants for Jesus' sake. For God, who said, "Let light shine out of darkness," has shone in our hearts to give the light of the knowledge of the glory of God in the face of Jesus Christ.

The god of this world, Satan, has blinded the minds of unbelievers so that they cannot understand the truth of the gospel or see the glory of Christ. This blindness does not mean that a sinner cannot understand the bare facts of the gospel when you present them clearly. A sinner may have full mental assent to the biblical information, but he or she lacks both the spiritual and moral ability to repent and believe in Jesus and bow to him as the ultimate Lord and King.

This passage shows us the total inability of sinners to see the glories of Christ due to spiritual and moral blindness, but in verse 5, Paul gives us our responsibility in declaring the gospel to sinners. What are we responsible for doing? We can't open blind eyes. We can't enliven dead hearts. We can't replace hearts of stone with hearts of flesh. We cannot cause a person to spiritually understand the truth in such a way that they genuinely want to know Jesus as Savior and Lord. Paul tells us that our responsibility is to preach Christ as Lord. We testify about Jesus. We share the gospel about the death, burial, and resurrection of Jesus as the Lord of lords and King of kings who demands repentance and faith. What does God accomplish when we share the gospel to blind sinners who are spiritually dead and morally incapable of coming to faith in Christ? In verse 6, we see the sovereign power of God at work when we take up the responsibility to preach the gospel. He opens the eyes of the heart, reaches down into the spiritually dead person's soul, and does a re-creation. In Genesis, on the first day of creation, God said, "Let there be light!" He does this creative work of regeneration in the soul of an unsaved person. God overcomes their deadness, defeats the blindness, and irresistibly draws people to Christ so that their wills are no longer in bondage to sin and Satan. The Holy Spirit effectively calls non-Christians and causes them to be born again. Now liberated from sin, they freely come to Jesus in repentance and faith. No one will be saved unless the Holy Spirit sovereignly brings sinners to spiritual life.

There are two fundamental realities you need to understand. First, people who are not Christians are genuinely lost, spiritually dead, enslaved to sin, blinded by Satan, unable to come to Christ in their power, and desperately need sovereign grace to overcome that sin. You can't accomplish these even on your best day. The greatest evangelists who ever lived, such as George Whitefield, John Wesley, Charles Spurgeon, or Billy Graham, could not do this sovereign work of grace on their best day. Only the Spirit of God can regenerate lost sinners and overcome their spiritual deadness and moral inability to repent and believe. Second, God will empower you to proclaim the gospel through the Holy Spirit as the means to bring about the conversion of a lost person. This means that you desperately need the Holy Spirit to empower your witness and the lost person desperately needs the Holy Spirit to cause the new birth. In other words, the Holy Spirit is indispensable to your witnessing and the salvation of non-Christians.

In Colossians 4:2–6, Paul provides some practical application in doing evangelism:

> Continue steadfastly in prayer, being watchful in it with thanksgiving. At the same time, pray also for us, that God may open to us a door for the word, to declare the mystery of Christ, on account of which I am in prison—that I may make it clear, which is how I ought to speak. Walk in wisdom toward outsiders, making the best use of the time. Let your speech always be gracious, seasoned with salt, so that you may know how you ought to answer each person.

Paul exhorts us with three specific ways we can obey the Great Commission with an evangelistic lifestyle.

CONSTANT PRAYER

In verse 2, Paul commands us to continue steadfastly in prayer. First of all, we should pray regularly for opportunities to share the gospel with lost people. The steadfast devotion to prayer marked the early church in Acts.

> All these with one accord were *devoting* themselves to prayer. (Acts 1:14)

> And they *devoted* themselves to the apostles' teaching and fellowship, to the breaking of bread and the prayers. (Acts 2:42)

> But we will *devote* ourselves to prayer and to the ministry of the word. (Acts 6:4)

As we follow the example of Acts, we should continually devote ourselves to earnest prayer and never give up—especially for evangelistic effectiveness. Romans 12:12 says, "Be constant in prayer," while 1 Thessalonians 5:17 reiterates this command: "pray without ceasing." The Scriptures command us to be those whose lifestyle demonstrates constant, fervent, and earnest prayer for those who are separated from God in their sins and desperately need his salvation.

In addition to earnest prayer, Paul urges us to be watchful while we pray. We should watch out for the onslaughts of the devil. We should watch so we don't fall into temptation. We should wait for opportunities to share Christ with others. First Thessalonians 5:6 reads, "So then let us not sleep, as others do, but let us keep awake and be sober." First Peter 5:8 exhorts us: "Be sober-minded; be watchful. Your adversary the devil prowls around like a roaring lion, seeking someone to devour." While we continue steadfastly in prayer, we need to do this all with an attitude of watchfulness and thanksgiving. We need to be thankful that God does answer prayer as our loving Father.

Paul asks his readers to pray for him that God may open a door for the word so that he would have opportunities to share the gospel with clarity. He wants to be able to declare the mystery of Christ clearly and accurately so that his message is not confusing or convoluted. In Ephesians 6:19-20, Paul also prays for boldness: "Pray also for me, that words may be given to me in opening my mouth boldly to proclaim the mystery of the gospel, for which I am an ambassador in chains, that I may declare it boldly, as I ought to speak." We should pray for strength to open our mouths and share the gospel of Jesus with clarity and boldness. Clarity involves making sure that you have the message correct about the person and work of Christ (see chapter 2). Even if you stumble over your words and do not give the most precise, textbook definition of the gospel, the Holy Spirit can still use your verbal witness to bring clarity to the person with whom you're sharing. This divine intervention is not an excuse to be purposely unclear, but it does give us confidence in the Spirit's ability to overcome our weaknesses. This word "boldness" signifies that the Holy Spirit grants us an unhindered ability to speak with supernatural courage and an authority that comes quickly off the tongue. How we desperately need both clarity and boldness when we declare the gospel!

Here's the encouragement for you: God will most often use your testifying of the gospel, your sharing about Jesus, your proclaiming Christ as Lord, as the powerful means to bring about the salvation of a non-Christian. The Spirit of truth, the helper who indwells us, supplies the power for us to testify to the truth about Jesus. In Matthew 10:19–20, Jesus proclaims, "When they deliver you over, do not be anxious how you are to speak or what you are to say, for what you are to say will be given to you in that hour. For it is not you who speak, but the Spirit of your Father speaking through you." Have you ever had those rare moments when you shared the gospel or gave testimony to Christ, and it was almost like the words coming out of your mouth weren't your words, but supernatural boldness? The Holy Spirit supernaturally empowered you at that moment with the courage to proclaim the gospel. In essence, the Holy Spirit was speaking through you.

Paul gives a qualifying statement at the end of the verse in that he "ought" to testify to the gospel, which means that sharing our faith is a nonnegotiable obligation. In his sermon "Bringing Sinners to the Savior," Charles Spurgeon tells a story of a man who told him that he had been praying twenty years for the salvation of his friend. He was complaining to Spurgeon that his prayers didn't work because God had not saved his friend after all these years of concern. Listen to Spurgeon's response:

> "Have you spoken to your friend personally about his soul? Have you made it your business to go down to his house, and tell him that you are concerned about him?" "No," he replied, "I cannot say that I have done so." "Well, then," I asked, "do you expect God to hear prayers of that kind? Suppose I were to pray that there might be a good harvest in a particular field, and yet, for twenty years, I did not sow any corn there; the probability is that, when I did sow some, I would get my prayers answered, and gather in the harvest." If we pray for anything, God expects us to use the proper means of obtaining it; and if we neglect the means, we have no right to expect him to believe in the sincerity of our prayer. If a father and mother pray for their children, but never pray with them, or speak to them personally about the welfare of their souls, then they must not wonder if they are not brought to Christ.[11]

---

11. Spurgeon, "Bringing Sinners to the Savior."

Obedience in evangelism means that we open our mouths to share the gospel with both clarity and boldness.

KAIROS MOMENTS

Paul describes the second way we can practice evangelism by capturing the unique moments God gives you to engage non-Christians. In verse 5, Paul commands us to walk in a manner that shows wisdom toward outsiders. How do you engage those in your life who are unsaved? How do you show wisdom in your interaction with those who find the gospel repulsive? Or those who express ambivalence toward your message? These outsiders may be a relative or a close friend which makes evangelism all that more difficult at times. In the early church, outsiders often slandered Christians with all types of derogatory names. Believers were called atheists because they didn't worship the pantheon of Greek gods. They were called unpatriotic because they did not burn incense once a year on the altar pledging allegiance to the Roman emperor, calling him Lord and God. They were called cannibals because outsiders misunderstood the Lord's Supper, thinking Christians were literally eating the flesh and drinking the blood of a man named Jesus. They were accused of incest because they often referred to each other as brother and sister. They were considered immoral because they would often meet behind locked doors for fear of persecution. Not much has changed in over 2,000 years. The culture still maligns us, mistreats us, and misunderstands us at times. Regardless of how the outsiders treat us, we need to be wise in how we treat them. They may mock, reject, or laugh at us with contempt. They may not care about our message and think we're irrelevant. In anger, they may never want us to bring up the subject of Jesus again. No matter how they treat us, we need to treat them with wisdom, respect, and genuine compassion. Jesus warns us in Matthew 10:16: "Behold, I am sending you out as sheep in the midst of wolves, so be wise as serpents and innocent as doves."

In addition to positively engaging non-Christians with the gospel, Paul tells us to "redeem" the time. This word picture means to buy up intensively or to snap up every opportunity. Paul also uses this phrase in Ephesians 5:15-16: "Look carefully then how you walk, not as unwise but as wise, making the best use of the time, because the days are evil." The word Paul uses for "time" here is *kairos*, which means a unique opportunity or an opportune moment that you may not have again. God in his providence has given you unique opportunities to share Christ, and you must not miss out on these when they present themselves. Take advantage of them. Don't let them slip through your fingers. God sovereignly places you in unique situations where you interact with unsaved people whereby he ordains many divine appointments and open doors for you to share the gospel. Are you living in an attitude of prayer and watchfulness for these *kairos* moments? Are you asking the Holy Spirit to open your eyes to these unique opportunities that you may never have again? Are you praying daily for non-Christians by name? Are you praying for opportunities to share? Once you begin to pray for clarity, boldness, wisdom, and *kairos* moments, you will be amazed at how God specifically opens doors or creates unique opportunities for you to share. In the heat of the moment, when you're faced with the decision of whether you will open your mouth and testify about Jesus, do you begin to rationalize why you shouldn't share the gospel? Do you become paralyzed in fear, and not open your mouth to speak? This fear is why we desperately need the power of the Holy Spirit to equip us. Do you see how it all works together? When you are praying and watching for open doors, God in his sovereignty will give you these golden moments where you can redeem the time and share the gospel with confidence. Jeff Iorg states,

> Experienced witnesses know the Holy Spirit's power is actuated during a witnessing encounter—not before. It's futile to pray for spiritual power, waiting for a holy buzz or spine tingling urge to settle on you, before you try to witness. Instead, trust the Spirit's power to be evident in the moment and start sharing the gospel. When you do this, you will discover spiritual power is accessed by stepping forward in faith. Step out boldly, trusting that the Spirit's power will sustain you.[12]

GRACE-FILLED WORDS

This passage in Colossians shows us the third way we can practice evangelism by gracing others with our words. We should always season our speech with salt so that what comes out of our mouths is grace filled. Does what come out your mouth exude grace? Jesus told us this truth in Matthew 5:13: "You are the salt of the earth, but if salt has lost its

---

12. Iorg, Live *Like a Missionary*, 80–81.

taste, how shall its saltiness be restored? It is no longer good for anything except to be thrown out and trampled under people's feet." Do you pay attention to how you speak around non-Christians? Does what comes out of your mouth spew poison and toxic venom, or is it sweet, savory grace and love? Are you speaking in ways that edify and show evidence of God's grace in others or are you tearing down, backbiting, complaining, and gossiping? How many times have our words damaged our witness?

Paul's verb choice (perfect tense) of the word "seasoned" means that your speech was seasoned at one point in time and it continues to remain seasoned with salt. It's not like you put a dab of salt on your French fries and then forget about it. It means that your speech is perpetually in a state of being seasoned with salt to give grace to all that hear. It's a lifestyle of having grace-filled speech. First Peter 3:15–16 gives us a clear model of what it looks like to answer someone with grace-filled words seasoned with salt: "but in your hearts regard Christ the Lord as holy, always being prepared to make a defense to anyone who asks you for a reason for the hope that is in you; yet do it with gentleness and respect, having a good conscience, so that, when you are slandered, those who revile your good behavior in Christ may be put to shame." We should always be prepared to defend the truth of the gospel with the readiness and preparedness that come from exposure to God's word. You cannot share what you do not know. We must always saturate ourselves in the gospel so that we can be prepared to share it. The more we preach the gospel to ourselves every day (see chapter 3) the more we prepare our minds and hearts to make a defense. This defense is where we get our word "apologetics," to make an apologetic. It doesn't mean that we apologize for being a Christian, but that we can make a clear and concise defense of the truth of the gospel. We don't waver. We don't water it down. We don't try to mince our words and lighten the blow of the gospel, but instead we make a defense. Defending Christianity involves communicating the truth of the gospel—not just some warm fuzzy ideas or some personal testimonies that don't tie back to the person and work of Christ. It's not wrong to share your testimony, but your testimony is not the gospel. It is not what saves people. If you don't share the death, burial, and resurrection of Christ and his call for all sinners everywhere to repent and trust solely in him, you haven't defended or communicated the gospel.

We should also share the faith with gentleness and respect. When discussing the gospel with nonbelievers, we should never be condescending. We should never try to win an argument by screaming at them in arrogance. Instead, we need to be gracious, humble, and respectful; not belligerent, overbearing, and obnoxious. The word "respect" in the original language means we defend the faith with "fear." This fear carries two meanings: first, we should respect the person we are sharing the gospel with as one who is created in the image of God. Second, we should also fear God and not man by boldly testifying to the truth. In addition, we need to display godly lifestyles that back up our verbal witness with clear consciences. Our behavior should never contradict the truth we share. Paul says in Acts 24:16, "So I always take pains to have a clear conscience toward both God and man." When we combine both Paul and Peter's instructions on evangelism we see that sharing our faith should become a natural part of our lives. We need to pray for open doors to share the gospel with boldness and clarity as we engage non-Christians with compassion and respect.

SUCCESSFUL EVANGELISM?

What is successful evangelism? Is it effective only if a sinner responds in repentance and faith? Is it efficacious if someone weeps and wails in travail of the soul? Is it only valid if a sinner attends church with you? These may occur when you declare the gospel, but effective evangelism means that you are obedient to the Lord by sharing the full gospel verbally and then leaving the results up to him. St. Francis of Assisi's statement has done us no good when he supposedly said, "Preach the gospel always, if necessary use words." That's like saying, play basketball always, if necessary use a ball. Go hunt elk with a rifle, and if necessary use bullets. Bake chicken parmesan, and if necessary use chicken. Paint your nails, and if necessary use nail polish!

You are successful in evangelism when you share the gospel with clarity, boldness, and respect and leave the results up to God. An unsaved person may not pray to receive Christ right there. They may laugh in your face. They may have more questions. They may not understand a word you're saying. They may scoff at you and call you names, but regardless of the response, you have been successful because you've shared the gospel. Once the gospel leaves your mouth, it's the Holy Spirit's job to bring about the conversion of a sinner. It's the Holy Spirit's job to penetrate deep into their hearts, bringing conviction of sin. It is his responsibility to open their eyes to the truth, to replace their hearts of stone with hearts of flesh, and to bring them from spiritual death to spiritual life.

First Corinthians 3:7 says, "So neither he who plants nor he who waters is anything, but only God who gives the growth." We plant, water, sow, share, love, declare, and disciple. The one thing we absolutely cannot do is cause spiritual growth. Only God can do that. He is the one who brings to life those who are dead in their trespasses. He is the one who converts sinners to Christ. Listen to J. I. Packer: "Were it not for the sovereign grace of God, evangelism would be the most futile and useless enterprise that the world has ever seen, and there would be no more complete waste of time under the sun than to preach the Christian gospel. Why is this? Because of the spiritual inability of man in sin."[13] This truth should give us great confidence! The pressure is off of us to act like salespeople using slick, marketing techniques, or relying on our charismatic personality or trusting in any other worldly means to somehow coax a decision out of a sinner.

Can I take the pressure off you in evangelism and engaging the culture? You don't save anyone. You can't save anyone. All you have to do is share the good news. All you have to do is open your mouth and tell others about Jesus. As your lifestyle consistently backs up your message, God will do his sovereign work of bringing sinners to Christ. This reality should free you up to share the gospel with confidence knowing that God is in control. We need to engage our culture, present the whole gospel, and do this in winsome and creative ways to build bridges of understanding. I encourage you to take a risk with the gospel and realize its inherent power. When you testify about Jesus, sometimes you will receive seething hatred. Other times curiosity. Other times ambivalence. Thankfully there are those times when you see God convert a sinner by his grace alone. God is sovereign, and he is using you to share the gospel faithfully to a lost culture which desperately needs the hope of redemption only found in Jesus Christ. Would you take your mission seriously as one sent by Jesus to call sinners to repentance and faith? Would you rest securely in God's sovereignty in evangelism and define success by your obedience, not necessarily the positive response to your message? As one who is chosen, adopted, and accepted in the Father; purchased, forgiven, and righteous in the Son; and regenerated, indwelt, and sanctified by the Spirit, would your heart break for those who do not yet have this glorious

---

13. Packer, *Evangelism and the Sovereignty of God*, 106.

identity? Would you weep for those still trapped in the bondage of sin? Would you pray for the salvation of those in your life who desperately need the identity you have in the Trinity? Would you rely on the power of the Holy Spirit to share the gospel clearly and boldly in obedience to the Great Commission?

15

Your Identity in Suffering

"I have said these things to you, that in me you may have peace. In the world you will have tribulation. But take heart; I have overcome the world."

JOHN 16:33

I AM THE PROUD parent of a special-needs child, and I thank God for sovereignly choosing my wife and me to be his parents. Our youngest son, Zachary, has a rare chromosome disorder which causes severe autism, epilepsy, and developmental delays, such as being nonverbal. When he was first diagnosed with this disorder as a one-year old, we as parents experienced the full range of emotions—fear, sorrow, doubt, anger, and many sleepless nights. But there was one day during the midst of this time where God showed up in power and proved his faithfulness to me. As I was crying out to God in prayer one morning, he reminded me that I was not in charge of my son. He reminded me that my son was a gift and I was only to be a steward of that gift. God was sovereign over Zachary's life, and he would glorify himself through Zachary. At that moment, I gave up all rights to my son and offered him up to the Lord to use in whatever way he saw fit to bring the most glory to himself.

To this day, I cannot say that it has been easy raising a special needs son, but there is one thing I can say—Zachary has brought me more joy than anything I can express. He is a beautiful boy with a contagious smile, infectious curiosity, and childlike innocence. I get the privilege of seeing a side of Zachary that nobody probably will as I tuck him in bed at night, as I feed him breakfast, as I know the joy in his eyes when he gets a new toy, or when he flaps his arms and speaks gibberish in a high-pitched frenzy! I would not trade any of these precious moments as God has given Zachary to me as a gift to be cherished. He is not an accident or a surprise to God. He is not a genetic mistake or a freak of nature (hurtful words spoken to us as parents by those who do not fully understand God's plan). Listen to how Psalm 139:13–14 describes my son: "For you formed my inward parts; you knitted me together in my mother's womb. I praise you, for I am fearfully and wonderfully made. Wonderful are your works; my soul knows it very well." God formed Zachary, and his chromosome disorder was part of his sovereign plan. My son may not be able to talk or express his joy verbally, but I have confidence that Jesus has given him a deep pleasure that I don't think we can fully understand. I believe God has reached down in his heart to reveal himself and that Zachary may know our Savior in a way we won't comprehend. For that I am thankful. I am also grateful that in heaven, Zachary will be complete and in the presence of his true Father and I will have gotten the privilege of being able to raise him as his earthly father.

GOD WILLS FOR YOU TO SUFFER

God ordains for us to experience suffering, trials, and difficulties to grow us in our identity in the Trinity. This reality proves counterintuitive, countercultural, and strikes against the spirit of this age which values comfort and convenience above all else. Acts 14:22 says "that through many tribulations we must enter the kingdom of God." The apostle Peter does not mince words about the reality of suffering in the life of a believer. He doesn't put a spin on it, lighten the blow, or equivocate. He lays this truth out there for us to struggle with the reality that it is God's will for Christians to suffer. First Peter 4:12–19 reads,

> Beloved, do not be surprised at the fiery trial when it comes upon you to test you, as though something strange were happening to you. But rejoice insofar as you share Christ's sufferings, that you may also rejoice and be glad when his glory is revealed. If you are insulted for the name of Christ, you are blessed, because the Spirit of glory and of God rests upon you.

> But let none of you suffer as a murderer or a thief or an evildoer or as a meddler. Yet if anyone suffers as a Christian, let him not be ashamed, but let him glorify God in that name. For it is time for judgment to begin at the household of God; and if it begins with us, what will be the outcome for those who do not obey the gospel of God? And if the righteous is scarcely saved, what will become of the ungodly and the sinner? Therefore, let those who suffer according to God's will entrust their souls to a faithful Creator while doing good.

In this passage, Peter provides four commands that illustrate how we should respond to suffering and trials in our lives.

First, don't be surprised when you experience sufferings or trials

Don't be surprised, as if something strange were happening to you. Peter calls it a "fiery trial" God ordains to test us. What's the purpose of this testing? Why can't the Christian life be stress-free, pain-free, and disease-free, with unlimited health, wealth, and prosperity? Peter already addressed this back in 1 Peter 1:7 when he says, "So that the tested genuineness of your faith—more precious than gold that perishes though it is tested by fire—may be found to result in praise and glory and honor at the revelation of Jesus Christ." In the process of refining gold, the dross and impurities rise to the top so that the final product will be purified. This fiery trial of testing is a form of purification, not punishment. We may think at the time it is a form of punishment, but in reality, God orchestrates suffering in our lives to purify us.

Centuries ago, when massive ships sailed the ocean, sailors would use a flat piece of stone, called a holy stone to scour the decks. The reason it was called a holy stone is that when a sailor was on his knees scrubbing the ship, he looked like he was praying and thus this practice was associated with holiness. Sailors had to clean the deck of the ship with this hard stone, not another piece of wood, to prevent the ship from rotting. This ancient practice illustrates how we cannot cleanse ourselves from the corruption of sin with anything that resides within ourselves. God uses a metaphorical holy stone to scour us so that we can be clean. This purification process often proves to be painful and rigorous, but it is necessary to prevent us from rotting and falling apart spiritually. God ordains these trials as a way to test the genuineness of our faith. God works out this painful process as the master potter to make you look more like Jesus. This experience may be painful like a fiery trial, but it is for our good. Jeff Iorg asserts, "God sometimes allows challenging circumstances, not because we have done anything wrong, but as a part of his process of shaping us into the image of Jesus."[1]

Second, rejoice in this suffering

The New Testament repeats this theme of rejoicing in times of difficulties. Paul urges us in Romans 5:3–5: "More than that, we rejoice in our sufferings, knowing that suffering produces endurance, and endurance produces character, and character produces hope, and hope does not put us to shame, because God's love has been poured into our hearts through the Holy Spirit who has been given to us." James 1:2–4 says, "Count it all joy, my brothers, when you meet trials of various kinds, for you know that the testing of your faith produces steadfastness. And let steadfastness have its full effect, that you may be perfect and complete, lacking in nothing." Peter tells us in verse 13 that we share in Christ's sufferings. This doesn't mean that we somehow can atone for our sins or that our pain will be as agonizing as the cross. It does mean that when we become a Christian, we will share in insults, hardships, misunderstandings, and betrayals in many of the ways Jesus himself suffered.

Romans 12:12 says, "Rejoice in hope, be patient in tribulation, be constant in prayer." Paul's word for "tribulation" means to be squeezed through a narrow strait very similar to a vice grip. We can have confidence that when his glory is revealed (1 Pet 4:13) at the second coming, Christ will right all wrongs, and we will be vindicated of our present suffering. Revelation 21:4 gives us great hope: "He will wipe away every tear from their eyes, and death shall be no more, neither shall there be mourning nor crying nor pain anymore, for the former things have passed away."

What's the source behind the fiery ordeal? What exactly is the nature of these sufferings? We get a clue by the word Peter uses in verse 14 where he says that we are insulted for the name of Christ. For his original audience, this outbreak of hostility toward these struggling believers was verbal abuse, not physical torture. They had to endure the spreading of lies, gossip, slander, and mischaracterizations that came with claiming the name of Christ. Today, people spread lies about us, slander us, use

---

1. Iorg, *Painful Side of Leadership*, 11.

false labels against us, lampoon us, and mischaracterize us all for the name of Christ! If we proclaimed a message about a vague and generic "God" our experience would be much different. Our culture is perfectly fine with a nonthreatening, banal god who sits up in heaven like a happy grandfather. The moment you start talking about Jesus, or saying Jesus is the only way or that Christ alone is Lord, you immediately become a target for verbal abuse. Peter also says that we are blessed because the Spirit of glory and God rests upon us. This word "rests" conveys the idea that the Holy Spirit gives us a supply of refreshing grace. The gracious Spirit provides us with the power to survive these verbal attacks. He is proof that God has not abandoned us. He is the helper who lives in us and empowers us. Remember that we are regenerated, indwelt, and sanctified by the Spirit!

Third, do not be ashamed of being a Christian

In the New Testament, believers were rarely called Christians. Acts 11:26 states, "And in Antioch the disciples were first called Christians." Early believers were called followers of the Way, or they were called believers or brothers or the family of God, but the word "Christian" was very rarely used. The word "Christian" means "follower of Christ" or one who imitates Christ. To be called a Christian means that you follow Jesus, love him, live for him, and embrace him as Lord and Savior. In our culture, you don't suffer much when you mark "Christian" on a form or survey when they ask you about your religious affiliation. When you begin to live for Christ as distinct from the world, the culture begins to mark you out as a target of their hostility. Instead of being ashamed of Jesus, we should glorify God in that name. We bear the name "little Christ" as a badge of honor. Jesus warns us in Mark 8:38: "For whoever is ashamed of me and of my words in this adulterous and sinful generation, of him will the Son of Man also be ashamed when he comes in the glory of his Father with the holy angels." Second Timothy 1:8 reiterates this truth: "Therefore do not be ashamed of the testimony about our Lord, nor of me his prisoner, but share in suffering for the gospel by the power of God." In Acts 5:41, the apostles left the presence of the council, rejoicing that they were counted "worthy to suffer dishonor for the name."

Fourth, we must keep on entrusting ourselves to our faithful Creator

In verse 19, Peter uses the word "entrust," which is a banking term. This term means to put your money on deposit for safekeeping. In our economy today, this can be very shaky. We put our money in stock portfolios, and 401(k)s hoping that it is safe, but nothing is for sure in a volatile market. Not so with God. In 1 Peter 2:23, Jesus also "entrusted" himself to the Father while hanging on the cross. We too should continually entrust ourselves to our Creator who providentially controls the universe. Nothing catches him off guard. Nothing happens which he does not ordain to happen. He is intricately involved in every aspect of our lives. We can continue to rest in him because he is faithful and sovereign. We can cast all our anxieties on him, because he cares for us (1 Pet 5:7). Do you embrace the truth that suffering is a reality of life? Do you rejoice in your pain? Are you ashamed of being a Christian? Do you entrust yourself to your faithful Creator?

JACOB'S WRESTLING MATCH

In high school, I enjoyed watching Game 6 of the 1988 NBA finals—a thrilling matchup between the Los Angeles Lakers and the Detroit Pistons. At the end of the third quarter, Isiah Thomas, all-star point guard for the Pistons, landed on Michael Cooper's foot and severely sprained his own ankle. He reentered the game thirty-five seconds later and went on a rampage, scoring eleven of the next thirteen points, setting an NBA Finals record for points in a quarter. Playing on an injured foot, you could see him grimace throughout, but yet he played like he was unconscious. The Pistons ultimately lost the game, and the Lakers went on to win the 1988 championship, but Thomas finished the game with a jammed left pinkie, a poked eye, a scratched face, a ballooned ankle, and yet had forty-three points, six steals, and a career performance. He did all this while hobbling around on one foot. It's no fun being injured. It's no fun breaking a bone, shattering a hip, or cracking an ankle. It leaves you limping and you have to walk with crutches or maybe have a replacement surgery and then endure the pain of physical therapy. None of us would voluntarily want to walk with a limp. But what if walking with a limp is precisely where God wants us to be, spiritually?

Genesis 32:24–32 records the account where Jacob wrestled with a mysterious man who changed his life forever:

> And Jacob was left alone. And a man wrestled with him until the breaking of the day. When the man saw that he did not prevail against Jacob, he touched his hip socket, putting it out of joint as he wrestled with him. Then he said, "Let me go, for the day has broken." But Jacob said, "I will not let you go unless you bless me." And he said to him, "What is your name?" And he said, "Jacob." Then he said, "your name shall no longer be called Jacob, but Israel, for you have striven with God and with men, and have prevailed." Then Jacob asked him, "Please tell me your name." But he said, "Why is it that you ask my name?" And there he blessed him. So Jacob called the name of the place Peniel, saying, "For I have seen God face to face, and yet my life has been delivered." The sun rose upon him as he passed Peniel, limping because of his hip.

This scene takes place at the Jabbok river, which is an essential detail in this narrative because it's the boundary to the promised land. The name Jabbok is a play on words with Jacob's name. Do you see it? "Jacob/Jabbok!" The word "Jabbok" means "wrestling" or "twisting river." For his entire life, Jacob was the epitome of a fierce wrestler as well. He wrestled with Esau in the womb and came out grabbing his heel. Later on, he again wrestled with Esau and cheated him twice. Jacob also wrestled with his uncle Laban and tricked him. At this wrestling river called Jabbok, Jacob is about to have the ultimate wrestling match of his life. In the solitude of darkness, this mysterious man begins wrestling him, and this struggle continues with intensity all night. Right before dawn, this man touches Jacob's hip socket and wounds him. The word used for "touch" here means a soft touch. It wasn't a powerful torque or a punch, but simply a touch. In other words, God gently, yet powerfully, wounds Jacob's hip and leaves him writhing in pain! As the day breaks, this mysterious man urges Jacob to let him go, but Jacob is relentless and won't let go until he gets blessed. This is somewhat shocking. What would we expect? We would expect Jacob to be bowled over in agony because God knocked his hip out of its socket. Wouldn't Jacob want this man to let him go so he could nurse his wound? Instead, he grabs on more tightly and won't let go until he's personally blessed.

What has Jacob wanted all his life? The favor and blessing of others. He looked for acceptance in his father Isaac who never really gave Jacob the time of day since he favored Esau. He looked for approval in his wife Rachel—the drop-dead gorgeous woman he idolized. But when fathers and wives disappoint, all that's left is Christ, and he is more than enough! At this moment, Jacob grabs on to God for dear life. He doesn't care if he dies or that he might get wounded more fiercely. He's finally gotten a hold of the living God, and that's all that matters to him.

This story still carries more tension as the mystery man asks Jacob for his name. Why would he need to know Jacob's name? Was God in need of some information? In this definitive moment of truth, Jacob would have to finally admit to the living God his real identity—his identity as a deceiver. What does the name Jacob mean? Deceiver! Heel Grabber! Jacob would have to come clean and admit that he was a wicked con man and a master manipulator. You can picture it in your mind, can't you? Jacob is dripping with sweat, writhing in pain, breathing heavily, and then he pauses—it hits him—he comes face to face with the sinister meaning of his name. In agony, he whispers "Jacob. My name is Deceiver! Heal grabber! Sinner! Unworthy wretch!" In another powerful turn of events, God changes Jacob's name to Israel because he fought with God and won. Only the living God has the power to change Jacob's name and his identity.

Jacob then calls the place Peniel which means "face of God." He has seen God face to face. He wrestled with God and wasn't annihilated. The LORD didn't scorch him with holy fire. The LORD didn't obliterate him into a million pieces. In mercy, God wounded Jacob, and he came out with a limp, even though the LORD spared his life. And more importantly, his name was changed. He had a new identity, Israel, which was profoundly significant. Jacob stood on the border of the promised land as the only one who wrestled with God. This new identity as Israel would serve as a foreshadowing of the life of the nation from there on out—a people that wrestled with God. For the rest of his life, Jacob walked with a limp as a daily reminder that God had touched him, changed him, wounded him, broken him. Does this make any sense? How does God bless Jacob? By wounding him. How does God strengthen Jacob? By humbling him. How does God transform Jacob? By wrenching his hip, breaking him, and ultimately giving him a new name. Sometimes God must wound us before he can use us. Does God desire for us to live in prideful self-sufficiency where we have life all figured out? Does God prefer that we are in charge of our lives as we walk confidently in our power? Or does God will that we would walk with a limp? That we would walk in weakness and utter dependence upon him. Does this attitude describe you? A. W. Tozer said, "It is doubtful whether God can bless a man greatly until he has hurt him deeply."[2] Have you been hurt deeply through enduring sufferings and trials so that God can use you mightily for his glory?

SUFFICIENT GRACE

Remember Paul's testimony? God ordained for him to experience the suffering of a "thorn in the flesh" that was so excruciatingly painful, Paul desperately prayed that God would take it away. Second Corinthians 12:7–10 says,

> So to keep me from becoming conceited because of the surpassing greatness of the revelations, a thorn was given me in the flesh, a messenger of Satan to harass me, to keep me from becoming conceited. Three times I pleaded with the Lord about this, that it should leave me. But he said to me, "My grace is sufficient for you, for my power is made perfect in weakness." Therefore I will boast all the more gladly of my weaknesses, so that the power of Christ may rest upon me. For the sake of Christ, then, I am content with weaknesses, insults, hardships, persecutions, and calamities. For when I am weak, then I am strong.

We don't know what this thorn in the flesh was that severely plagued Paul, but God chose not to remove it. In essence, you could say, Paul walked with a limp. Are you walking with a limp? Has God wounded you so that he can use you? Has God changed your name from wretched sinner (Jacob) to child of God (Israel)? This changing of Jacob's name is a beautiful picture of the gospel. In brokenness, we come to Christ confessing our unworthiness as sinners who don't deserve his love. We cling on to him for dear life as our only hope of salvation. In a powerful act of mercy, God invades our lives, changes our names, and takes control through his lordship and changes us forever. We walk with a spiritual limp. We walk dependent on him, yet with confidence because we know that he will never leave us nor forsake us.

In difficulties and trials, we can rest secure in the words of Jesus in John 10:27–29: "My sheep hear my voice, and I know them, and they follow me. I give them eternal life, and they will never perish, and no one will snatch them out of my hand. My Father, who has given them to me,

---

2. Tozer, *Root of Righteousness*, 137.

is greater than all, and no one is able to snatch them out of the Father's hand." What confidence do we have? We will *never* perish. That word "never" in the Greek is a double-negative and could be translated "no, not ever, ever!" It is the strongest way of showing that we will never perish. The word "perish" means to spend eternity in hell. As his sheep, Jesus will ensure that we will never ever experience God's eternal wrath against sin.

But you may ask: What if I could lose my salvation? Or what if I do something so terrible that God stops loving me? Or what if the devil comes and wants to take me for himself? No one can snatch us out of the hand of Jesus. The word "snatch" is where we get the word "raptured"—to be snatched up forcibly. Why will we never be snatched out of God's hand? God is greater than any power or any force that would come against us. In election, God gave you to Jesus in eternity past, and he promises to keep you to the end. Even you are not powerful enough to snatch yourself out of the Father's hand. Do you see the double grip described here? You are utterly and eternally secure in both the sovereign hands of Jesus the Son and God the Father. You are in the double grip! You are chosen, adopted, and accepted in the Father and purchased, forgiven, and righteous in the Son.

Paul continues this theme in Romans 8:35–39:

> Who shall separate us from the love of Christ? Shall tribulation, or distress, or persecution, or famine, or nakedness, or danger, or sword? As it is written, "For your sake we are being killed all the day long; we are regarded as sheep to be slaughtered." No, in all these things we are more than conquerors through him who loved us. For I am sure that neither death nor life, nor angels nor rulers, nor things present nor things to come, nor powers, nor height nor depth, nor anything else in all creation, will be able to separate us from the love of God in Christ Jesus our Lord.

Because we are his sheep, God will sustain us to the end. He alone is faithful to make sure we are fully and finally saved. Rest confidently in God's power to keep you saved to the end. Hold fast to this truth that God will never let you go, that you are sovereignly and securely in his grip, that he will sustain you to the end through suffering. He will complete what he started in you as you experience trials. He can keep you from stumbling. Rejoice in the words of Isaiah 43:1–2: "But now thus says the Lord, he who created you, O Jacob, he who formed you, O Israel: 'Fear not, for I have redeemed you; I have called you by name, you are mine. When you pass through the waters, I will be with you; and through the rivers, they shall not overwhelm you; when you walk through fire you shall not be burned, and the flame shall not consume you.'" God never promises to take us out of suffering, but he does promise to be with us through it.

Throughout the Bible, people have cried out in anguish to the Lord as they have experienced severe trials. Job lamented the day he was born. David cried out in despair while hiding for his life in desert caves. Habakkuk questioned the goodness of God. Elijah experienced bouts of depression. Jeremiah accused God of tricking him by having him endure a prophetic ministry of imprisonment and slander. Many of the psalms express outright anger at God in the midst of suffering. Let me be very clear here: there is nothing wrong with asking God "Why?" and pouring our heart out to him in pain, frustration, and discouragement. You have permission to cry out to God with the confidence that he hears you and cares about you deeply. Psalm 86:6–7 says, "Give ear, O Lord, to my prayer; listen to my plea for grace. In the day of my trouble I call upon you, for you answer me." I must warn you about a danger, however. If you're not careful, this doubt and frustration can soon lead to bitterness and despair which are spiritually dangerous. You don't want to get that far off the path. You don't want to give into bitterness, you don't want to fall into despair, and most importantly, you don't want to succumb to unbelief. So how do you, by God's grace, deal with overwhelming discouragement, disappointment, suffering, and trials? Reminding yourself of God's sovereign goodness helps you overcome the pain of despair and misery.

When you face trials of various kinds, remind yourself of the gospel truth that God is *good*:

> "I say to the Lord, you are my Lord; I have no good apart from you." (Ps 16:2)

> "Oh, how abundant is your goodness, which you have stored up for those who fear you and worked for those who take refuge in you, in the sight of the children of mankind!" (Ps 31:19)

When you face trials of various kinds, remind yourself of the gospel truth that God is *trustworthy*:

> "The Lord is my strength and my shield; in him my heart trusts, and I am helped; my heart exults, and with my song I give thanks to him." (Ps 28:7)

> "In God, whose word I praise, in God I trust; I shall not be afraid. What can flesh do to me?" (Ps 56:4)

When you face trials of various kinds, remind yourself that God has *a plan and purpose* for you:

> "For I know the plans I have for you, declares the Lord, plans for welfare and not for evil, to give you a future and a hope." (Jer 29:11)

> "And we know that for those who love God all things work together for good, for those who are called according to his purpose." (Rom 8:28)

When you face trials of various kinds, remind yourself that God is *powerful*:

> "Awesome is God from his sanctuary; the God of Israel—he is the one who gives power and strength to his people. Blessed be God!" (Ps 68:35)

> "Great is our Lord, and abundant in power; his understanding is beyond measure." (Ps 147:5)

In other words, you need to daily preach the gospel to yourself and remind yourself of the God you worship!

Paul makes a striking statement about suffering in Philippians 3:10–11: "That I may know him and the power of his resurrection, and may share his sufferings, becoming like him in his death, that by any means possible I may attain the resurrection from the dead." In this passage, Paul mentions this passionate desire to know Jesus more deeply and the power of his resurrection. Paul had a holy dissatisfaction with his present condition. Spiritual discontent is healthy because it drives us to want more of Christ. Also, Paul makes a surprising and unsettling statement that he wants to share in Christ's sufferings. That's a bold statement. We like experiencing the awesome power of God! We enjoy knowing Jesus more deeply! But do we truly desire to share in his suffering? What if I told you that for God to bring true revival in your life, it would involve a significant interruption that might bring misery? Would you welcome it with joy or run as far from it as you could? I don't know the secret things of God, so I don't know what he might do, but it is within his divine prerogative to ordain suffering for his children.

What is our ultimate hope in the gospel? Do you long to experience the life-changing power of salvation, to be declared not guilty, to be born again, and to know Christ? I hope it is. But for Paul, his ultimate hope was final salvation with a resurrected body in the very presence of

Christ in heaven. Paul wants to "become like him" in his death. Having a new identity in the Trinity means deeply knowing Jesus, experiencing his power at work in us, and suffering well for his glory. Finally, at the resurrection, we will become like Jesus in his death where he victoriously rose from the grave. We too will one day rise from the grave with new bodies to be with Christ forever. Paul anticipates this future in Philippians 3:20–21: "But our citizenship is in heaven, and from it we await a Savior, the Lord Jesus Christ, who will transform our lowly body to be like his glorious body, by the power that enables him even to subject all things to himself." As you walk with a limp, experience various fiery trials, and endure the hardships of following Christ, rejoice in suffering, knowing that the reward of heaven awaits you on that final day! One day we will experience a powerful transformation! In the twinkling of an eye, we will receive our glorified bodies! We will inherit eternal life! Would you rest confidently in this truth and embrace the words of Paul in 2 Corinthians 4:16–17 when he says, "So we do not lose heart. Though our outer self is wasting away, our inner self is being renewed day by day. For this light momentary affliction is preparing for us an eternal weight of glory beyond all comparison?"

Conclusion

We've come to the end of our journey in discovering your identity in the Trinity which all started with the centrality of the glory of God. Do you make it your holy ambition to display God's fame as a lifestyle of worship? Also, the gospel is the central message that undergirds everything about who we are in Christ. The gospel is the good news of the death, burial, and resurrection of Jesus. Nothing is more precious than the gospel, which is the power of God for salvation, the word of truth, and life itself! We also explored gospel grammar in that the indicatives always come before the imperatives in Scripture. God always starts with what he alone has done in our salvation as the foundation for our identity. We need to understand that who we are in the Triune God serves as the grounds and motivation for our obedience. If we get the moral imperatives before the gospel indicatives, we have a recipe for disaster. We think we can obey perfectly which leads to inflated pride, or we shrink in despair because we melt under the weight of our inability to follow his commands. Instead, we obey the Lord joyfully out of our identity in the Trinity.

We also examined the insidious nature of indwelling sin, as well as the internal battle that rages between the flesh and the Spirit. We analyzed the importance of killing sin through the power of the Holy Spirit. We also learned about the means of grace God has given us to grow in our obedience and strengthen our identity, which are (1) Scripture saturation, (2) prayer, (3) the ordinances of baptism and the Lord's Supper, (4) fellowship, and (5) evangelism. We also delved into how God ordains suffering to shape us more into the image of Christ.

As we come to the end of this book, we have to ask the question: Why do so many Christians live in quiet desperation? Why do so many believers either struggle with works-based legalism on the one hand or an overwhelming sense of guilt and despair on the other? The answer is that many believers do not fully understand their identity in the Trinity. The remedy to this problem is to preach the gospel to ourselves every day. When I use the phrase "preach the gospel" to ourselves, I do not envision a pastor standing in the pulpit on Sunday mornings, but a call to every believer to meditate upon, reflect on, think deeply about, and immerse him or herself in the glorious truths of the gospel daily. By doing this, we can avoid the dangerous traps of legalism on one hand and despair on the other. We need to continually remind ourselves that we are chosen, adopted, and accepted in the Father; purchased, forgiven, and righteous in the Son; and regenerated, indwelt, and sanctified by the Spirit.

Titus 3:3–7 gives us what I call the gospel in a nutshell. In these five verses, we find some glorious gospel declarations that tell us what God has done for us in Christ and how we can be assured of his love for us. This passage succinctly summarizes your identity in the Trinity. Paul writes:

> For we ourselves were once foolish, disobedient, led astray, slaves to various passions and pleasures, passing our days in malice and envy, hated by others and hating one another. But when the goodness and loving kindness of God our Savior appeared, he saved us, not because of works done by us in righteousness, but according to his own mercy, by the washing of regeneration and renewal of the Holy Spirit, whom he poured out on us richly through Jesus Christ our Savior, so that being justified by his grace we might become heirs according to the hope of eternal life.

I want to encourage you with seven gospel declarations that emerge directly from this passage of Scripture that I pray you can use to saturate your heart and soul with the good news of God's love for you in Christ. These declarations will help strengthen you in your identity.

Gospel declaration #1: *The gospel tells me of my former identity as an enslaved sinner before trusting Christ.* Paul reminds us that we were *once* foolish, disobedient, enslaved to passions and pleasures, and engulfed in our sin. In other words, that is not our identity anymore. The gospel tells me that I have a new identity. Praise you, Jesus, that you have taken me out of the kingdom of darkness and brought me into the kingdom of light.

Gospel declaration #2: *The gospel tells me that God's awesome mercy and love have come to me personally through Jesus Christ.* I'm not the source of salvation. Salvation starts in the heart of God for lost sinners, and he chooses to shower us with goodness, lovingkindness, and mercy through sending Jesus.

Gospel declaration #3: *The gospel tells me that I can in no way contribute to my salvation since God saved me by His grace alone.* How do you preach this to yourself? You always remind yourself that God is sovereign in your salvation and that you can't do any good work to make God love you more or love you less. As a believer God loves you perfectly—on your best day when you're doing everything great for Jesus and on your worst day when you fail miserably, God's love for you is constant. It doesn't change based upon your performance one way or the other.

Gospel declaration #4: *The gospel tells me that I have been born again as a new creation in Christ.* Remind yourself daily that God has washed you. God has regenerated your heart. God has caused you to be born again. You are a new creation in Christ

Gospel declaration #5: *The gospel tells me that God has richly given me the indwelling Holy Spirit.* We have the Holy Spirit living inside of us as the very presence of Christ. He empowers me to obey Jesus and promises to conform me to the image of God's Son.

Gospel declaration #6: *The gospel tells me that God accepts me, and I have a clean record before him.* That's what it means for God to justify you by his grace. God declares us as righteous. He wipes our record clean and gives us the record of Christ. We stand not guilty, clothed in Christ's righteousness and not our own, and God accepts us on the basis of Christ, not our performance.

Gospel declaration #7: *The gospel tells me that I have the hope of eternal life.* Remind yourself daily that this is not your real home. You have a home in heaven. You will one day see Christ face to face. He has an inheritance waiting for you. He holds you in his grip and will never let you go. He will ensure that you make it to heaven. Allow the power of the gospel to affect your thinking, your affections, and your actions as you celebrate God's amazing grace for sinners in his Son Jesus Christ.

In 1 Timothy 1:15–17, Paul provides another summary statement of what it means to have a glorious gospel identity in the Trinity:

> The saying is trustworthy and deserving of full acceptance, that Christ Jesus came into the world to save sinners, of whom I am the foremost. But I received mercy for this reason, that in me, as the foremost, Jesus Christ might display his perfect patience as an example to those who were to believe in him for eternal life.

> To the King of the ages, immortal, invisible, the only God, be honor and glory forever and ever. Amen.

What is the trustworthy saying that deserves our full attention? Jesus Christ came into the world as our Messiah to secure our eternal redemption. In John 12:46, he says, "I have come into the world as light, so that whoever believes in me may not remain in darkness." The angel announces his birth in Matthew 1:21 when he says, "She will bear a son, and you shall call his name Jesus, for he will save his people from their sins." Mark 10:45 reads, "For even the Son of Man came not to be served but to serve, and to give his life as a ransom for many."

Paul uses a rare term to refer to himself as the worst or "foremost" of sinners. He had this lingering amazement that God forgave him of his past egregious sins, and he never got over this amazing grace in the gospel. In Paul's blasphemous rebellion, Christ invaded his life and displayed perfect patience. The Father showered this outrageous sinner with complete patience to serve as an example of how he saves you and me. Here's a great theological truth: Soteriology leads to doxology. What the Bible says about our salvation should always lead to adoration. Fundamentally, our identity in the Trinity is not a doctrine we examine much like dissecting a frog in a laboratory, but instead, it should lead us to worship our great God with awe and wonder. In other words, when you think about God's amazing grace and mercy in your salvation (soteriology), it can only lead you to erupt in an outburst of praise and adoration (doxology).

In verse 17, Paul bursts into a song and gives four great descriptions of the character and nature of God as King.

First, God is the King eternal. Psalm 90:2 says, "Before the mountains were brought forth, or ever you had formed the earth and the world, from everlasting to everlasting you are God."

Second, God is the King immortal or unchangeable. Numbers 23:19 affirms this truth: "God is not man, that he should lie, or a son of man, that he should change his mind. Has he said, and will he not do it? Or has he spoken, and will he not fulfill it?" Malachi 3:6 echoes this: "For I the Lord do not change; therefore you, O children of Jacob, are not consumed."

Third, God is the King invisible. First Timothy 6:15–16 says, "He who is the blessed and only Sovereign, the King of kings and Lord of lords, who alone has immortality, who dwells in unapproachable light, whom no one has ever seen or can see. To him be honor and eternal dominion.

Amen." Remember from chapter one, Moses' desire to see God in all of his glory? The LORD reminds him in Exodus 33:20 that "You cannot see my face, for man shall not see me and live."

Fourth, our God is the only true God. Deuteronomy 6:4–5 declares, "Hear, O Israel: The Lord our God, the Lord is one. You shall love the Lord your God with all your heart and with all your soul and with all your might." To this King belongs honor and glory forever and ever. Amen. Psalm 34:3 calls us to "magnify the Lord with me, and let us exalt his name together!"

I hope through this journey of understanding your identity in the Trinity, you have grown in your assurance of salvation. I pray that you have seen a small glimpse of the absolute sovereignty and majesty of our great God. I hope that this book has not just filled your mind with theological doctrine that will help you win a Bible trivia contest. I pray that this book has not only filled your head with information, but that the Holy Spirit has used these truths for your transformation. I hope that God has solidified his word in your heart through becoming more strengthened in your identity, by learning how to mortify sin, and by practicing the means of grace. My longing is that you have a more profound love for the Triune God. Since you are chosen, adopted, and accepted in the Father; and purchased, forgiven, and righteous in the Son; and regenerated, indwelt, and sanctified by the Spirit, you can join with the angelic host in Revelation 4:11 and cry out: "Worthy are you, our Lord and God, to receive glory and honor and power, for you created all things, and by your will they existed and were created."

Soli Deo Gloria!

Bibliography

Alexander, Eric J. *Prayer: A Biblical Perspective*. Carlisle, PA: The Banner of Truth Trust, 2012.
Allison, Gregg R. *Sojourners and Strangers: The Doctrine of the Church*. Wheaton, IL: Crossway, 2012.
Arndt, Danker, et al. *A Greek-English Lexicon of the New Testament and Other Early Christian Literature*. Chicago: University of Chicago Press, 2000.
Augustine. *Confessions*. Translated by Henry Chadwick. Oxford University Press, 2008.
Bar, Norma, and Laura Roberson. "Where Sit Happens." http://www.menshealth.com/health/most-active-cities.
Barcellos, Richard C. *The Lord's Supper as a Means of Grace: More than a Memory*. Fearn, UK: Mentor, 2013.
Barker, K. L. *New American Commentary Vol. 20: Micah, Nahum, Habakkuk, Zephaniah*. Nashville: B & H, 1999.
Bavinck, Herman. *Reformed Dogmatics: Holy Spirit, Church, and New Creation, IV*. Translated by John Vriend. Grand Rapids: Baker Academic, 2008.
Beeke, Joel. "Hallowing God's Name." In *Let us Pray: A Symposium on Prayer by Leading Preachers and Theologians*, edited by Don Kistler, 37–56. Orlando: Northampton, 2011.
Beeke, Joel, and Brian G. Najapfour. *Taking Hold of God: Reformed and Puritan Perspectives on Prayer*. Grand Rapids: Reformation Heritage, 2011.
Berkhof, Louis. *Systematic Theology: New Combined Edition*. Grand Rapids: Eerdmans, 1996.
Bickel, Bruce, and Stan Jantz. *Knowing the Bible 101: A Guide to God's Word in Plain Language*. Eugene, OR: Harvest House, 1998.
Blomberg, Craig. *Matthew: New American Commentary*. Nashville: B & H, 1992.
Boettner, Loraine. *The Reformed Doctrine of Predestination*. Phillipsburg, NJ: P & R, 1932.
Bolton, Samuel. *The True Bounds of Christian Freedom*. Carlisle, PA: The Banner of Truth Trust, 2001.
Bonhoeffer, Dietrich. *Life Together*. New York: HarperCollins, 1954.
Boston, Thomas. *The Works of Thomas Boston*. 6 Vols. Carlisle, PA: Banner of Truth Trust, 1980.
Bratt, James D. *Sphere Sovereignty: Abraham Kuyper, A Centennial Reader*. Grand Rapids: Eerdmans, 1998.

Bridges, Jerry. *The Gospel for Real Life: Turn to the Liberating Power of the Cross Every Day.* Colorado Springs, CO: NavPress, 2003.

———. *The Pursuit of Holiness.* Colorado Springs, CO: NavPress, 1996.

Bridges, Jerry, and Bob Bevington. *Bookends of the Christian Life.* Wheaton, IL: Crossway, 2007.

Brooks, Thomas. *Precious Remedies against Satan's Devices.* Carlisle, PA: Banner of Truth Trust, 2001.

———. *The Works of Thomas Brooks.* 6 Vols. Carlisle, PA: Banner of Truth Trust, 2001.

Bruce, F. F. *The Epistle to the Hebrews. The New International Commentary on the New Testament.* Grand Rapids: Eerdmans, 1990.

Bunyan, John. *The Works of John Bunyan.* 3 Vols. Carlisle, PA: The Banner of Truth Trust, 2001.

Calvin, John. *Acts-Romans Calvin's Commentaries.* Grand Rapids: Baker, 2005.

———. *Commentary on the Harmony of the Evangelists, Matthew, Mark, and Luke.* Grand Rapids: Baker, 2005.

———. *Galatians-Philemon. Calvin's Commentaries.* Grand Rapids: Baker, 2005.

———. *Institutes of the Christian Religion.* Grand Rapids: Eerdmans, 1989.

———. *Instruction in Faith.* Translated by Paul T. Furhmann. Philadelphia: Westminster, 1949.

———. *John 12–21 and Acts. Calvin's Commentaries.* Grand Rapids: Baker, 2005.

———. *Sermons on Election and Reprobation.* Translated by John Fields. Grand Rapids: Reformation Heritage, 1996.

Carson, D. A. *The Difficult Doctrine of the Love of God.* Wheaton, IL: Crossway, 2000.

———. "Reflections on Assurance." In *Still Sovereign: Contemporary Perspectives on Election, Foreknowledge, and Grace,* edited by Thomas R. Schreiner and Bruce Ware, 247–76. Grand Rapids: Baker, 2000.

Chapell, Bryan. *Christ-Centered Preaching: Redeeming the Expository Sermon.* Grand Rapids: Baker, 1994.

———. *Praying Backwards: Transform Your Prayer Life by Beginning in Jesus' Name.* Grand Rapids: Baker, 2005.

Cheeseman, John. *Saving Grace.* Carlisle, PA: The Banner of Truth Trust, 1999.

Chester, Tim, and Marcus Honeycutt. *Gospel Centered Preaching.* Surrey, UK: Good Book, 2014.

Chester, Tim, and Steve Timmis. *Total Church: A Radical Reshaping around Gospel and Community.* Wheaton, IL: Crossway, 2008.

Clowney, Edmund P. *The Church.* Downers Grove, IL: InterVarsity, 1995.

Comfort, Ray. *Hell's Best Kept Secret.* New Kensington, PA: Whitaker, 1989.

Davis, Andrew. *An Approach to Extended Memory of Scripture.* http://www.fbcdurham.org/wp-content/uploads/2015/07/Scripture-Memory-Booklet-for-Publication-Website-Layout.pdf.

Descartes, Rene. *A Discourse on the Method.* Translated by Ian McLean. Oxford: Oxford University Press, 2006.

Dever, Mark. *The Church: The Gospel Made Visible.* Nashville: B & H Academic, 2012.

DeYoung, Kevin. *The Good News We Almost Forgot: Rediscovering the Gospel in a 16th Century Catechism.* Chicago: Moody, 2010.

DeYoung, Kevin, and Greg Gilbert. *What Is the Mission of the Church?* Wheaton, IL: Crossway, 2011.

Duvall, J. Scott, and J. Daniel Hays. *Grasping God's Word: A Hands-On Approach to Reading, Interpreting, and Applying the Bible*. Grand Rapids: Zondervan, 2012.

Edwards, Jonathan. "Advice to Young Converts." https://www.monergism.com/advice-young-converts.

———. *Religious Affections*. Grand Rapids: Sovereign Grace, 1971.

———. *Sermons on the Lord's Supper*. Orlando: Northampton, 2007.

———. *The Works of Jonathan Edwards*. 2 vols. Peabody, MA: Hendrickson, 1998.

"Election." In *The Valley of Vision: A Collection of Puritan Prayers and Devotions*, edited by Arthur Bennett, 88–89. Carlisle, PA: Banner of Truth Trust, 2009.

Fee, Gordon D., and Douglas Stuart. *How to Read the Bible for All Its Worth*. Grand Rapids: Zondervan, 2014.

Field, Carla. "Ten Tragic Lottery Stories Prove Money Doesn't Buy Happiness." https://www.wyff4.com/article/10-tragic-lottery-stories-prove-money-doesnt-buy-happiness/12060337.

Feinberg, Paul D. "The Meaning of Inerrancy." In *Inerrancy*, edited by Norman L. Geisler, 267–306. Grand Rapids: Zondervan, 1980.

Ferguson, Sinclair B. *The Christian Life*. Carlisle, PA: The Banner of Truth Trust, 1981.

———. *John Owen on the Christian Life*. Carlisle, PA: Banner of Truth Trust, 1987.

Frame, John M. *The Doctrine of God*. Phillipsburg, NJ: P & R, 2002.

Friedrich, Gerhard. *Theological Dictionary of the New Testament*. 10 Vols. Edited by Gerhard Kittel. Grand Rapids: Eerdmans, 1956.

Grudem, Wayne. *Systematic Theology*. Grand Rapids: Zondervan, 2000.

Hammett, John S. *Biblical Foundations for Baptist Churches: A Contemporary Ecclesiology* Grand Rapids: Kregel, 2005.

Henley, William Ernest. *A Selection of Poems*. Worcestershire, UK: Read, 2015.

Hodge, Charles. *Romans*. Wheaton, IL: Crossway, 1993.

Hopkins, Hugh Evans. *Charles Simeon of Cambridge*. Grand Rapids: Eerdmans, 1977.

Horton, Michael. *A Better Way: Rediscovering the Drama of God-Centered Worship*. Grand Rapids: Baker, 2002.

———. *The Gospel-Driven Life, Being Good News People in a Bad News World*. Grand Rapids: Baker, 2009.

———. *In the Face of God: The Dangers and Delights of Spiritual Intimacy*. Dallas: Word, 1996.

———. *The Law of Perfect Freedom: Relating to God and Others through the Ten Commandments*. Chicago: Moody, 1993.

———. *Putting Amazing Back into Grace*. Grand Rapids: Baker, 2002.

Iorg, Jeff. *Live Like a Missionary: Giving Your Life for What Matters Most*. Birmingham, AL: New Hope, 2011.

———. *The Painful Side of Leadership: Moving Forward Even When It Hurts*. Nashville: B & H, 2009.

Jamieson, Bobby. *Going Public: Why Baptism is Required for Church Membership*. Nashville: B & H Academic, 2015.

Kaiser, Walter C., Jr. *Toward an Exegetical Theology*. Grand Rapids: Baker Academic, 1981.

Keil, C. F., and Franz Delitzsch. *Commentary on the Old Testament, Vol. 1: Pentateuch*. Peabody, MA: Hendrickson, 2006.

———. *Commentary on the Old Testament, Vol. 5: Psalms*. Peabody, MA: Hendrickson, 2006.

Keller, Timothy. *Counterfeit Gods: The Empty Promises of Money, Sex, and Power, and the Only Hope that Matters.* New York: Dutton, 2009.

———. *Prayer: Experiencing Intimacy with God.* New York: Dutton, 2014.

———. *Preaching: Communicating Faith in an Age of Skepticism.* New York: Viking, 2015.

Kittel, Gerhard, and Gerhard Friedrich. *Theological Dictionary of the New Testament.* 10 Vols. Grand Rapids: Eerdmans, 1967.

Kochhar, Rakesh. "How Americans Compare with the Global Middle Class." http://www.pewresearch.org/fact-tank/2015/07/09/how-americans-compare-with-the-global-middle-class/.

Lane, William L. *The Gospel of Mark: The New International Commentary on the New Testament.* Grand Rapids: Eerdmans, 1974.

Larsen, David. *The Company of the Preachers, Vol. 1: A History of Biblical Preaching from the Old Testament to the Modern Era.* Grand Rapids: Kregel, 1998.

Larson, Craig Brian. "What Gives Preaching its Power?" https://www.christianitytoday.com/pastors/2004/spring/2.30.html.

Leiter, Charles. *Justification and Regeneration.* Hannibal, MO: Granted Ministries, 2009.

Lewis, C. S. *Prince Caspian.* New York: Harper Collins, 1951.

———. *The Weight of Glory.* New York: Harper Collins, 1976.

Lloyd-Jones, D. Martyn. *The Cross: God's Way of Salvation.* Wheaton, IL: Crossway, 1986.

———. *An Exposition of Ephesians 4:1–16.* Grand Rapids: Baker, 1980.

———. *Romans: Exposition of Chapters 3:20—4:25.* Carlisle, PA: Banner of Truth Trust, 2007.

———. *Studies in the Sermon on the Mount.* Grand Rapids: Eerdmans, 1960.

Lovelace, Richard. *Dynamics of Spiritual Life: An Evangelical Theology of Renewal.* Downers Grove, IL: IVP Academic, 1979.

Luther, Martin. *Galatians.* Wheaton, IL: Crossway, 1998.

MacArthur, John. *The Gospel According to Jesus.* Grand Rapids: Zondervan, 1994.

———. "The Mandate of Biblical Inerrancy: Expository Preaching." In *Preaching: How to Preach Biblically,* edited by John MacArthur and the Master's Seminary Faculty, 17–26. Nashville: Thomas Nelson, 2005.

———. "Preaching." In *Pastoral Ministry: How to Shepherd Biblically,* edited by John MacArthur and The Master's Seminary Faculty, 204–13. Nashville: Thomas Nelson, 2005.

———. "What's Inside the Trojan Horse?" https://www.gty.org/resources/print/articles/A333.

Mahaney, C. J. *Humility: True Greatness.* Sisters, OR: Multnomah, 2005.

———. *Living the Cross Centered Life.* Sisters, OR: Multnomah, 2006.

Marshall, Walter. *The Gospel Mystery of Sanctification.* Grand Rapids: Reformation Heritage, 1999.

Martinez, Edecio. "Lynn France Learns of Husband John France's 2nd Wedding . . . On Facebook." http://www.cbsnews.com/8301-504083_162-20012786-504083.html.

McConnell, Mariana. "Interview: Wall-E's Andrew Stanton." https://www.cinemablend.com/new/Interview-WALL-E-Andrew-Stanton-9323.html.

Mohler, Albert R., Jr. *He Is Not Silent: Preaching to a Postmodern World.* Chicago: Moody, 2008.

———. "When the Bible Speaks, God Speaks: The Classic Doctrine of Biblical Inerrancy." In *Five Views on Biblical Inerrancy*, edited by J. Merick and Stephen M. Garrett, 29–58. Grand Rapids: Zondervan, 2013.
Murray, John. *The Epistle to the Romans*. Grand Rapids: Eerdmans, 1965.
———. *Redemption Accomplished and Applied*. Grand Rapids: Eerdmans, 1955.
Naselli, Andy. *No Quick Fix: Where Higher Life Theology Came From, What It Is, and Why It's Harmful*. Bellingham, WA: Lexham, 2017.
O'Brien, Peter. *The Letter to the Hebrews: Pillar New Testament Commentary*. Grand Rapids: Eerdmans, 2010.
Owen, John. *Communion with God: Fellowship with Father, Son, and Spirit*. Fearn, UK: Christian Focus, 2007.
———. *The Glory of Christ: His Office and Grace*. Fearn, UK: Christian Focus, 2004.
———. *The Holy Spirit: Abridged and Made Easy to Read*. Carlisle, PA: Banner of Truth Trust, 1984.
———. *The Mortification of Sin*. Fearn, UK: Christian Heritage, 2002.
———. *The Works of John Owen*. 16 vols. London: Banner of Truth Trust, 1965–68.
Packer, J. I. *Concise Theology*. Carol Stream, IL: Tyndale, 2001.
———. *Evangelism and the Sovereignty of God*. Downers Grove, IL: InterVarsity, 1961.
———. *Keep in Step with the Spirit*. Grand Rapids: Revell, 1984.
———. *Knowing God*. Downers Grove, IL: InterVarsity, 1993.
———. "Preaching as Biblical Interpretation." In *Inerrancy and Common Sense*, edited by Roger R. Nicole and Ramsey Michaels, 189–203. Grand Rapids: Baker, 1980.
———. *A Quest for Godliness: The Puritan Vision of the Christian Life*. Wheaton, IL: Crossway, 1990
———. *Truth and Power: The Place of Scripture in the Christian Life*. Wheaton, IL: Harold Shaw, 1996.
Packer, J. I., and Mark Dever. *In My Place Condemned He Stood*. Wheaton, IL: Crossway, 2007.
Peterson, David. *Possessed by God: A New Testament Theology of Sanctification and Holiness* Downers Grove, IL: InterVarsity, 1995.
Pink, Arthur W. *An Exposition of the Sermon on the Mount*. Bellingham, WA: Logos, 2005.
———. *The Sovereignty of God*. Grand Rapids: Baker, 1984.
Piper, John. *Desiring God*. Sisters, OR: Multnomah, 1996.
———. *Let the Nations Be Glad*. Grand Rapids: Baker Academic, 1993.
———. *The Supremacy of God in Preaching*. Grand Rapids: Baker, 2004.
Plummer, Robert L. *40 Questions about Interpreting the Bible*. Grand Rapids: Kregel, 2010.
Ravenhill, Leonard. *Revival God's Way*. Minneapolis: Bethany, 1983.
Reisinger, Ernest. C. *Law and Gospel*. Phillipsburg, NJ: P & R, 1997.
———. *Today's Evangelism: Its Message and Methods*. Phillipsburg, NJ: P & R, 1982.
Renihan, Samuel. *God without Passions*. Palmdale, CA: Reformed Baptist Academic, 2015.
Rideout, Victoria J., et al. "Generation M2: Media in the Lives of 8 to 18 Year-Olds." https://files.eric.ed.gov/fulltext/ED527859.pdf.
Ryle, J. C. *Expository Thoughts on the Gospels: Matthew-Luke*. Grand Rapids: Baker, 2007.
———. *Holiness*. Darlington, UK: Evangelical, 1879.

Sanders, Fred. *The Deep Things of God: How the Trinity Changes Everything*. Wheaton, IL: Crossway, 2010.
Scougal, Henry. *The Life of God in the Soul of Man*. Blacksburg, VA: Wilder, 2011.
"The Second Helvetic Confession." In *Thy Word is Still Truth: Essential Writings on the Doctrine of Scripture from the Reformation to Today*, edited by Peter A. Lilliback and Richard B. Gaffin, 155–69. Phillipsburg, NJ: P & R, 2013.
Smeaton, George. *The Apostles' Doctrine of the Atonement*. Carlisle, PA: Banner of Truth Trust. 1870.
"Sloths." In *The Encyclopedia of Mammals*, edited by David. W. Macdonald, 120–23. Oxford: Oxford University Press, 2009.
Sproul, R. C. "Why Pray?" In *Let us Pray: A Symposium on Prayer by Leading Preachers and Theologians*, edited by Don Kistler, 1–8. Orlando: Northampton, 2011.
Spurgeon, Charles, H. "Bringing Sinners to the Savior, sermon no. 2731." http://www.spurgeongems.org/vols46-48/chs2731.pdf.
———. *C. H. Spurgeon's Autobiography: Compiled from His Diary, Letters, and Records*. London: Passmore and Alabaster, 1899.
———. *The Complete Sermons of C. H. Spurgeon, Book 1, Vols. 1–3*. Louisville: David Attebury, 2015.
———. *Lectures to My Students*. Grand Rapids: Zondervan, 1954.
———. "Pride and Humility." www.spurgeon.org/resource-library/sermons/pride-and-humility#flipbook/
———. "Revival Promise." https://www.spurgeongems.org/vols19-21/chs1151.pdf.
———. *The Soul Winner*. Pasadena, TX: Pilgrim, 1978.
———. *Spurgeon at His Best*. Grand Rapids: Baker, 1988.
———. *Spurgeon's Sermons on the Death and Resurrection of Jesus*. Peabody, MA: Hendrickson, 2005.
Stott, John R. *Between Two Worlds: The Challenge of Preaching Today*. Grand Rapids: Eerdmans, 1982.
———. *The Cross of Christ*. Downers Grove, IL: InterVarsity, 2006.
———. *The Living Church*. Downers Grove, IL: InterVarsity, 2007.
———. *The Message of Galatians*. Downers Grove, IL: InterVarsity, 1968.
———. *The Message of Romans*. Downers Grove, IL: InterVarsity, 1994.
Strauch, Alexander. *Biblical Eldership: An Urgent Call to Restore Biblical Church Leadership*. Colorado Springs, CO: Lewis and Roth, 1995
Stuart, Douglas K. *New American Commentary: Exodus*. Nashville: B & H, 2006.
Swindoll, Charles. *So You Want to Be Like Christ?* Nashville: W, 2005.
Tozer, A. W. *Keys to the Deeper Life*. Grand Rapids: Zondervan, 1957.
———. *Man: The Dwelling Place of God*. Camp Hill, PA: Wing Spread, 1997.
———. *The Root of Righteousness*. Harrisburg, PA: Christian, 1955.
———. *A Treasury of A. W. Tozer*. Grand Rapids: Baker, 1980.
Trumbull, Charles. *Victory in Christ*. Fort Washington, PA: CLC, 1972.
Vincent, Milton, *A Gospel Primer for Christians: Learning to See the Glories of God's Love*. Bemidji, MN: Focus, 2008.
Vos, Geerhardus. *Biblical Theology*. Grand Rapids: Eerdmans, 1948.
———. *Redemptive History and Biblical Interpretation, The Shorter Writings of Geerhardus Vos*. Edited by Richard B. Gaffin. Phillipsburg, NJ: P & R, 2001.
Ward, Timothy. *Words of Life: Scripture as the Living and Active Word of God*. Downers Grove, IL: IVP Academic, 2009.

Ware, Bruce A. *Father, Son, and Holy Spirit: Relationship, Roles, and Relevance.* Wheaton, IL: Crossway, 2005.
Warfield, Benjamin B. *The Works of Benjamin B. Warfield.* 10 Vols. Grand Rapids Baker, 2003.
Watson, Thomas. *The Godly Man's Picture.* Carlisle, PA: The Banner of Truth Trust, 2007.
———. *The Ten Commandments.* Carlisle, PA: The Banner of Truth Trust, 2009.
"The Westminster Larger Catechism." In *Thy Word is Still Truth: Essential Writings on the Doctrine of Scripture from the Reformation to Today,* edited by Peter A. Lilliback and Richard B. Gaffin, 223–33. Phillipsburg, NJ: P & R, 2013. http://www.westminsterconfession.org/confessional-standards/the-westminster-shorter-catechism.php.
Whitney, Don. *Spiritual Disciplines for the Christian Life.* Colorado Springs, CO: NavPress, 1991.
———. *Spiritual Disciplines Within the Church.* Chicago: Moody, 1996.
Wiles, Russ. "A Winner's Guide to Managing Your Powerball Jackpot." http://www.azcentral.com/story/money/business/consumers/2016/01/08/winners-guide-managing-your-powerball-jackpot/78408648/.

Subject Index

Adoption, 10, 23, 26, 33–34, 38–42, 46, 8, 153–154, 156–157, 193
Arianism, 32
Assurance, 26–29, 41, 45–46, 53, 60–61, 89, 180–181
Atonement, 15, 49–53, 178
Baptism, believer's, 170–175, 205
Born again, 70, 73–75, 86, 105, 191, 209, 234
Burdens, bearing others, 194–195
Calling, effectual, 72
Christ, *see Jesus*
Communion, see Lord's Supper
Conversion, 140, 210, 216,
Condemnation, 11, 16, 20, 40, 61, 85–86, 121, 123
Covenant of Redemption, 38
Cross, the, 21, 33, 40–41, 49–52, 66–67, 110, 153, 177–178, 190, 196–197, 203–204
Devil, the, *see Satan*
Elders, 145, 193
Election, 35–39, 42, 44–46, 228
Encourage/Encouragement, 197–198
Eternal life, 19–20, 39–40, 77–78, 231, 234
Eternal Security, 78–79
Evangelism, 203, 205–207, 213–218
Evil, 13, 41, 52, 89, 92, 94–95, 108, 115, 117–118, 120, 144, 166
Fall, the, 92–94, 99
Faith, 15, 27–29, 38, 40, 59–60, 67, 71–72, 74–75, 120, 124, 130, 134, 140, 154, 160, 164, 171, 173–175, 180, 209, 221–222

Forgiveness, 53–54, 62, 165–166, 177, 195–197
God
  Faithfulness of, 8–9, 46, 82–83, 157–158, 168, 224, 228
  Glory of, 1–8, 24–25, 47, 57–58, 108, 158, 168, 204, 235–236
  Holiness of, 5, 8, 30, 43–44, 50, 53, 62, 81, 110, 154–157
  Love of, 8–10, 23, 26, 33, 35, 38–39, 41–46, 86, 153, 158, 180, 191, 228, 233–234
  Mercy of, 9, 15, 36, 39, 42, 45, 63, 73, 106, 111, 164–165, 227, 233–234
  Providence of, 5, 32, 160, 214
  Sovereignty of, 3–6, 30, 36–40, 44, 153–154, 157, 160–161, 203, 208–210, 217
  Will of, 81, 141–142, 160–162, 220–221
  Wrath of, 10, 15, 20, 39, 50–52, 62–63, 97, 115, 176, 198–199, 228
Gospel, 12, 14–21, 24–26, 34, 49, 80–81, 85, 109–110, 133–134, 160, 174, 188, 199, 203–204, 208–209, 211–212, 215, 229–230, 232–234
Grace, 14, 19, 20–21, 27, 33, 44–45, 56, 58, 72–73, 75, 80, 84, 106, 122, 124, 165, 173, 175, 189, 191, 196, 210, 214, 217, 227, 229, 234–235
Glorification, 114
Great Commission, 171, 204, 210, 218
Heidelberg Catechism, 59
Heaven, 19, 48, 56, 68, 77, 114, 153–156, 180, 184, 203, 223, 231, 234

Subject Index

Hell, 20, 39–40, 45, 51, 97, 112, 115, 123, 177, 190, 208, 228
Holy Spirit
    Divine Person, 31–32, 76–78
    Drawing work of the, 71–75, 209
    Indwelling of, 37, 75–78, 82, 122, 180, 191, 212, 234
    Illuminating work of the, 135, 137
    Sealed with, 18, 78–79, 156,
Holiness, 27, 46, 80–83, 85, 88, 101, 104–106, 109–110, 134, 141, 167
Humility, 45, 94, 155
Imputation/imputed, 27, 50, 57–58, 61, 80, 126
Inability, spiritual, 70–73, 75, 208–210
Jesus
    Ascension of, 32, 77, 203
    Baptism of, 31, 172
    Death of, *see* Atonement and Cross
    Deity of, 32, 76
    Incarnation of, 31, 33, 190
    Resurrection of, 14–15, 18–19, 56, 60, 77, 110, 156, 174, 207, 230–231
Judgment, 56, 63, 80, 113, 145
Justification, 26–27, 57–61, 63, 80, 165
Keswick, 104, 107–108, 110–111
Kingdom of God, 73, 159–160, 201, 220
Law, of God, 40, 46, 50–51, 62–63, 85–87, 109–110 114, 161
Legalism, 16–17, 55, 232–233
Love, 54–55, 84–86, 140–143, 185, 188–192, 195, 198, 200
Lord's Prayer, The, 151–169
Lord's Supper, The/Communion, 125, 170–171, 176–184, 198, 203, 213, 232
Lordship, of Christ, 14, 67, 80, 204, 227
Means of grace, 25, 124–126, 128, 134, 146–147, 169, 171, 175–176, 178, 184, 198, 200, 203, 232, 236
Missions, 34, 202
Modalism, 31
Monergism/monergistic, 105, 121
Mortification of sin, 115–122, 124
New Covenant, the, 85, 172, 176–178
Obedience, 23, 25–28, 46, 48, 57, 81, 84–87, 89, 93, 95, 105, 110, 114, 122, 130, 139–141, 143, 162, 167, 172, 174–175, 205, 216–218, 232
Perseverance. 139, 147, 183, 198
Persecution, 129, 198, 213, 227–228
Prayer, 24, 135, 147–151, 199–201, 210–214
Preaching/proclamation of gospel, 17, 25, 125, 128–134, 146, 198, 203–204, 206, 215–216
Predestination, 22, 33, 36, 39, 42, 44, 46, 161
Propitiation, 47, 51, 57, 62–63, 178, 189
Reconciliation, 60, 80, 172, 178, 182, 190, 199
Redemption/redeem, 32–33, 39, 41, 49, 53, 57, 105, 177, 180, 190, 213–214, 217, 228, 235
Regeneration, 17, 70–75, 85–86, 165, 191, 209–210
Repentance, 14, 54, 67, 120–121, 165–166, 173, 206–207, 215
Revival, 150–151
Righteous/Righteousness, 25–27, 57–63, 70, 80, 110, 126, 165, 234
Salvation, doctrine of, 15, 26, 28, 33, 38, 42, 56, 58–60, 67, 79, 83, 85, 105, 125, 174, 189, 205, 228, 234–235
Sacrifice, 20, 51, 62, 82, 176–177
Sanctification, 26–27, 80–83, 85, 100–101, 104–109, 121, 126
Satan/Devil, the, 17, 39, 42, 52, 72, 83, 89, 93–96, 119, 148, 159, 167–168, 208, 210–211, 228
Scripture
    Authority of, 130–132
    Inspiration of, 126–127
    Inerrancy of, 132–133
    Meditating on, 137–139
    Memorizing of, 137
    Obeying, 139, 143–146
    Reading of, 135
    Studying of, 136
Second Helvetic Confession, 130
Second London Baptist Confession, 38, 100
Sin, 9, 20–21, 26, 39–40, 49–53, 58–59, 62–63, 71–72, 82, 89, 92, 94–98, 101–103, 108, 113–121, 165–167, 177–178, 190–191, 193–197, 210

SUBJECT INDEX   247

Sinful nature/the flesh, 102, 124, 167
Spiritual deadness, 42, 52, 72, 75, 84, 191, 209–210
Submit, submission to Jesus, 66–68, 132–134, 160, 172–173
Suffering, 97, 129, 220–224, 228–231
Synergism/synergistic, 105–106, 121–122
Temptation, 97, 102–103, 116, 166–168
Total depravity, 38, 49
Tribulation, 219–220, 222
Trinity, the
    Baptism into, 172–173
    Definition of, 29–32, 76

    Economic function, 32–33
    Ontological essence, 32–33
    Praying, Trinitarian, 155
Victory/Victorious Christian Life, 101, 103–105, 108–111
Westminster Larger Catechism, 134
Westminster Shorter Catechism, 1, 125
Witness, witnessing, 207–208, 210–211, 215–216
Worship, 2, 5–6, 10, 29–30, 48, 48, 81, 129, 129, 140–143, 157, 168, 183, 2022
Wrath, *see God, wrath of*
YHWH, 3–5, 157

Scripture Index

OLD TESTAMENT

Genesis
1:1	157
3:1–5	92
3:6	140
6	36
12	36
32:24–32	225

Exodus
3:5	154
12:24–27	176
15:11	30
33:12–23	6
33:14	3
33:18	1, 7
33:20	236
34:6–8	8
35:8	10

Leviticus
19:18	189

Numbers
14:11	91
14:27	91
23:19	235

Deuteronomy
6:4–5	30, 236
7:6–8	36–37
26:16	162
29:29	160
30:6	86

Joshua
1:8	137

2 Samuel
11:1–5	97

1 Chronicles
29:11	168

Nehemiah
9:6	153
9:17–19	8

Job
20:12–14	119
26:14	4
42:2	36, 161

Psalms
1:1–2	137
19:7–9	139
29:2	5
31:19	8

Psalms (continued)

32	61–63
34:3	236
34:8	181
42:1–2	65
73:25–26	65, 150
86:6–7	229
86:8–12	10
86:11–12	150
90:2	4, 235
95:7–11	90–91
102:25–27	4
119:9–11	137, 162
119:18	135
119:99	137
135:6	36
139:13–14	220

Proverbs

5:3–8	120
27:6	194

Ecclesiastes

3:14	161
5:2	152

Isaiah

6:3	158
6:3–5	154–55
40:11	10
42:8	5
43:1–2	228–29
43:6–7	3
43:25	62
45:21–22	30
46:9–10	36
53:6	49
63:7	8
64:6	57

Jeremiah

29:11	230
31:3	46
31:33–34	85, 177

Ezekiel

36:26–27	73

Daniel

9:4	153

Joel

2:12–13	8

Jonah

4:2	8

Micah

7:19	177

Habakkuk

2:14	158

Zephaniah

3:17	43

Malachi

3:6	235

NEW TESTAMENT

Matthew

1:21	235
3:16–17	31
4:17	159
5:13	214
5:23–24	182
5:43–47	190
6:7–13	151
6:8	162
7:11	41
10:16	213
10:19–20	212
10:29–30	163
13:44–46	64
18:15–17	194
26:26–28	177

Scripture Index

26:33–35	55	14:16	77
26:40–41	116	14:16–17	75
26:41	103	15:5	24
27:45–46	50	15:26–27	208
28:19	171	16:13–14	135
28:19–20	204	16:23	156
		16:33	219
Mark		17:17	145
1:9–11	171	18:18	54
1:10	172	18:36	159
1:14–15	206	20:21	206
1:38–39	206	20:28	31
8:38	223	21:15–17	54
9:43	112, 123		
10:45	235	**Acts**	
12:28–30	47	1:8	207
14:38	167	1:14	210
16:15	205	2:41	171, 174
		2:42	211
Luke		2:42–47	125, 147, 186, 203
1:74	87	4:24	153
9:23–25	67	5:41	223
11:1–2	148	6:4	211
24:46–47	206	8:35–39	171–72
		11:26	223
John		14:22	221
1:1	30	16:14	73
1:12	40, 153	16:30–33	171
1:29	48, 177	17:24–25	4
3:5–8	73	19:9	91
3:36	50	20:24	20
6:35	179–80	24:16	216
6:37	74		
6:37–39	38	**Romans**	
6:44	71–72	1:16	15
6:53–57	180	1:29	121
6:63	72	2:5	97
6:65	71	3:21–26	57
8:31–32	143	3:23	57
8:44	93	3:24	58
10:27–29	227	4:5–8	63
10:27–30	28	5:1–2	60–61
12:23–25	66	5:3–5	222
12:46	235	5:5	41, 79
13:34	195	5:8	42
13:43	189	5:9	199

Romans (continued)

5:10	190
5:12	52
5:17	52
6:3–4	174
6:12–13	101
8:1	61
8:6–8	71
8:8–9	78, 102
8:13	113, 115–116, 121–122
8:14	102
8:15–16	154
8:26	156
8:29	22
8:32	52
8:34	56
8:35–39	228
11:34–36	4
12:1–2	6, 81, 140
12:9	118
12:12	211, 222
13:8–10	189
15:1	195
15:7	192

1 Corinthians

2:14	71, 208
3:1–4	131
3:7	217
5:6	119
5:7	177
10:12–13	168
10:16–17	179
10:17	181
10:31	6
11:23–26	178
11:27–29	181
15:1–4	14

2 Corinthians

1:21–22	79
2:11	94
3:18	24
4:3–6	159, 209
4:4–7	17
4:16–17	231
5:9–10	80
5:17	75, 205
5:21	49
10:5	102
12:7–10	227
13:11	195
13:14	33

Galatians

3:13	52
3:17	102
3:26	40
3:28	192
4:6–7	40
5:16–17	101
6:1–3	194–195
6:7–8	96
6:14	45

Ephesians

1:3–6	36
1:4	37
1:4–5	38
1:5	42
1:6	44
1:11	161
1:13–14	18, 78
2:1–3	39
2:4–7	42, 73
2:8–9	60
4:14–16	144
4:19	92
4:30	165
4:32	195
5:15–16	213
6:18	150
6:19–20	211

Philippians

1:6	23, 28, 84, 111
1:29	60
2:12–13	104
3:8	65
3:10	7
3:10–11	250

Scripture Index 253

3:20-21	231
4:6-7	150
4:8	138

Colossians

1:5-6	18, 25
1:13-14	159
1:21-22	60
2:9	32
2:12	174
2:13-14	165
3:5-8	114
3:6	115
3:16	143
3:17	6
4:2	148
4:2-6	210

1 Thessalonians

2:8-9	188
4:1-3	81
5:6	211
5:9-11	198
5:17	150, 211
5:22	120
5:23	82
5:23-24	28, 82

2 Thessalonians

| 2:13-14 | 37 |

1 Timothy

1:15-17	234
1:18	111
2:5-6	156
4:7-8	106
6:15-16	235
6:16	7

2 Timothy

1:8	223
1:8-10	19, 37
3:15-17	126
3:16	128
4:1	144

| 4:1-3 | 128 |

Titus

2:11-12	140
3:3-7	233
3:4-6	8
3:5	73

Hebrews

3:12-13	89
3:13	197
4:12	131
4:15	49-50
4:16	41, 153
5:14	144
7:25	56
10:24-25	198
11:24-25	95
12:2	68
12:11	46
12:15	201
12:28	159
13:17	145

James

1:2-4	222
1:13-14	166
1:14-15	102
1:17	41, 164
1:22-25	139
2:1-4	193
4:7	168
4:8	154
5:16	199

1 Peter

1:7	221
1:14-16	46, 81
1:18-19	52
2:23	224
2:24	51
3:15-16	215
3:18	20
4:12-19	220
4:13	222
5:8	211

2 Peter

1:3–4	191
1:5–8	107
1:20–21	127
3:18	29

1 John

1:8	116
1:8–10	109
1:9	166
2:15–17	81, 142
3:1–2	42
3:18	198
3:24	78
4:7	191
4:7–11	188
4:10	47, 189
4:13	78
5:2–4	140
5:14–15	162

Jude

3	145
24–25	28

Revelation

4:11	236
11:15	160
13:8	37
19:9	183
21:4	222

www.ingramcontent.com/pod-product-compliance
Lightning Source LLC
Chambersburg PA
CBHW050844230426
43667CB00012B/2136